Conversations with William S. Burroughs

Literary Conversations Series

Peggy Whitman Prenshaw
General Editor

D1570206

Books by William S. Burroughs

Junkie (as William Lee). New York: Ace Books, 1953.
The Naked Lunch. Paris: Olympia Press, 1959. First U.S. edition (titled *Naked Lunch*), New York: Grove Press, 1962.
Minutes to Go (with Brion Gysin, Sinclair Beiles, and Gregory Corso). Paris: Two Cities, 1960.
Exterminator (with Brion Gysin). San Francisco: Auerhahn, 1960.
The Soft Machine. Paris: Olympia Press, 1961. First U.S. edition, New York: Grove Press, 1966.
The Ticket That Exploded. Paris: Olympia Press, 1962. First U.S. edition, New York: Grove Press, 1967.
Dead Fingers Talk. London: Calder, 1963.
The Yage Letters (with Allen Ginsberg). San Francisco: City Lights, 1963.
Nova Express. New York: Grove Press, 1964.
Valentine's Day Reading. New York: American Theater for Poets, 1965.
Roosevelt after Inauguration. New York: Fuck You Press, 1965.
Time. New York: 'C' Press, 1965.
Health Bulletin: APO-33, a Metabolic Regulator. New York: Fuck You Press, 1965; Reprinted Beach Books, 1966.
The Soft Machine. New York: Grove Press, 1966; Revised and published by Calder in London, 1968.
So Who Owns Death TV? (with Claude Pelieu and Carl Weissner). San Francisco: Beach Books, 1967.
The Dead Start. San Francisco: Nova Broadcast Press, 1969.
Entretiens avec William Burroughs (WSB interviewed by Daniel Odier). Paris: Pierre Belfond, 1969; Issued in English, revised and enlarged, as *The Job: Interviews with William S. Burroughs.* New York: Grove Press, 1974.
The Last Words of Dutch Schultz. London: Cape Goliard, 1970; Reprinted in the U.S. (revised) by Viking, New York, 1975.
Jack Kerouac (in French, with Claude Pelieu). Paris: L'Herne, 1971.
Ali's Smile. Brighton: Unicorn, 1971; Reprinted with *Naked Scientology* in Bonn by Expanded Media Editions, 1991.
The Wild Boys. New York: Grove Press, 1970.
Electronic Revolution (with Brion Gysin and Henri Chopin). Cambridge, Massachusetts: Blackmoor Head Press, 1971.
Brion Gysin Let the Mice In (by Brion Gysin, texts by WSB), West Glover, V.: 1973.
Exterminator! New York: Viking Press, 1973.
White Subway. London: Aloes seolA, 1973.
Mayfair Academy Series More or Less. Brighton: Urgency Rip-Off Press, 1973.
Port of Saints. London: Covent Garden, 1973; Reprinted in Berkeley by Blue Wind Press, 1980.
The Book of Breathing (with Bob Gale). Ingatestone, England: OU, 1974.
Sidetripping (text to book of photographs by Charles Gatewood). New York: Strawberry Hill, 1975.
Snack. London: Aloes, 1975.
Cobble Stone Gardens. Cherry Valley, New York: Cherry Valley Editions, 1976.

The Retreat Diaries. New York: City Moon, 1976.

Colloque de Tanger (with Brion Gysin). 2 vols. Ed. Gerard-George Lemaire. Paris: Christian Bourgois, 1976, 1979.

Letters to Allen Ginsberg. Geneva: Givaudon/Am Here, 1976; reprinted in New York by Full Court Press, 1982.

Junky (unexpurgated). New York: Penguin, 1977.

The Third Mind (with Brion Gysin). New York: Viking, 1978.

Blade Runner, A Movie. Berkeley: 1979.

Dr. Benway. Santa Barbara: Brad Morrow, 1979.

Ah Pook Is Here. London: Calder, 1979.

Streets of Chance. New York: Red Ozier, 1981.

Early Routines. Santa Barbara: Cadmus, 1981.

Cities of the Red Night. New York: Holt Rinehart, 1981.

Sinki's Sauna. New York: Pequod, 1982.

A William Burroughs Reader. London: Picador, 1982.

The Place of Dead Roads. New York: Holt Rinehart, 1983.

Ruski. New York: Hand Job, 1984.

The Four Horsemen of the Apocalypse. Bonn: Expanded Media, 1984.

The Burroughs File. San Francisco: City Lights, 1982.

The Adding Machine: Collected Essays. London: Calder, 1985; published in New York by Seaver Books, 1986.

Queer. New York: Viking Penguin, 1985.

The Cat Inside (with Brion Gysin). New York: Grenfell Press, 1986; reprinted in revised form in New York by Viking Penguin, 1992.

The Western Lands. New York: Viking, 1987.

The Whole Tamale. np: Horse Press, nd.

Apocalypse (with Keith Haring). New York: Mulder Fine Arts, 1988.

Interzone. Ed. James Grauerholz. New York: Viking Press, 1989.

Seven Deadly Sins. Los Angeles: Lococo-Mulder Fine Arts, 1992.

The Letters of William S. Burroughs: 1945–1959. Ed. Oliver Harris. New York: Viking Press, 1993.

Ghost of Chance. New York: High Risk Books/Serpent's Tail, 1995.

My Education: A Book of Dreams. New York: Viking Penguin, 1995.

Photo credit: Ira Cohen

Conversations with William S. Burroughs

Edited by
Allen Hibbard

University Press of Mississippi
Jackson

www.upress.state.ms.us

Copyright © 1999 by University Press of Mississippi
All rights reserved
Manufactured in the United States of America

07 06 05 04 03 02 01 00   4 3 2 1
∞
Library of Congress Cataloging-in-Publication Data

Burroughs, William S., 1914–
    Conversations with William S. Burroughs / edited by Allen Hibbard.
        p.   cm.—(Literary conversations series)
    "Books by William S. Burroughs": p.
    Includes index.
    ISBN 1-57806-182-2 (alk. paper)—ISBN 1-57806-183-0 (pbk. : alk. paper)
        1. Burroughs, William S., 1914—Interviews.   2. Novelists, American—20th
    century—Interviews.   3. Fiction—Authorship.   I. Hibbard, Allen.   II. Title.   III. Series.
    PS3552.U75 Z465   1999
    813'.54—dc21
    [B]   99-052249

British Library Cataloging-in-Publication Data available

Contents

Introduction

When he died in 1997, William S. Burroughs was one of the most widely recognizable figures in contemporary American literature. His image circulated on album jackets, in Nike commercials, in films, and photographs accompanying news articles and interviews. The image was cultivated and refined: the gaunt, hollow-cheeked face, the glasses, the proverbial suit and tie, the hat out of the '20s, and (sometimes) the overcoat that made him look more like a private eye or businessman than a writer. Indeed, the very proliferation of Burroughs's image was proof of his notion that images and words are viruses, invading any receptive host, taking hold, and replicating themselves.

"It is the *idea* of Burroughs that appeals, not the man; the popular Burroughs, the cult icon, reaches them via printed and electronic media," writes Burroughs biographer Barry Miles.[1] Burroughs has always made good copy. He has enjoyed a celebrity status akin to that of a rock star. People like to read about him. But what is it about this writer that has fascinated and held the attention of so many? There are, first of all, the Burroughs legends: his various connections to the Beats, the famous William Tell incident in Mexico which left his wife dead, his mystique as an outlaw, the time he spent in Tangier, his association with various rock stars, and (we must not fail to mention) his distinctive twangy voice. The controversial nature of his work and legal attempts to suppress it have no doubt also generated interest in the man behind it all. What is more, so much biographical detail is tangled and twisted in the fabric of his fiction, creating among readers and fans the wish to determine what is autobiographical and what is fabrication. Finally, the outlines of Burroughs's life narrative and the kind of life he lived might represent to some the ultimate in freedom, situating his personal journey at the very center of a long-standing American tradition stretching back to Thoreau. Burroughs shirked dominant social values and not only got away with it but triumphed with the mocking cosmic smile of a satirist. What some may forget, of course, in their adulation and worship, is the tremendous price he paid for freedom: the pain and loneliness he suffered frequently and intensely. But, perhaps that, too, is part of it.

Burroughs is the quintessential postmodern writer, bridging "high" and "low" culture. He is an underground figure who in the later phases of his life made a memorable appearance as the junky priest in Gus Van Sant's *Drug Store Cowboy* and became associated with Kurt Cobain, popular leader of the Seattle grunge band Nirvana. The sometime heroin addict, homosexual, bad boy of American literature was begrudgingly voted into the American Academy of Arts and Letters in 1983 (largely as a result of Ginsberg's heavy lobbying apparently).

It is safe to say that William S. Burroughs has had more influence on contemporary popular music than has any other American writer. Patti Smith dubbed him "the father of heavy metal." Indeed, the very term heavy metal has been ascribed to him. Names of bands such as The Soft Machine, Insect Trust, and Steely Dan (the name of the dildo in *Naked Lunch*) are derived from Burroughs's work. These tributes have simply come his way; he has not gone out of his way to garner them. Punk, new wave, and heavy metal musicians—those rebellious forces that shake up the order of things and challenge systems of control—have found in Burroughs a kindred spirit who had been there long before.

Burroughs's appeal to both avant garde and popular or mass audiences can be seen in the range of places these interviews appeared. He has been featured in *The Guardian, Rolling Stone, Oui, Penthouse,* and *Esquire* as well as fly-by-night, alternative, underground, difficult-to-find rags such as *Rat* and *The Soho Weekly.* Academic and literary journals such as *The Paris Review, Modern Language Studies,* and *The Review of Contemporary Fiction* have also recognized his place in the contemporary literary scene and published interviews with him. In an interview for *The L.A. Weekly* (the last in this volume) Burroughs was asked how he reconciled this posture of attacking the system and reaping its benefits at the same time. "There's no contradiction to subverting something and profiting by it at the same time," he replied. "I say, you gotta play the cards you got."

Burroughs instinctively knew that the interview was one means by which images and ideas were disseminated. It worked according to the laws of commercial advertising. People are not likely to buy what they haven't heard of. The object of advertising, of course, is to pique interest in the product. Burroughs was not unaware of the need to remain an economically viable proposition. He sought, as an organism, to survive the onslaught of life-threatening forces that besieged him: drugs, political and moral intolerance, poverty, environmental degradation, enemies, parasites, the law, the hegemonic nature of language.

Burroughs was known to be rather private and reserved. Maurice Girodias, editor of the legendary Olympia Press which first published *Naked Lunch* and a host of other controversial novels, once noted that he "was very hard to talk to because he didn't say anything."[2] Yet, talk he does, as this collection of interviews demonstrates. Far from remaining elusive or reclusive, Burroughs seemed downright promiscuous when it came to giving interviews. What emerges, as one reads the interviews cumulatively, is a consistent picture of a genial, polite, intelligent man with a wry mid-Western sense of humor. "He is not a formidable presence," one of his interviewers has noted. "He is, rather, a formidable *absence,* an individual who by the very tenuousness of his corporeal presence suggests the proximity of Elsewhere."[3] As undemonstrative as he might be, he is at the same time exceedingly open. One rarely senses in his responses any dodging, guardedness, apology, dissembling, or cover-up. Of course, this candor is itself part of the persona Burroughs created. In interview situations, he listens and responds honestly to whatever questions are posed. (Of course, there are always the questions which—due to modesty, respect, or shyness—are not posed.) He seems interested in engaging the other through conversation. Somewhat ironically, this man who has maintained an almost nineteenth century decorum in his manner (but certainly not in his art!) seems almost to be a man without secrets. What you see is what you get. Ultimately, the public and private man merge as private conversations and letters are published and circulate.

The interview, for Burroughs, is but another mode of performance, another art form. And, it is a form perfectly suited to him for—like so much of his work—it is collaborative. Two people come together to talk, each bringing something to the scene, and what emerges belongs wholly neither to the one nor to the other. Each contributes and shapes the work, making it ultimately a product made by both participants. Burroughs, likely more than most writers, fed off intercourse with the creative spirits around him. Well-known are his collaborative projects with his St. Louis friend Kells Elvins, with Allen Ginsberg, with Jack Kerouac, with Brion Gysin, with James Grauerholz, and with a host of musicians and visual artists. The body of Burroughs's work, given the circumstances of its production, along the lines theorized by poststructuralist thinkers like Derrida, Barthes, and Foucault, challenges the very notion of autonomous authorship.

That Burroughs gave great interviews is amply demonstrated by this collection. I have sought to put together a volume which represents the progression of Burroughs's thought over a long stretch of time, from an early interview conducted by Ginsberg and Corso (published in 1961) to an interview in *The L.A. Weekly* published in 1996, just a year before his death. I have sought, as well, to choose interviews that would show Burroughs responding to a wide array of topics. One of the distinguishing qualities of his mind was the way in which it roamed freely, unimpeded by fences, disciplinary boundaries, or culturally established taboos. He was as willing to answer questions about the Carter presidency and gun control as ones pertaining to his books and literary influences.

While expectedly, from interview to interview, Burroughs often goes over the same ground, interviewers tend to approach their subject with particular questions and concerns, dictated by timely events, interests of the interviewer, or the nature of the forum for which the interview was conducted. Thus, each interview has its own character. Ginsberg and Corso's playful exchange with Burroughs is set very much within the Cold War context; it deals with questions concerning political power, language, consciousness, science, and the specter of apocalypse—themes Burroughs would return to over and over again in his career. In his *Rolling Stone* interview, Robert Palmer gets Burroughs's comments on the music industry, film experiments, *The Job,* the E-Meter, drugs, the Beat Hotel, the cut-up technique, *The Wild Boys,* and global politics. David Bowie and Burroughs rap casually about *Nova Express* and *Ziggy Stardust,* performance, love and sexuality, Andy Warhol and pop culture.[4] In his conversation with Gerard Malanga, Burroughs talks about his writing, overpopulation, New York, dreams, his experience teaching at CCNY, sex, Paul Bowles, the media, ESP, and property.[5] Laura Delp pushes Burroughs to clarify his thoughts and views on women. Jennie Skerl begins her interview by asking what it was like to come back to the U.S. in 1974, after such a long period of expatriation. Philippe Mikriammos gets Burroughs to talk about the picaresque tradition, especially his relation to Petronius and Céline. Interviews published by the Gay Sunshine Press focus on Burroughs's attitudes toward and experiences with homosexuality.[6] Vale is interested in Burroughs's ideas on overpopulation and possibilities for human colonization of outer space. Barry Alfonso draws Burroughs out on evolution and spiritual matters. Von Ziegesar solicits Burroughs's reactions to the publication of *Queer.* Larry McCaffery and Jim McManamin's interview focuses on the writer's connection to sci fi.[7] Regina Weinreich's interview, as well as Lynn Snowden's piece featuring David Cronenberg talking with Burroughs, gets responses to Cronenberg's film version of *Naked Lunch,* which was coming out around the time of the interviews. Interviews in *Cover, Contemporanea,* and *The L.A. Weekly,* responding again to contemporary events, dwell on Burroughs's growing acclaim as a visual artist.

As I sat down to arrange interviews, I began to see a larger, fuller, more colorful tapestry yielding patterns and shapes I had not seen before. Their placement one beside another, in chronological order, created—much in the way many of Burroughs's works took their form—something new and unexpected. There emerged a counterpoint between expansive interviews and shorter ones that zeroed in on one or two specific matters. I became interested in where each interview had been conducted and what was going on with Burroughs and his work at the time. I noted that the bulk of the interviews were clumped around the mid-seventies to the mid-eighties when Burroughs really became an icon. I also noted the various ways interviewers presented backdrops, dramatic settings, for their pieces, in an attempt to draw their audience into the private world of their subject. I saw, for instance in pieces by Anne Morrissett and Edmund White, how interview material had been creatively manipulated to produce quite novel forms. Readers will no doubt tease out and conjure their own figures from the carpet.

Burroughs fans will be aware of two full-length works comprising interviews with Burroughs. *The Job,* a joint project undertaken by Daniel Odier and Burroughs, was first published in Paris in 1969. The book is built around interviews Odier conducted with Burroughs, but it is much more than that. It is a book constructed of various material, including essays and short fiction. Jennie Skerl calls it "the quintessential Burroughs book": "It is fragmentary; both fact and fiction; a collaborative effort; a combination of old and new, previously published and unpublished material; both improvisational and edited. *The Job* shows Burroughs's artistic process and his definition of art *as* process more clearly than any other work."[8] Indeed, the book is a great place for one to get an introduction to Burroughs's philosophy and creative process.

There is also Victor Bockris's *With William Burroughs: A Report From the Bunker,* first published in 1981 and revised in 1996, a full-length book devoted to conversations with Burroughs. In his introduction to the revised edition Bockris states his motives for the project: "A book was needed to introduce William to his public as a humorous, sharp-minded individual, not some heavy metal character like the dread Dr. Benway himself. I thought such a book would allow people to hear the tone of his voice as they read and so find the writer and his books less threatening" (xii–xiv). Bockris followed Burroughs around with a microphone and tape player sporadically over a six-year period, from 1974–1980, just after Burroughs had moved back to New York after a long period of expatriation. (The revised edition contains conversations from 1986 and 1991 as well.) By catching (and even setting up) conversations with luminaries such as Susan Sontag, Lou Reed, Patti Smith, David Bowie, Terry Southern, Tennessee Williams, Debbie Harry, Andy Warhol, Christopher Isherwood, and Mick Jagger, the book certainly bestows celebrity status on Burroughs. These conversations are more spontaneous, more natural-flowing than most of those collected in this volume which were conducted on specific occasions for specific purposes, often by people who may not have been on familiar terms with the writer. Conversations in Bockris's book slide from banal banter to topics such as literary influence, biographical narrative, views on the writing process, drugs, sex, dreams, politics, women, etc. At one point, Burroughs states his oft-repeated philosophy that "the function of the poet is to make us aware of what we know and don't know we know" (21).

Conversations with William S. Burroughs has been long in the making, and would never have become a concrete reality without the encouragement and tangible help of many friends and colleagues. The idea of compiling the book first came to me when Gena Dagel Caponi's book on Paul Bowles in this series, containing an interview I had conducted with Bowles, came out in 1993. I remember thinking at that time, "Why not a collection of Burroughs interviews?" So, I wrote to Seetha Srinivasan asking if the press would be interested. She responded positively and encouraged me to submit a proposal. I thank both Seetha, Anne Stascavage, Elizabeth Young, and others at the University Press of Mississippi for their faith, their patience, their advice, and their prodding. I am grateful to both Barry Alfonso and Regina Weinreich for their willingness to supply me with transcriptions of previously unpublished interviews and consent to their use here. Jennie Skerl, whose early critical study of Burroughs remains the foundation for Burroughs scholars, has been extraordinarily generous and helpful, coaching me along the way and digging through her files to find interviews I was having trouble tracking down. Graduate assistants here at Middle Tennessee State University also have been involved with the project at one stage or another. John Greer found and made copies of interviews; Charles Johnson helped me set up a system for seeking and accounting for permissions requests. The Interlibrary Loan staff at MTSU, notably Karin Hallett and Karen Martin, diligently sought interviews in obscure, out-of-the way, defunct little magazines. Darlene Fults, in the English Department, came to my rescue at critical junctures. I am grateful to Jeffrey Posternak, Burroughs's agent at Andrew Wylie, for his interest and support. Ira Cohen responded quickly to my frantic plea for a photo of Burroughs. (Thanks, Ira. You always come through when I need you.) My colleague Will Brantley, who has done a book on Pauline Kael for this series, reminded me how pleased I would be when the book was actually published and I could cradle it in my hands. My friends Nora Hibbard, Josh Russell, and Mark Forshee provided essential encouragement and support for the project.

Poised as we are at the close of one millennium and the dawn of another, I am thrilled by the prospect of having this collection of interviews fall into the hands of so many avid Burroughs fans, and into hands of readers for whom this might be their first exposure to one of the most inventive, radical American literary personalities of the twentieth century. Speaking of the *Paris Review* interview, Alfred Kazin calls Burroughs "an engineer of the pen, a calmly interested specialist of the new process. When Burroughs makes philosophic and scientific claims for his disorderly collections of data, we happily recognize under the externally calm surface of the interview, the kind of inner frenzy that is his genius."[9] These interviews give a window into that genius.

Notes

1. Barry Miles, *William Burroughs: El Hombre Invisible* (New York: Hyperion, 1993) 5. Another, more comprehensive biography of Burroughs is Ted Morgan's *Literary Outlaw: The Life and Times of William S. Burroughs* (New York: Henry Holt, 1988).

2. Quoted in Victor Bockris, *With William Burroughs: A Report From the Bunker,* Rev. ed. (New York: St. Martins, 1996) 26.

3. Craig Karpel, "With the Goat God," *Oui,* 28 August 1973, 70.

4. "Beat Godfather Meets Glitter Mainman: William Burroughs, Say Hello to David Bowie." Craig Copetas, interviewer. *Rolling Stone,* 155 (February 28, 1974), 24–27.

5. Gerard Malanga, "An Interview with William Burroughs." *The Beat Book,* ed. Arthur and Glee Knight, (California, PA: the unspeakable visions of the individual series, 1974) 90–112.

6. In two interviews: Laurence Collinson and Roger Baker's 1973 interview and John Giorno's 1977 interview, both published in *Gay Sunshine Interviews.* Vol. 1. Ed. Winston Leyland, (San Francisco: Gay Sunshine Press, 1978).

7. So, too, does "The Hallucinatory Operators Are Real," an interview that appeared in *Science Fiction Horizons,* 2 (1965) 3–12.

8. *William S. Burroughs* (Boston: Twayne, 1985) 75–6.

9. Introduction, *Writers at Work: The Paris Review Interviews,* Third Series. (New York: The Viking Press, 1967) xii–xiii.

Chronology

1914 Born February 5, in St. Louis, Missouri, second son of Mortimer and Laura Lee Burroughs.

1920 Goes to Community School.

1925 Enrolls in John Burroughs School (named after the naturalist, no relation).

1929 Sent to Los Alamos Ranch School in New Mexico.

1931 Returns to St. Louis and finishes high school at The Taylor School.

1932–36 Attends Harvard University where he majors in English and receives B.A.

1936–37 Goes to medical school at the University of Vienna; marries Ilse Herzfeld Klapper, a Jew who had fled Nazi Germany, in order to help her come to the U.S.

1938 Enters graduate school in anthropology at Harvard, for lack of anything better to do; with Kells Elvins, his roommate whom he had known in St. Louis, writes "Twilight's Last Gleamings," later included in *Nova Express*.

1939 In Chicago enrolls in Alfred Korzybski's seminar on general semantics; returns to New York and enters analysis; severs the tip of his finger; stays briefly at Payne-Whitney psychiatric hospital.

1940 Returns home to St. Louis for a while, then goes to Lockport, Illinois, and takes flying lessons.

1941 Returns briefly to St. Louis in June; goes to New York and works for ad agency.

1942 Drafted into U.S. Army; given honorable discharge in September; moves to Chicago where he lives briefly and works at detective agency, then at an exterminator company.

1943   Settles in New York in the spring; meets Allen Ginsberg, Jack
           Kerouac, and Kerouac's girlfriend Edie Parker late in the year.

1944   Serves as material witness in Carr/Kammerer case, in which Carr
           argued he killed Kammerer, a known homosexual, in self-de-
           fense; Ginsberg and Kerouac introduce Burroughs to Edie Par-
           ker's roommate Joan Vollmer Adams, a student in journalism at
           Columbia.

1945   Collaborates with Kerouac on "And the Hippos Were Boiled in
           Their Tanks," a work based on the Carr/Kammerer case.

1946   Meets Herbert Huncke who introduces him to morphine to which
           he becomes addicted; moves in with Joan Vollmer; arrested for
           obtaining narcotics through fraud; returns to St. Louis for sum-
           mer; divorces Ilse Burroughs in Mexico; Joan Vollmer (his com-
           mon-law wife) and her young daughter move to Texas where
           Burroughs and Elvins had set up on a farm in the Rio Grande
           Valley.

1947   Son William, Jr. born; Huncke joins the Burroughses in Texas,
           then later Neal Cassady and Allen Ginsberg visit.

1948   Seeks help for drug addiction at the Federal Narcotics Farm in
           Lexington, Kentucky; moves to Louisiana, near New Orleans,
           after having a run-in with the Texas law.

1949   Kerouac and Cassady stop to see Burroughs in Louisiana; Burro-
           ughs busted on drug charges; moves to Mexico City; Kells Elvins
           visits Burroughs in Mexico City; Burroughs begins work on
           Junkie.

1951   Travels with Lewis Marker through Central and South America;
           accidentally shoots wife Joan to death in legendary William Tell
           scene; children sent back to live with grandparents.

1952   Kerouac visits Burroughs in Mexico; Burroughs begins working
           on *Queer* (not published until 1985).

1953   Travels in South America in quest for yage and corresponds with
           Ginsberg; stops off to see Ginsberg in New York during the fall
           and they work at editing the correspondence to produce "In
           Search of Yage"; *Junkie* first published in London by Ace Books,
           in a double-header volume with *Narcotic Agent* by Maurice Hel-
           brant; heads off to Europe with Alan Ansen.

1954   Burroughs lands in Tangier in January where he meets Paul
            Bowles and Brion Gysin both of whom, over time, become close
            friends; also hooks up with Spanish boy named Kiki; Kells Elvins
            visits; in October visits Kerouac in New York, then his parents in
            Palm Beach; returns to Tangier by November.

1955   Begins working on *Naked Lunch.*

1956   Goes to London and undergoes apomorphine treatment with Dr.
            Yerbury Dent to cure heroine addiction; visits Alan Ansen in Ven-
            ice; returns to Tangier by September, via Tripoli and Algiers.

1957   First Kerouac, then Ginsberg and Peter Orlovsky, then Alan
            Ansen descend on Tangier and help type, edit, and assemble
            Naked Lunch, referred to then as *Word Hoard;* parts of *Naked
            Lunch* published in *The Black Mountain Review;* Burroughs
            learns that Kiki (now an ex) was stabbed to death in Madrid.

1958   Moves from Tangier to Paris in January, and lives in what be-
            comes known as the Beat Hotel where Allen Ginsberg had already
            established himself; Gysin moves into the Beat Hotel, too; parts
            of *Naked Lunch* published in *Chicago Review,* causing outrage.

1959   Parts of *Naked Lunch* appear in *Big Table* and the issue is held up
            by Chicago postal officials on obscenity charges; eventually it is
            judged not obscene; *Naked Lunch* published by Olympia Press in
            Paris; begins working with Brion Gysin on cut-up method; Gysin
            also introduces Burroughs to Scientology and the myths of Has-
            san I. Sabbah; Burroughs meets Ian Sommerville who becomes a
            close associate.

1960   Portions of cut-up experiments published in *Minutes to Go* (Paris)
            and *The Exterminator* (U.S.); goes to see Sommerville in England
            and meets Mikey Portman; London becomes his base.

1961   *Floating Bear,* with Burroughs's "Roosevelt after Inauguration,"
            held up by postal inspectors on obscenity charges; *The Soft Ma-
            chine* published in Paris; goes to Tangier in April where he meets
            Timothy Leary for the first time; Burroughs then visits Leary at
            Harvard.

1962   Burroughs gets a lot of attention at conference of writers in Edin-
            burgh; learns of Kells Elvins's death; *The Ticket That Exploded*
            published; *Naked Lunch* published by Grove in U.S.

1963   *Yage Letters* (with Allen Ginsberg) published; proceedings against *Naked Lunch* begin in Boston courts; *Dead Fingers Talk* published in London; goes to Tangier in June with Portman, Gysin and Sommerville; Billy Burroughs joins them in Tangier for a spell.

1964   *Nova Express* published in the U.S.; Burroughs leaves for New York late fall; visits St. Louis.

1965   Resides temporarily in New York: Burroughs's father dies in January; trial over *Naked Lunch* begins in Boston; the book is declared obscene and the decision is appealed; returns to London in September; works with Antony Balch and Brion Gysin on experimental films: *Towers Open Fire, The Cut Ups,* and *Bill and Tony;* goes to Tangier at the end of the year.

1966   Returns to London in January; Massachusetts Supreme Court rules that *Naked Lunch* is not obscene; *The Soft Machine* published in the U.S.; spends Christmas with his mother Laura and his son Billy in Palm Beach.

1967   By March Burroughs is back in London; *The Ticket That Exploded* published in the U.S.

1968   Covers the Democratic National Convention in Chicago for *Esquire* along with Jean Genet and Terry Southern.

1969   Jack Kerouac dies, October 20.

1970   Visits New York in summer; Burroughs's mother dies in fall; *The Job* published in the U.S.; *The Last Words of Dutch Schultz* published in London.

1971   *The Wild Boys* published in U.S.

1972   Goes to Hollywood at Terry Southern's urging to check out movie possibilities.

1973   Travels to Morocco in January with John Brady to cover Joujouka musician festival (described in an article in *Oui*); *Exterminator!* published in U.S.

1974   Moves to New York from London in February; teaches at City College in New York; meets James Grauerholz who becomes important collaborator and manager for the rest of Burroughs's life; begins doing readings.

1975   Lectures at the Naropa Institute; *Ports of Saints* published in London; *The Last Words of Dutch Schultz* published in the U.S.; in November moves into space at 222 Bowery which came to be known as The Bunker.

1976   Ian Sommerville killed in car crash; *Cobble Stone Gardens* and *The Retreat Diaries* published in the U.S.

1977   *Junky,* unexpurgated and with the spelling of title changed, published in U.S.

1978   *The Third Mind,* written in collaboration with Brion Gysin, published; The Nova Convention held in New York in honor of Burroughs.

1979   Grauerholz moves to Lawrence, Kansas.

1980   *Ports of Saints* published in U.S.

1981   Burroughs appears on *Saturday Night Live;* moves to Lawrence, Kansas; William Burroughs, Jr., dies March 3; *Cities of the Red Night* published in the U.S.

1982   *Letters to Allen Ginsberg* published in U.S.

1983   Burroughs's brother, Mortimer, dies. Burroughs inducted into the American Academy and Institute of Arts and Letters; Brookner documentary of Burroughs premieres.

1984   *The Place of Dead Roads* published; *The Burroughs File* published.

1985   *The Adding Machine: Collected Essays* published; *Queer* (written in the early fifties) published.

1986   Brion Gysin dies; *The Cat Inside* published; Burroughs makes brief appearance in Laurie Anderson's film *Home of the Brave.*

1987   *The Western Lands* published; exhibition of Burroughs's paintings at the Tony Shafrazi Gallery in New York.

1989   *Interzone,* edited by James Grauerholz, published; Burroughs makes a memorable appearance as junky priest in Gus Van Sant's film *Drug Store Cowboy;* collaborates with Tom Waits on Robert Wilson's *Black Rider,* an opera performed in Hamburg, Germany.

1990   *Blade Runner, a Movie* (not to be confused with Ridley Scott's *Bladerunner*) comes out.

1991   *Ali's Smile* and *Naked Scientology* published; Burroughs under-
        goes triple-bypass heart surgery and cracks his hip.

1992   David Cronenberg's film version of *Naked Lunch* is released;
        Ministry's Just One Fix released.

1993   Collaborates with Kurt Cobain on *The "Priest" They Called Him;*
        Tom Waits's *The Black Rider,* with Burroughs material, released.

1995   *Ghost of Chance* published; *My Education: A Book of Dreams*
        published.

1996   Exhibition of Burroughs's art, *Ports of Entry,* runs at Los Angeles
        County Museum of Art; catalog of exhibit, *Ports of Entry: Wil-
        liam S. Burroughs and the Arts,* published.

1997   Allen Ginsberg dies in Greenwich Village on April 5; Burroughs
        dies in Lawrence, Kansas on August 2.

Conversations with William S. Burroughs

Interview with William Burroughs

Gregory Corso and Allen Ginsberg / 1961

Originally published in *Journal for the Protection of All Beings,* no. 1. San Francisco: City Lights, 1961: 79–83. Reprinted by permission of City Lights.

Corso: What is your department?
Burroughs: Kunst unt Wissenschaft.

Corso: What say you about political conflicts?
Burroughs: Political conflicts are merely surfaced manifestations. If conflicts arise you may be sure that certain powers intend to keep this conflict under operation since they hope to profit from the situation. To concern yourself with surface political conflicts is to make the mistake of the bull in the ring, you are charging the cloth. That is what politics is for, to teach you the cloth. Just as the bullfighter teaches the bull, teaches him to follow, obey the cloth.

Corso: Who manipulates the cloth?
Burroughs: Death.

Ginsberg: What is death?
Burroughs: A gimmick. It's the time birth death gimmick. Can't go on much longer, too many people are wising up.

Corso: Do you feel there has been a definite change in man's makeup? A new consciousness?
Burroughs: Yes, I can give you a precise answer to that. I feel that the change the mutation in consciousness will occur spontaneously once certain pressures now in operation are removed. I feel that the principal instrument of monopoly and control that prevents expansion of consciousness is the word lines controlling thought feeling and apparent sensory impressions of the human host.

Ginsberg: And if they are removed, what step?
Burroughs: The forward step must be made in silence. We detach ourselves from word forms—this can be accomplished by substituting for words, letters, concepts, verbal concepts, other modes of expression; for example, color. We can translate word and letter into color (Rimbaud stated that in his color vowels, words quote "words" can be read in silent color.) In other

words man must get away from verbal forms to attain the consciousness, that which is there to be perceived at hand.

Corso: How does one take that "forward step," can you say?

Burroughs: Well, this is my subject and is what I am concerned with. Forward steps are made by giving up old armor because words are built into you—in the soft typewriter of the womb you do not realize the word-armor you carry; for example, when you read this page your eyes move irresistibly from left to right following the words that you have been accustomed to. Now try breaking up part of the page like this:

Are there   or just   we can translate
many solutions?   for example color   word color
      in the soft typewriter   into
    political conflicts   to attain consciousness
                      monopoly and control

Corso: Reading that it seems you end up where you began, with politics and its nomenclature: conflict, attain, solution, monopoly, control—so what kind of help is that?

Burroughs: Precisely what I was saying—if you talk you always end up with politics, it gets nowhere, I mean man it's strictly from the soft type-writer.

Corso: What kind of advice you got for politicians?

Burroughs: Tell the truth once and for all and shut up forever.

Corso: What if people don't want to change, don't want no new conscious-ness?

Burroughs: For any species to change, if they are unable and are unwilling to do so—I might for example however have suggested to the dinosaurs that heavy armor and great size was a sinking ship, and that they would do well to convert to mammal facilities—it would not lie in my power or desire to reconvert a reluctant dinosaur. I can make my feeling very clear, Gregory. I feel like I'm on a sinking ship and I want off.

Corso: Do you think Hemingway got off?

Burroughs: Probably not.

(NEXT DAY)

Ginsberg: What about control?

Burroughs: Now all politicians assume a necessity of control, the more efficient the control the better. All political organizations tend to function like a machine, to eliminate the unpredictable factor of AFFECT—emotion. Any machine tends to absorb, eliminate, Affect. Yet the only person who can make a machine move is someone who has a motive, who has Affect. If all individuals were conditioned to machine efficiency in the performance of their duties there would have to be at least one person outside the machine to give the necessary orders; if the machine absorbed or eliminated all those outside the machine, the machine will slow down and stop forever. Any unchecked impulse does, within the human body and psyche, lead to the destruction of the organism.

Ginsberg: What kind of organization could a technological society have without control?

Burroughs: The whole point is I feel the machine should be eliminated. Now that it has served its purpose of alerting us to the dangers of machine control. Elimination of all natural sciences—If anybody ought to go to the extermination chambers, definitely scientists. Yes I'm definitely antiscientist because I feel that science represents a conspiracy to impose as the real and only universe, the universe of scientists themselves. They're reality-addicts. They've got to have things real so they can get their hands on it. We have a great elaborate machine which I feel has to be completely dismantled—in order to do that we need the people who understand how the machine works—the mass media—unparalleled opportunity.

Ginsberg: Who do you think is responsible for the dope situation in America?

Burroughs: Old Army game, "I act under orders." As Captain Ahab said, "You are not other men but my arms and legs—" Mr. Anslinger has a lot of arms and legs, or whoever is controlling him, same thing as the Eichman case, he's the front man, the man who has got to take the rap, poor bastard; I got sympathy for him.

Corso: Could you or do you think it wise to say who it will be or just what force it will be that will destroy the world?

Burroughs: You want to create a panic? That's top secret—want to swamp the lifeboats?

Corso: O.K. How did them there lifeboats get there in the first place?

Burroughs: Take for instance some Indians in South America I seen. There comes along this sloppy cop with his shirt buttons all in the wrong

hole, well then, Parkinson's law goes into operation—there's need not for
one cop but seven or eight, need for sanitation inspectors, rent collectors,
etc.; so after a period of years problems arise, crime, dope taking and traffic,
juvenile delinquency—So the question is asked, "What should we do about
these problems?" The answer as Gertrude Stein on her deathbed said comes
before the question—in short before the bastards got there in the first place!
that's all—

Ginsberg: What do you think Cuba and the FLN think about poets? And
what do you think their marijuana policy is?
Burroughs: All political movements are basically anti-creative—since a
political movement is a form of war. "There's no place for impractical
dreamers around here." That's what they always say. "Your writing activities
will be directed, kindly stop horsing around." "As for the smoking of marijuana, it is the exploitation for the workers." Both favor alcohol and are
against pot.

Corso: I feel capital punishment is dooming U.S.A.
Burroughs: I'm against capital punishment in all forms, and I have written
many pamphlets on this subject in the manner of Swift's modest proposal
pamphlet incorporated into *Naked Lunch;* these pamphlets have marked
Naked Lunch as an obscene book. Most all methods of capital punishment
are designed to inflict the maximum of humiliation—note attempts to prevent
suicide.

Ginsberg: What advice do you have for American youth who are drawn
to political action out of sympathy for the American revolution—
Burroughs: "I wouldn't be in your position"—old saw. If there is any
political move that I would advocate it would be an alliance between America
and Red China, if they'd have us.

Corso: What about the Arab peoples—how are they faring?
Burroughs: They're stuck back thousands of years and they think they're
going to get out with a TV set.

Corso: What about the Negros, will they make it—not only the ones in
the South, but everywhere?
Burroughs: Biologically speaking the Afro-Asiatic block is in the ascendancy. Always remember that both Negro and White are minority groups.
The largest race is the Mongoloid group. In the event of atomic war there is

a tremendous biological advantage in the so-called undeveloped areas that have high birth rate and high death rate because, man, they can plow under those mutations. The country with a low birth rate and low death rate will be the hardest hit—and so the poor may indeed inherit the earth, because they're healthier.

Ginsberg: What do you think of white supremacy?

Burroughs: The essence of white supremacy is this: they are people who want to keep things as they are. That their children's children's children might be a different color is something very alarming to them. In short they are committed to the maintenance of the static image. The attempt to maintain a static image, even if it's a good image, just won't work.

Corso: Do you think Americans want and could fight the next war with the same fire and fervency as they did World War II?

Burroughs: Undoubtedly, yes—because they remember what a soft time they had in the last one—they sat on their ass.

An Account of the Events Preceding the Death of Bill Burroughs

Ann Morrissett / 1963

Originally appeared in *Evergreen Review,* no. 29 (March–April 1963), 103–08.

Nine Lies-the-Heart: the door opens on a narrow cell with a bright window. A high figure is silhouetted against the light. Gradually I make out its features. Stretched over the skeleton and meat is a fine yellow parchment on which have been written many things now carefully erased. Dark-rimmed glasses are painted around the eyes.

Will you have some tea, he says, bowing. I am only three feet tall and I see it is no use appearing taller. We let down our defenses a little so we will not have to let them down further.

A fat brown pot sits cold on the gas burner. Wedged in the radiator on the other side of the window is a thin smoldering stick. I feel we must get to the point.

Is that the machine? I ask, pointing to the machine on the table.

The muscles in his face work slightly and I think he is going to say something rude, or refuse to answer. Instead he replies politely, Yes.

Is it hard? I demand.

At first, he says almost apologetically. His look is haughty and yet his manner is strangely humble, as if he thinks I have a right to ask these questions.

When you press the keys it gets softer, a sort of soft machine you might say? I suggest. My tone is perhaps becoming imperious; I am like a little Caesar, though I am disguised as a soft woman.

We seat ourselves, my face to the light and his in the shadow: my mistake. This makes him loom large and faceless which I counter with bigger and more drastic demands: I must be careful. Still, this way he thinks me defenseless. He sits silent, his arms and legs loosely crossed and his shoulders hunched.

And it all comes out just like that, I say with a slight irony, ignoring that he has not answered my last question. We have ways of making them talk, but we do not always use them.

6

He remains silent. His eyes do not quite meet mine, and I see them come to focus on another machine at the side of the room.

Sometimes I use that one, he confesses.

The one that talks?

Yes, he says; it also makes noises like streets and cafés.

We lapse into silence.

When did you become addicted to them? I ask finally, my voice neutral but with a shade of sympathy.

Not until I was 35, he says. It started with *Junky.*

Before that you were only on junk?

Oh yes, bored to death, he sighs.

Now you're never bored?

No.

I smile a little and make a mental note. I do not believe him but I do not know how bored he might have been before.

It would be simpler if you fill out this questionnaire, I say, handing him my hand. On its lines he traces perfunctorily: Born 1914 of Burroughs Adding Machines. Boarding school in Los Alamos where they now make bombs. Harvard. Advertising in New York. Mother one of thirteen children of a minister: most of them in public relations and advertising. Uncle Ivy Lee did PR for John D. Rockefeller, handing out the dimes. In the army for four months, discharged as psychologically incompatible. No conscientious scruples, just didn't suit me. OK for those who like it; inefficient for modern warfare. Back to odd jobs in New York. Junk a matter of association. On it ten years. Psychological approach bunk. Only apomorphine cures. Wife never on it. Like Mexico: wife accident. Son 14, with grandparents in Florida. Never remarry. Like living alone. Conventional brother still in St. Louis. Never go back. Midwest a wasteland. Would like to go to the Far East. Have no base, but not much of a voyager. Tangiers OK but had enough. New York awful. Etc.

I do not smile, though his finger tickles. I make more mental notes: there are already numerous counts to be used against him for the indictment. I turn my hand over and play it back. He listens in passive attention.

The skeleton is there, but guts missing. All dried out? My case is nothing without the crap. Whose side is he on? I tap my fingers.

The door opens and an Arab boy dances into the room, whirling and immobile, staring intensely at the seated figure. Something passes between them without words. He rises, accompanies the boy to the door, and closes it behind them. I am disturbed: normally we cannot allow mixing business with business. I decide it is better to let the reins loose than draw them too tight. Enough rope.

He returns soon, calm, straightening his old school tie. They have no shame, he says with a flicker of fatherly pride. He tucks his hands into the long black academic robe he is now wearing. They are not neurotic, the Arabs, he announces. Sometimes they are psychotic, but they are not confused about who they are and what they are supposed to do. It is all laid out in the Koran. They can shift from homosexuality to heterosexuality without fears or guilts. They don't understand the Western fascination for pornography. For them it is not interesting. In the West conflicting signals make people neurotic, the way conflicting signals make a rat neurotic.

He pulls a rat from his gown and throws it down on the floor. The rat runs frantically to one side of the room and hits the wall. Then it runs to the other side of the room and hits the wall. After several tries it sinks into an apathetic stupor.

You see? he says, picking up the immobile rat and tucking it back into his gown. He spreads the gown to sit down again and for a moment I glimpse the rat's trembling pink nose and blinking eyes. Then everything melts away into the gown's folds and with his deft fingers, including the stumped one, he neatly folds them all away. Then he folds the stump away.

There is a methodist neatness in every move which I do not think we can get around. I sense that all his mechanical manipulations are like this, even the messiest ones. We must find another tack. I try to soften him up with mother memories.

You never ever feel you want someone just for you? I croon.

The parchment mask flinches but does not dissolve. The mouth moves, forming the words "Western concept."

Sex and Spiritual Love never go together, I say.

Not for me, he says.

I try a more mental (metal) approach: This may be all very well for Arab men, I rap out, but what about the women?

Nobody knows about them, he says. An Arab man often won't eat his own wife's cooking for fear it's poisoned.

You contradict yourself, I say. And what about their opiates?

It is a matter of association and availability, he says. In China when everyone could get opium everyone was always doped. You can't do anything that way: only manual labor, but nothing creative. In New York everyone is on psychoanalysis and they never get anything done, they never get off it. Worse

than junk. And as expensive. All they need to do is develop a few interests.
Junk isn't bad for your health, as people think; it's just such a *bore*. Only
apomorphine cures.

I recognize the voice of the Old Doctor, number two on our list. Faintly
Boston, but nasal and midwest in origin. An obscene old quack who hates
obscenity; we have never decided whose side he is really on. So they are one
and the same: a real catch!

Now about these plays, I say. When did you decide to dramatize—I wave
at the machines—all this stuff?

Few weeks ago. Mike Blake came looking for material for his Anglo-
American theatre. I gave him some excerpts to read to jazz. The mime needs
to be more integrated. I think they could use puppets and tapes too; the cook
is a puppeteer. I'd like to direct myself. I'll be doing the reading for an actor
who dropped out. I'm getting interested in this theatre racket. If they wouldn't
be so busy hustling drinks.

And how would you sum up what your plays—or readings—are all about?
My voice is casual, suggesting I already know: we have our own ideas.

Just an intergalactic conflict, he says shrugging. The Nova mob versus the
Nova police.

What's this Nova mob trying to do?

Blow up the planet. They grab everything and then blow up what's left so
they don't have to pay.

And—which side are you on? My voice is still casual.

I create the conflict, I do not take sides.

But inevitably there are heroes and villains, I press him (though it does not
matter what he answers; we are by definition out to get him). Do you feel
you would like one side or the other to win—or that you want the audience
to feel this?

That depends on them, he says cagily.

And who *does* win in the end?

I don't know yet, I haven't come to that. Maybe no one; there are just
temporary gains and defeats, but it goes on and on.

Like a comic strip, I suggest.

Yes, he says, like a comic strip.

And this weapon they use, I say, closing in; what do you mean by Obscenity as a total weapon?

That's just one of them, he says evasively. There are others from other
planets with other weapons.

And the police, they also come from different planets?

Yes.

So that one from a certain planet is put on the tail of the criminal from the *same* planet?

Yes, because he knows their ways.

All right, that's enough, I say wearily. I expose my Nova police badge, a large scar on my left thigh. Confiscate this stuff, I tell my invisible lieutenants. The machines disappear, but my victim's mask hardly twitches. Now would you mind telling me where I can find the w.c.? I know I can count on him as a gentleman for correct information of this sort. He motions down the hall.

When I come back two boys are carrying him out on a slab of gray stone. He is stiff and gray.

Typewriter withdrawal? I say in a low voice to the beardless youth behind. He nods, his eyes downcast and his hair curling around his ears.

I do not feel personally responsible: I am only following orders, and my lieutenants are only following mine.

I watch the boys carry him down the hall and out the door. I presume they will turn right and dump him in the Seine at the corner.*

Oh what a brilliant mind is here o'erthrown, I say, removing my wig and revealing my bald head. Despite my official duties, I too am a lover of the arts, a well-turned phrase, machines, madness, and rebellion. But we must fight them with their own weapons.

I try to feel more personally sad for my victim, but I cannot remember what his face looks like.

---

*Editorial note: As it turned out, this was obviously a ruse. A man purporting to be an inspector from the Nova police turned up the following week on a stool in the dim recesses of a junky sanitarium called La Boheme behind the Gare Montparnasse. His voice was that of the Old Doctor.

Rencontre avec William Burroughs
Eric Mottram / 1964

Originally appeared in *Les Langues Modernes* (Paris) Jan/Feb 1965:
79–83. Reprinted by permission.

Eric Mottram: Burroughs creates conflict through opposition to authority,
and this includes the authority of established methods of plot, time, and space
in novels and the readers' response to them. Burroughs's anarchic freedom
takes the form of complete parody of people in power situations *and* also of
authoritatively accepted literary forms. Human conduct in his fiction is a web
of resistances, dominations, and surrenders, and the way they are dramatized:
as war, capitalism, psychological medicine, and other metaphors of the
human condition as he sees it. A world without love or true community,
projected through a new mythology with a moral purpose.

    Burroughs: In *The Naked Lunch* and *The Soft Machine* I have diagnosed
an illness, and in *The Ticket That Exploded* and *Nova Express* is suggested a
remedy. In this work I am attempting to create a new mythology for the space
age. I feel that the old mythologies are definitely broken down and not ade-
quate at the present time. In this mythology, I have Nova conspiracies, Nova
police, Nova criminals. I do definitely have heroes and villains with respect
to overall intentions with regard to this planet. Love plays little part in my
mythology, which is a mythology of a war and conflict. I feel that what we
call love is largely a fraud—a mixture of sentimentality and sex that has been
systematically degraded and vulgarized by the virus power. Heaven and hell
exist in my mythology. Hell consists of falling into enemy hands, into the
hands of the virus power, and heaven consists of freeing oneself from this
power, of achieving inner freedom, freedom from conditioning. I may add
that none of the characters in my mythology are free. If they were free they
would not still be in the mythological system, that is, in the cycle of conditioned action.

    Eric Mottram: In the first two novels, this mythology is worked out as a
monstrous, ambivalent parody of organization, commerce, fertility, and
travel, through forms of prose and plot which are themselves experimental
acts of revolt. His techniques of re-assembling cut-up and folded versions of

paragraphs have the intention of "altering and expanding states of conscious-ness in himself, he hopes, and in the readers as well." Burroughs feels himself to be in the continuity of the "verbal innovators and experimenters" of the Twenties—Gertrude Stein and James Joyce—trying to discover "what words actually are, and exactly what is the relationship to the human nervous sys-tem." Burroughs also admires, and recalls in his novels, T. S. Eliot of *The Waste Land:* in one sense his own work is a vision of a waste land: [in his own words], "a new mythology for the space age." This replaces "broken-down old mythologies." He uses routines drawn from science fiction, pulp thrillers, and violent strip cartoons, and in doing so opens up the political and psychological drives they conceal. The result is an honesty about power and obsession which most contemporary writers do not even attempt. Admittedly, Burroughs's repetitive narcotic and homoerotic fantasies become tedious in sections of his third novel, but it is from these obsessions that his most power-ful work develops.

Burroughs: The virus power manifests itself in many ways. In the con-struction of nuclear weapons, in practically all the existing political systems which are aimed at curtailing inner freedom, that is, at control. It manifests itself in the extreme drabness of everyday life in Western countries. It mani-fests itself in the ugliness and vulgarity we see on every hand, and of course, it manifests itself in the actual virus illnesses. On the other hand, the partisans are everywhere, of all races and nations. A partisan may simply be defined as any individual who is aware of the enemy, of their methods of operation, and who is actively engaged in combating the enemy.

Eric Mottram: Burroughs's central analogy is the relationship between addict and agent or pusher—who is himself an addict—where addiction is the compulsive consumption not only of heroin but also of aspirin, tobacco, alcohol, religion, T.V., sex, and the rest. The central relationship is between consumer, product, and agent in a loveless and parasitic system in which people manipulate each other. Burroughs's irony is that this conflict relation-ship is needed and developed by human beings, and could even be extended as it is in *The Ticket That Exploded* and *Nova Express,* to inter-galactical warfare.

Burroughs: So we start right to work, making our headquarters in the land of the free where the call came from, and which is really free and wide open for any life form, the uglier the better. Well, they don't come any uglier than the intolerable kid and your reporter. When a planet is all prime to go up, they call in "I and I," to jump around from one faction to the other, agitating and insulting all the parties before and after the fact, until they all say "By God, before I give an inch, the whole planet goes up in chunks." Where we came in. You have to move fast on this job and I and I is fast. Jumping in and out of a hundred faces, in a split second, spitting his intolerable insults. We have the plan, what they call the Board Books, to show us what is what on this dead whistle stop. Three life forms, uneasily parasitic on a fourth form, that is beginning to wise up, and the whole planet absolutely flapping. Hysterical with panic. The way we like to see them. "This is a dead easy pitch," the Kid says. "Yeah," I say, "a little bit too easy. Something here. Something wrong, kid. I can feel it." But the Kid can't hear now. "Well," he said, "We need a peg to hang it on. Something really ugly, like virus." So he takes over this news magazine. "Now," he said, "I'll by God show them how ugly the ugly American can be," and he breaks out all the ugliest pictures in the image park and puts it all out on the subliminal, so one crisis piles up after the other, right on schedule, and I and I's whizzing around like a buzz-saw and that black Nova laugh of his, you can hear it now down all the streets, shaking the buildings and skyline like a stage prop. But me, I am looking around, and the more I look the less I like what I see. For one thing, the Nova police are moving fast and heavy, like I never see it anywhere else. But I and I says I have the copper jitters and turns back to his view screen. "They're skinning the Chief of Police alive in some jerkwater place. Want to sit in?" "No," I said, "only interested in my own skin." And I walk out thinking who I would like to see skinned alive.

Eric Mottram: It's clear from that parody of popular thrillers, that Burroughs's warfare is a kind of pleasure, a power situation which relies on the interaction of relief and dependence. This is his standard relationship. Heroin or Junk, as it is called, transforms the body's cells, and already in his first work, *Junkie,* Burroughs used this change as an allegory of the transformations of power. Similar metaphors of control can be found in Poe, Hawthorne, and Henry James; they seem to be a peculiarly American fictional material. The receiving homosexuals therefore become types of puppet men under ventriloquist power—the dummy and his controller. The typical scene comes to a climax in both *The Naked Lunch* and *The Soft Machine* in the executioner enacting with the victim a complex pleasure-pain ritual of power which involves useless orgasm which is permitted by the state. Their act obscenely parodies sacrificial fertility rituals. It therefore exposes what those rites become in a society whose moral standards are based on expediency and hollow traditions. Burroughs satirizes all forms of licensed crime-executions, war-killing, extreme capitalist exploitation, the use of one man by another—and their hypocritical justification by an endlessly self-justifying state.

His extreme term for this pride is a phrase similarly used by Alexander Pope in his satirical poetry: "insect lust." But Burroughs invents a range of imagery which reduces the humans not only to the insect, but to the Crustacean, the parasite and virus images of human lust which culminate in the ultimate virus of cancer, the central modern image of predatory disease. The actions of Burroughs's novels take place in the jungles of cannibalistic, South American horror, or in cities which are a maze of tensions and pleasure-seeking. His decaying interlocking buildings and streets read like a heightened version of Dickens's or Kafka's fantasies of urban tyranny. But within this double scene of jungle and city, Burroughs can be mercilessly, gruesomely funny; his sharp farcical humour operates against the agents of power in the addicted world, against lawyers and judges, financiers and priests, doctors and psychiatrists, in order to expose the ridiculous idea of absolutely free society. Ultimate freedom means a society constructed of sadist and masochist relationships, fantasy living through pleasure-pain situations of inflicting and receiving. Burroughs is acutely aware, as who is not in mid-century, of the meaning of concentration camps, armed service regimentation, censorship, racialist dreams, and entertainment industries, all working for similar ends—all, eventually, giving the consumer what he wants or training him to want what he is given: Burroughs is satirizing all forms of spurious security which dehumanize the human . . . Burroughs's image of junkie-dependence describes the nightmare force of totalitarian bureaucracy. The helplessness of the drug addict is the image of free enterprise and its effects in a range wide enough to include the preying inroads made on human life by psychiatrists, surgeons, and businessmen, by the deliberate encouragement of inflated sex for anti-life purposes, the fear and criminality of the American white South, and even the housewife trapped in her so-called choice of soap-powders. To construct a fiction revolutionary enough to penetrate our defenses, Burroughs uses a variety of composition methods.

Burroughs: A Russian scientist has said that we will travel, not only in space, but in time as well, that is, to travel in space is to travel in time, and if writers are to travel in space-time and explore the areas opened by the space age, I think they must develop techniques quite as new and definite as the technique of physical space travel. Brion Gysin, an American painter living in Paris, has used what he calls cut-up method to place at the disposal of writers the collage used in painting for fifty years. Pages of text are cut and re-arranged to form new combinations of word and image; that is, the page is actually cut with scissors, usually into four sections, and the order re-arranged. In writing my last two novels, *The Nova Express* and *The Ticket That Exploded,* I have used an extension of the cut-up method I call the fold-in method. A page of text, my own or someone else's, is folded down the middle and placed on another page, the composite text is then read across, half one text and half the other. The fold-in method extends to writing the flashback used in films, enabling the writer to move backwards and forwards on his time track . . . This method of course is used in music where we are continually moved backwards and forwards on the time track by repetition and rearrangements of musical themes. I am not a dadaist and I don't believe in being obscure: I feel that a writer should be comprehensible to any intelligent reader. Actually, perfectly clear narrative prose can be produced using the cut-up and fold-in methods. But what does any writer do but choose, edit, and re-arrange materials at his disposal? What I would like to emphasize is that this is a technique, and like any technique will of course be useful to some writers and not to others, and in any case it is a matter of experimentation, not argument.

William Burroughs Interview

Jeff Shero / 1968

This interview was originally published in three installments in *RAT: Subterranean News,* Oct 14–17, 1968 (pp. 1, 10–11); Oct. 18–31, 1968 (p. 10); Dec 13–Jan 2 1968/9 (pp. 5, 14).

William Burroughs, author of *Junkie, Naked Lunch, The Soft Machine,* and *Nova Express,* has control of English prose. Son of Burroughs Business Machine Inc., Burroughs alias Bill Lee, projects a conspiratorial image of the Universe. (The rulers of the planet will shrink history of the human race onto microfilm, shove it up their ass, split in space ships. The earth blows up beneath them.)

Burroughs's forthcoming book, *7 Hertz,* is based on his recent investigation of scientific research.

Burroughs has lived in London for the last years. He took part in the Chicago demonstration while covering it for *Esquire.* He was in the lines and was tear gassed in Grant Park. He observed that many people seemed to get "contact highs" and that tear gas didn't seem to be an effective weapon against determined people.

This interview took place in Terry Southern's apartment. Burroughs wore a crisp brown suit which he referred to as his costume. Taping was delayed by the obstinate *RAT* tape recorder so we walked to a nearby store and bought a tape for Burroughs's machine. We talked about the movement in this country.

Burroughs has decided to move his apartment from London to New York so he can directly involve himself in the movement.

After several hours we went for dinner where Burroughs talked about *7 Hertz.* A discussion on the importance of publication of secret research and a summary of *7 Hertz* will appear in the next issue of *RAT* containing the second half of the interview.

After dinner we continued our discussion mellowed by a few drinks. The *RAT* recorder decided to run so we did another hour of taping. This time the conversation though less analytical was more lively. William Burroughs spoke of his personal conflicts as well as rapping humorously on subjects such as the Queen of England. "Bugger the Queen."

RAT: Do you see the kind of revolts going on in the Western countries now as reformist in nature, or are they revolutionary?

Burroughs: I'd say revolutionary.

R: You think that in the end the struggle's going to be for power?

B: Well, I don't know about that. It seems to me to be the most anti-political revolt that I've ever seen and perhaps that there's ever been in history. That is, a revolt more aimed towards getting rid of something than simply substituting something else. When I was in college in the 1930s, there were only two alternatives—either you were a Marxist or you were supporting the establishment. But these people are not, by and large, Marxist.

R: Were you a Marxist?

B: I was not, no. Because it seemed to me just substituting something else. I've never been a Marxist.

R: Do you think—you've written a great deal about the future—do you believe that it's possible to make a revolution which has a decentralized character, which is in some way determined by participatory democracy in the kind of age in which a technology is being developed which tends to centralize coordination, communication . . .

B: Yes, because by the very fact that we have this communication system, it can be decentralized to any point if you seize the—of course, the first thing for any revolutionary party to do would be to seize communications. Who owns communications now, controls the country. Much more than it's ever been true in history. Of course, that's always been a revolutionary maxim.

R: More important than the army.

B: More important than the army. *Much* more important than the army.

R: If the French students . . . had controlled the TV and the radio, do you think they would have been more successful or won?

B: Possibly, if they had known exactly what to do with them.

R: And what kind of things should they do with them?

B: Well, there are highly developed techniques that are already in use. I've endeavored to describe some of them in this book I'm writing now. It's a little bit complicated to go into at this point. The techniques exist for manipulating the mass mind and they are very definite techniques.

R: More sophisticated than TV commercials.

B: Yes. Much more. But you don't really know what's going on on TV on a subliminal level. Of course, they aren't allowed to use subliminal techniques any more. But simply as a matter of juxtaposition.

R: Well, in our country, you view the kind of development at Chicago where the press essentially supported the demonstrations.
B: Precisely. There was an example of the students, the revolutionaries, winning an engagement by very definite steps to get the support of the press.

R: How do you see that developing? Because there's been considerable debate among the radicals.
B: Well, everything really played right into their hands from the very first day when the newsmen were beaten up by police.

R: In Chicago, you see the deciding factor being that the press got beat up.
B: Certainly.

R: That doesn't give us much of a basis for coverage in the future.
B: No, but of course in Chicago we have this Mayor Daley who's left over from the nineteenth century, an old political boss with the sort of pig idea of authority at the end of a nightstick. He was already, I understand, prejudiced against reporters, for some reason or other, was he not? Hasn't he previously had some bad publicity?

R: I'm sure of it.
B: So there was a set-up that I don't think exists here.

R: What does it say about power, how it's exercised in the United States, if the people who run the Party in power run this country, run the war, make such bad decisions about choosing the location for their convention, and choosing a strategy to contain demonstrations? Shows they're incapable, it seems to me.
B: Well, there's no question of that. No question of their inefficiency.

R: It seems to me that there are a lot of parallels between Chicago and Vietnam in that they applied the same strategy of massive pinpointing of force at every point of insurgency in hopes to eliminate the insurgency before it could grow. And they achieved exactly the opposite effect in both Chicago and Vietnam. . . . Were you surprised at the attitudes of most of the demonstrators?
B: No, the only thing that surprised me at all was that they seemed to be

much more organized and much more determined than I had anticipated, coming as I had from England. I've been away for three years now. Three years ago there was really nothing comparable. I would say that the whole picture has changed immeasurably in three years.

R: That was functional organization. It was organized not on a static bureaucratic level, where people gave orders down from the top.

B: Yes. There again was something I found quite impressive. And something that I had not seen before. Possibly something that has not existed before.

R: It seemed to me in Chicago there were a lot of people of liberal mythology. There were these kind of McCarthy kids who constantly said, "Well, let's not be provocative towards the police because they'll attack us." After the police had already attacked on about five different occasions without provocation. It seemed that there was this whole residue of the liberal ethos still maintained in a large part of the crowd.

B: True. That I agree with. But of course there's a tremendous contrast in my mind between say, the old Communist demonstrations in the 1930s which were also definitely organized to get incidents, incite incidents. They wanted the police to fire into the crowd or do something like that. But there you felt it was all being run on an absolutely bureaucratic basis. This man gave an order. That man gave an order. There was no question of these orders right down the line—right down to the people who were going to be the incident. I didn't feel any sort of bureaucratic, hierarchical control, and yet there was organization.

R: It's been thought a lot of times that the way the Movement in the United States is organized is a way that it's impossible for the authorities to contend with. Because, at any point, if they arrest a hundred leaders, it really doesn't affect the Movement.

B: Yes. Well you could see that from the results achieved. There's only one thing that has occurred to me and that is that the Yippies are rather too conspicuous.

R: What do you mean?

B: Well, they look like Yippies. Particularly to move from one place to another. Now, for example, anybody with a beard, anybody that looks like a Yippie is being turned back at the border of Mexico. They wouldn't let Allen Ginsberg in . . . until he went to the Consul. He finally did get in.

R: How important do you think the symbols of rebellion are?

B: It seems to me it depends on the state of the rebellion. When it gets to a certain point, the rebellion must go underground. How long does an underground last that has a uniform? Certainly to get from one place to another. If they want to get into Chicago or into another town, now what would the strategy be if this should start to happen in another city? The strategy would be to keep them out of the city. And how would they keep them out of the city? Because they would be able to spot them. Now if they all put on business suits and went into the city, by the time they were in there they could put on anything they liked. But to get in, they should look like anybody else. . . . Suppose they wanted to go to Mexico for a confrontation. If they did, that would be quite a different confrontation from Chicago. Mexican police are apt to use machine guns rather than clubs. But they wouldn't get in if they were there in trailer trucks with signs all over them and beards, etc. They'd be stopped at the border. Most countries in Europe are not letting them in now.

R: And you were inside the Convention Hall itself, too.

B: Yes, yes.

R: Did you ever talk to any of the delegates? Do you think they had any sense of the upheaval going on outside?

B: I didn't talk to any of the delegates. We tried to talk to Senator McCarthy and even tried to talk to Governor Maddox, but it was quite hopeless. You couldn't even get a call through to the Hilton. All the switchboards were jammed. Oh, I was there—it just seemed to me just a terrifically boring scene. You couldn't hear what was being said. And it was bullshit if you could hear it. But all the political reporters said the same thing. The speeches were just incredibly boring.

R: Do you think that people with power in this country have much understanding of the upheaval brewing beneath them, not just among the young people, but among the blacks? Do they have a real understanding?

B: I would say on a top level, very much so. I think that power in this country is held by very, very few people. Very few indeed. The people like presidents, and mayors and people like that do not hold power. They're only front people. The rich people have always let the politicians hold the ostensible positions of power so long as they did what they were told. And that has not changed a bit. The real orders are coming from an oligarchy of extreme wealth. And that would be very few people. And I think very definitely they know.

R: If that's the case, one can surmise that the eastern wealth was behind Nelson Rockefeller. And of course if Nelson was running for the presidency, you'd expect David Rockefeller and all the powers of the Chase Manhattan Bank to be behind it, and yet Nelson ran what could be called a pathetic campaign.

B: Well, I don't think that you could assume that they ever intended to put in Nelson Rockefeller. I mean what they intend is not apparent at all on the surface.

R: And so the forces of contradiction move forward. What do you think is going to be the overall strategy of the people in power? How do you think they're going to try to handle it?

B: It's hard to say. They've never been as threatened as they are right now from so many quarters. My guess will be they'll start a nuclear war.

R: You expect that.

B: Yes.

R: With China.

B: Yes.

R: In concert with Russia or with Russia sitting it out?

B: If they can get a nod from Russia that they'll stay out. Because if they took on both Russia and China, we would be pulverized.

R: And the function of such a war would be to maintain their absolute power like they did during the McCarthy era, after World War II. To develop complete obedience.

B: Well, of course, as soon as they'd declared war, it would be a police state, one hundred per cent.

R: Would you call America a police state now—with trappings—liberal trappings?

B: That's a difficult question. It's becoming more and more a police state. There still are forces in operation in opposition to the power of the police. And if it's what you might call one hundred per cent police state, that means that there are no forces of opposition.

R: At least overt opposition.

B: Or effective opposition. There may be an underground. But I mean there are no official forces. Nothing like, say, the civil liberties unions or anything like that to oppose this police power. There's very little that opposes police power in Russia. The writers' union is, I believe, the strongest semi-official agency in opposition to police power in Russia.

R: The Movement forces in this country tend to identify with Third World countries. Countries like Cuba and Vietnam. As opposed to the Soviet Union and Eastern European countries. And the kind of direction they'd like us to head is some way the direction that, say, Cuba and Vietnam are trying to head. Do you think that's applicable at all?

B: Well, I think there's a bit of romanticism in it. After all, Che Guevara and Castro—really their tactics date back to the nineteenth century: Effective in areas which are a hundred years back like Latin America but I don't think too effective in a highly industrialized country like America.

R: Is the outcome of our struggle based on the number of humans we can mobilize, or is it largely dependent on the new technology?

B: Well, I wouldn't say dependent on the new technologies. And rather not the people you can mobilize, but the number of people you can disconnect.

R: Were you surprised by that uprising in France?

B: I was surprised by it. I had been in France and I thought the French had the young people really down. I was surprised by it. I was delighted by it, in another sense, because I thought "By god, they're really breaking up."

R: You don't think the latent potential is sitting in England?

B: I hope so. I would love—I would love—to see something like that happen in England. But it must happen after they get rid of the idea of this bloody Queen. As long as they have any subservience to that image, it's hopeless. I think I can get 5,000 people in Trafalgar Square saying "Bugger the Queen." That bitch. Sitting there soaking up the energy of forty million people. People say, "The Queen isn't important. She's just a figurehead." A figurehead of subservience. A figurehead of kissing her ass. Worthless wench. She should be sweeping floors.

R: The Pope's that way, too. You think about the Encyclical about birth control. The Pope is even more evil because he influences more people.

B: I wouldn't say necessarily more evil. . . . Here's a woman who's fucked up a whole country. . . . That's what has held England back.

R: Well, the control by America to a great extent too. I mean like Wilson can't come out against the war because America is propping up the pound.

B: Yes, but forget about Wilson. Just think about the Queen for a moment. That is what is holding the whole of England back . . . the subservience on the part of a great majority of the English people to this bitch.

R: What do the young people think about it?

B: The young people. A lot of them of course are against the Queen. But as I say there's no hope for them until we have five thousand people out in Trafalgar Square screaming "Bugger the Queen."

R: That was a pretty effective chant, you know, in Chicago, "Fuck you, LBJ."

B: In America we don't hesitate to say "Bugger LBJ." But to get people in England to say "Bugger the Queen," that . . . (searching pause) . . . Oh my God. They've been so conditioned to revere this worthless bitch. It really shocks them, this idea of saying "Bugger the Queen." But until they can say that, there's no hope for them at all.

R: The royalty of Europe sticks together and . . .

B: If you ask me, at this point in history what could be more ridiculous than a Queen?

R: It's even against the law to say anything against the Queen. It's the only sacred thing. More sacred than God. You can say "Fuck God" but not the Queen. . . . How about the Rolling Stones, could they lead a movement like this?

B: I think it could be done. I think there are a lot of people in England who think it should be done. It would be the first indication that something was going to happen.

R: Do the Rolling Stones consider themselves to be revolutionary?

B: They really do, baby. They're all out to help, and on our side completely.

R: They can't come to this country, can they?

B: No, because they are facing drug charges. They're one hundred percent behind us. I know them all. . . . I talked with this student tactician. He said the only thing to be done was to put out a pamphlet covering the royal family with vile abuse, just saying the worst. And the reaction from the establishment would tell us where we'd have to go.

R: Just like the reaction in Chicago ripped the facade off the Democratic machine.

B: That's what he meant exactly.

R: People within the system, they're afraid of risking.

B: They're terrified. I don't care at all. I don't care if I die tomorrow, it's not important to me. . . . I find it increasingly difficult to write. I've written. I've written. I've written. I've written. Tired writing.

R: Is it even hard for you to write non-fiction?

B: Hard for me to write anything. I can write on order, that is to say if *Esquire* says can you write this piece, I can write it. But for years, for years, for years, I wrote all the time, all the time, all the time. But now, I just don't feel like writing.

R: You mean you'd wake up in the morning and write most of the day?

B: Yeah. I just don't want, I just don't feel like writing. I'm bored with it. I mean I'm finished. I don't want to write anymore.

R: And now maybe you're beginning your activist career.

B: I want action. I want to get out and do something. I'm tired of sitting on my ass. I want to get out and stir up some trouble. I want to make trouble for everybody!

R: Not for everybody.

B: For all the people in power. . . . I'm tired of sitting on my ass and writing. I want to get out and do something.

R: Writing has its force, but it's not as great as people think. Many times people just . . .

B: It's much greater than people think.

R: You think so?

B: Yeah. And I will continue to do that when it's necessary. You know I think that writers write what happens. Let's face it, things don't happen unless somebody writes it.

R: Well, you can get too far extended. Because the Yippies had a split. Abbie Hoffman believed that anything that became reported was reality, and began just creating things that never happened. But then your credibility is . . .

B: Maybe you can get out on a limb, but writers do write what happens. Now I remember—you see Graham Greene wrote *The Quiet American,* a great book. I hadn't read it before, but I got to the point of the milk bar.

R: The what bar?

B: The milk bar. You know the explosion in the milk bar. And he's looking around in this milk bar. And I said wait a minute, time to hit the floor. I knew when the explosion was going to take place. . . . I hadn't read it yet. And that was about two years before the same explosion happened in the milk bar in Algiers. I had been in Algiers eating in this milk bar. Two months after I had left there, about two years after Graham Greene had written this scene, the explosion occurred. There was this incredible scene with people with their legs all splattered with Maraschino cherries and ice cream and blood and brains and this and that. In this very milk bar where I would eat. A friend of mine who was there at that time got to the milk bar just at this time and saw this scene. Of people with their legs all splattered with Maraschino cherries, passion fruit, pieces of mirror . . . Wow! Graham Greene had written that.

You see, writers don't want to take responsibility for these things. They have to. A long time ago I said, "The soccer scores come in from the capital." You remember the soccer riot in Peru, 300 people dead. There'd be different scores coming in. 300 people. 320. 330. That's what it referred to. When the soccer scores come into the capital one must pretend an interest.

R: Why do you think Genet is the only one who has taken responsibility for his characters? What about Kesey? You know Kesey's book, *One Flew Over the Cuckoo's Nest*?

B: Sure. It was simply that Genet was one of the first ones to state this, that every author has the tremendous responsibility for his characters.

R: So . . . it was Genet that recognized it?

B: Genet recognized it, yes. Possibly before I did. But if the soccer scores are coming into the capital one must pretend an interest. That was ten years before this soccer riot happened.

R: Maybe the reason for you wanting to become more involved is Genet's idea?

B: Yes, because I realized what writers write happens. Therefore writers have responsibility to be there. And to do something about it.

R: How do you apply that to Styron in [*The Confessions of*] *Nat Turner*? He probably doesn't understand at all the revolt. Its feelings. Its internal sensibilities. He isn't there really.

B: Perhaps he doesn't realize the full responsibility writers have.

R: Do you agree with what I said about Styron? What do you think about him writing *Nat Turner*?

B: Well, excuse me. I'm not in a position to say much about that because I glanced at the book. That's all. But I do feel you see how in Chicago Genet said to writers they must support the youth movement, not just with their words, but with their presence. I agree with that one hundred percent.

R: Do you think it's going to press other writers in the country to make a commitment?

B: I think it should.

R: Maybe even women like Mary McCarthy.

B: Yes. I feel this very definitely, and I'm willing to say that wherever anything is going on I'm willing to support it with my presence.

R: There's this whole detached liberal literary scene here, where they all go to cocktail parties and intellectual events and talk to each other and express sympathy, but never do anything. Work for Eugene McCarthy—the level they get involved at is very respectable.

B: Well, I feel it's time for every writer who's worth his salt to put his ass where his mouth is. If he is standing for freedom, get out there and stand for it. I'm willing to do this.

R: In your life you've always been willing to live your life along the ideas you've developed. Was that true at Harvard?

B: At Harvard I was just a completely beat down person with no idea of who he was or what he was. And I'd rather not think about it ever since then. It's too disgusting to think about.

R: Have you ever been back there?

B: I've never been back there.

R: What did you think about World War II?

B: Nothing.

R: It didn't seem like a patriotic fight everyone should be involved in?

B: No. . . . What I was trying to convey is my whole past in something I have nothing to do with. I am now a completely different person. Anything in the past as far as I'm concerned is of no importance.

R: It's funny how lives build. For a lot of writers as they've gone on it became more and more difficult to write. A lot of them never did break with the past. Look at Fitzgerald. Fitzgerald kind of fell apart. Hemingway had more and more trouble writing.

B: Well, excuse me, Fitzgerald was a great writer, but he was completely tied up in the nineteen-twenties.

R: Well, take a guy like O'Neill. He dealt with the most basic themes.

B: . . . I'm not associated with any period. But Fitzgerald was a very great writer associated strictly with the nineteen-twenties. What a writer he was.

R: You represent something of an anachronism, because the revolt in America is very much the revolt of a generation. And yet you have more radical ideas than many of the people in the movement. How did that come about? You went to Harvard, you came out of a wealthy background, you were in Tangiers for a while. You've written about how you were hooked on drugs in Tangiers, and how you came out of that. What was the kindling of your ideas?

B: It was a long process. It certainly began with my middle class upbringing which I always found extremely stultifying and confining. I felt out of place, that I wasn't being offered anything of any value by my environment. And then when I began to write, the satisfaction crystalized into very definite criticisms. And I always went much further than so-called radicals. I felt that it wasn't a question of substituting one establishment for another. For example, the whole idea of a nation is an anachronism. That is, they take a piece of real estate, draw a line around it, and that's a nation. Immediately, they have trouble with the people on the other side of the line, and they have to spend all their money on armies and the police and so on. Now, this concept of a nation has outlived its usefulness by about three hundred years. It had a certain use in breaking up the feudal system. But now it's an absolute anachronism. And a league of nations, a world government, isn't the answer at all. That's merely perpetuating the error.

R: We must destroy nationalism?

B: Well, the basic formula of authority is a nation. . . . What is their authority based on? Their authority is based on the fact that they are the officials in one of these hunks of real estate called a nation, large or small. That is the authority formula; and that is the formula that must be broken. You have families, clans, countries, nations. The order is quite clear.

Of course in the old stone age tribes, they had bad folk on the other side of the river and they'd bash each other's heads in every now and then and it was comparatively harmless. But it's not harmless now. Like all basic formulas, it is very difficult to break down. It's hard for people even to think in other terms.

R: How would you start out?

B: With the possibility of any people withdrawing from the country, setting up as it were states within states. I think that is the line that is going to break it down more than anything else. Like say if the Black Muslims were to form a separate state, in this country, with international affiliations. And if a large number of people defy the whole question of boundaries, thousands of people walking across borders without passports. That sort of thing seems to me quite a useful form of demonstration.

R: The nation state is the ideological basis for authority of the people in power and we're living in a society in which that basic family unit from which it is copied is breaking down. Families are breaking down, marriage is becoming an obsolete institution. Do you think that that erodes away, on a basic level, the ideological basis?

B: To a considerable extent, but it can survive that. Because once the thing is set up they have the power. They have the police. They've got the communications, and so on.

R: In Chicago we differentiated a great deal between the police and the National Guard; The National Guard, many of them being guys who didn't want to go to Vietnam.

B: Certainly. I know John Brandt, one of our team, is in the National Guard. I was with *Esquire,* and he was a man from *Esquire.*

R: Our belief is that as the system breaks down we'll not ever be able to rely on the police, but the army or the National Guard will begin to become dysfunctional or disaffect to our side.

B: Well, that has always been true in all liberal revolutions. The army is much more liable to go to the people than the police. Now for example in Colombia—I was there during the Civil War—the reactionary government considered their army so unreliable they built up a second army of the Polizia Nacional. They were not police, properly speaking, but were like a special army. It's always been true in all Latin American countries that the police are sort of the palace guard of the establishment, or the people in power, and the army has always been considered potentially unreliable.

R: Do you think the war in Vietnam was necessary, or was it a mistake?

B: It's ridiculous. The French were in there for God knows how many years, and finally had to pull out and then repeated the same mistake in Algeria. And we step in when you could see right on the face of it from Algeria and the French occupation of Indo China it's a war that can't possibly be won. It shouldn't have been fought in the first place, but just even from that point of view, we can't even win it.

R: It's speeded up the breakdown in this country.

B: Of course.

R: We keep returning to the question of the elite. The people who manage the society aren't doing a good job of it.

B: Well, I don't think they are trying to do a good job. In other words, they're not trying to do a job that is good for you, or for anyone but their own very specialized interests.

R: But it doesn't seem like things are working in their interest.

B: Well, I don't know. They think in rather long range terms. Now, it's pretty necessary for the establishment to keep a war going somewhere. And you will find that since the end of WWII there has always been a war going on somewhere. I think someone wrote a book on that thesis, that society must have wars, economically for one thing. That was one of the reasons they were so reluctant to stop the war in Algeria; they were afraid of what would happen if they did.

R: Do you think socialist countries like the Soviet Union have the same needs?

B: Not to the same extent, no.

R: A great deal of what you write about deals with the microcosm, with the individual and how he functions. It seems to me you're saying a revolutionary has got to really understand the totality. A person who is going to be a revolutionary has to understand how technology can be used against him, to manipulate the individual.

B: Oh, certainly. And how they can be used to disrupt.

R: If you were going to give some pointers, say if you were going to teach a class and you were to say here are the ten most critical things . . .

B: I go into this very thoroughly in this book which I hope will be out quite soon. I haven't given it a title yet. It will be published first in France by

Delfon. He had the idea—sent someone over to see me. And I put the book together with the help of his man, who is translating it into French, and as soon as he's finished with the French translation, then we get the English version here and in England.

R: It seems to me that the establishment would be wary of publishing the book since in the short run it might make them some money, but in the long run it will be very damaging.

B: Well, but the people who are publishing it are not the establishment. The publishers are not the establishment at all. They are always publishing things that are contrary to the wishes and interest of the establishment and getting in trouble for it. In fact, I would say, by and large that publishers have done more against the establishment than many other groups. They completely broke down censorship here.

R: Would you say the same for universities?

B: Mostly negative, because they are getting all their money from the establishment. You see, publishers are not. They are getting their money from the reading public. But universities, being endowed, the board of trustees and all that have always very definitely been supportive of the establishment. They have to be.

R: What about high schools?

B: Much the same, with some exceptions, I suppose. Some are more liberal than others.

R: The whole schooling process inculcates the old values. Do you think we should attempt this setting of our own schools or do you think this would not succeed on a scale which . . .

B: I think that would be a very, very important step. If you could set up schools where they really taught people something.

R: What would we do in those schools? We don't want to have a teacher stand up and lecture the students.

B: Well, it all depends what the students want to learn. Of course there are definite techniques for learning things. The army found out a lot about learning and teaching in WWII when they had to have a whole bunch of people to do something in a very short time. For instance, they wanted people to learn a language. They had to teach it in six weeks. They didn't want people to know one word in that language. There are techniques for teaching but they're not using them in high schools. They're not trying to teach anything there. They're just fooling around.

R: And what would you think of a school that tried to combine experiences of the real world, that didn't set off school as kind of a safe island?

B: I think the whole educational system is about three hundreds years back. There's no application to what they're learning. Unless there is application, unless you are learning something you can use, there is not much point to it. The only education we have that is functioning is technical education, where there is definite criteria of whether it is a success or failure. If he's training to be an engineer he can either install an electrical system or build a bridge or he can't. But there is no such test as regards, say, the social sciences, sociology, anthropology, psychology, general education.

R: In the future as the struggle continues, it is being characterized a lot as the anti-authoritarians against the authoritarians.

B: I would agree with that. I think this is a liberal revolution, comparable to the revolution of 1848, and will probably precipitate as widespread a reaction, reactionary movements.

R: But it seems to me as the struggle goes on, people with power will use science to more thoroughgoingly possess the minds of the kids they are trying to teach, use all the latest techniques of psychology or electronics to . . .

B: Electronics particularly. They are doing it already and have been doing it for some time. All important discoveries in electronics and in psychology, advanced psychology or psychology that really works are all top secret.

R: And chemicals too. Give people chemicals that make it easier to induce certain ideas.

B: Of course. I've written a number of articles on this subject which are going to be collected into a book which will be published in France quite shortly, and then here very shortly afterwards, in which I have said that the Cold War is being used as a pretext to monopolize all sorts of fields of knowledge and new discoveries particularly along the lines of electronics and particularly along the lines of controlling thought. . . .

R: As the high school movement in this country develops, what sort of demands do you think they should make to the schools—for take-over? For dismantlement?

B: Well, school is a farce. As I say, the educational system is three hundred years back. The demands should be that all this knowledge which is now top secret classified should be made available to everyone. That is what the demands should be. They've got the knowledge.

R: Concretely, in a school like the Bronx High School of Science there is no way to mobilize the school around turning over electronics.

B: They don't even know what to ask for yet, but they can be told what to ask for: things like infra sound, for example. No one ever heard of it. It's low sound, not high sound. An infra sound installation turned up full blast can kill everyone within five miles and destroy all buildings, those red brick buildings. I don't know if it would knock down reinforced concrete. This is a very easy thing to make. Anybody can make one. On the other hand, what can be done with low concentrations is something that hasn't been fully investigated yet. The man who has done this work is Professor Gavereau of France.

R: They now have a technique developed for the anti-riot tanks, to use sound to immobilize demonstrators.

B: Well, that may well be infra sound.

R: It hasn't been put into effect yet.

B: You see, ultra sound, high sound, goes right through an object, through a person, but this you can't hear. It is below the level of hearing. It is below thirty vibrations per second.

R: Can the operator point it or direct it in any way?

B: Yes. There are ways in which he can be protected from the effects. On the other hand, it can be turned on from a distance. He wouldn't even have to be there.

R: As they begin to use clubs and mace the demonstrator becomes like a knight in armor.

B: He looks more and more like the police. The coming uniform is unquestionably blue crash helmet, shoulder pads, and aluminum jock straps. Of course those are very primitive weapons—mace, tear gas, and clubs, very primitive weapons indeed.

R: But built into the establishment are the rigid patterns of the past, and if you look at Chicago, it is much the same technique of suppression of demonstrators as anywhere in the world.

B: Certainly.

R: So do you really believe that they are going to institute these techniques they have developed?

B: Undoubtedly, undoubtedly. Certainly they will use them if the opposition finds out about them and starts using them too. The thing about infrasound is that there is nothing complicated about it. It is simply a large whistle connected to an air hose. Anybody can do it.

R: What sort of cost?

B: Oh, what you can get in a junk yard . . .

R: Is this Professor Gavereau a radical?

B: Well, nobody knows, but I saw an article about it in the *Sunday Times* in London which seems to me a real leak because I'm sure all governments will be experimenting with it if it works. Normally it would be top secret classified, surrounded by barb wire, security checks. So how it happened to leak out I don't know, but it did. These things do.

R: Do you think that middle class people are likely to give up the comfort they have been trained to desire all their lives, in any large scale?

B: I don't know how many millions have already done so. After all, all those Yippies and hippies come from middle class backgrounds for the most part. I mean they could be living quite comfortably if they wanted to, have good jobs, and have the suburban house. I think there are lots of people in this society that realize that this so called comfortable life is absolutely dull and so stultifying they simply don't want it.

R: If the schooling process is critical to the shaping of people's desires, much like advertising shapes your desires—you want to possess that thing they advertise so eloquently—if that's breaking down, if say at the age of eighteen, when a person is reached by the movement, if all those years of training can be broken down, then we're tremendously powerful.

B: Well, it's breaking down almost unbelievably, not only in America, but throughout the world. Now look, say twenty years ago, a young man in France of middle class family: there was just no question as to what he was going to do. He was going to become a lawyer or doctor or a professor and that was it. And the young people themselves were completely sold on it. This was the only alternative, the only thing for them to do. There was a lot of that too when I was in Harvard, that same attitude of, well, you graduate from Harvard and then you go into a career and that was it. The way in which that is broken down all over the world, say in the last twenty years I think is truly amazing. I don't think it has any parallel in history. Of course people say, oh well, these people will all be advertising executives in ten years. I don't believe it for one minute. I don't think so. If they'd have wanted to be advertising executives, they would have made those steps as soon as they graduated from college, or high school, or whatever.

R: . . . We have often judged that a good bit of our power doesn't come just from the ideas, but from the whole kind of sexual vitality of the movement, that the basic sexuality in the movement is lacking in America. Do you see that?

B: Yes. I wouldn't necessarily use the word sexual, but certainly you feel the vitality. I remember in the anti-birthday party you felt a tremendous vitality there. This seems to me is lacking completely in most American audiences, in most Americans for that matter.

R: How about this thing like the pig. Say, they're all pigs. Vote pig for president . . . And then we'll serve him to the people after the election, rather than have the people serve the pig.

B: Jokes have their place.

R: Do you think they're important politically?

B: They can be very important, yes. I'm working on a purple-assed baboon for president. They talk, they move their lips in speeches. You can't do that very well with a pig.

R: In Rio one time they elected a hippo or a rhinoceros. That caused great consternation among the officials so they had another election and he won again. And this was all on write-in vote. It was for something like Mayor.

B: Yes. Those political jokes I think have their place.

R: The movement is developing a different definition of news, a different description of what is important. If we controlled a television station, our news would be substantially different than Walter Cronkite.

B: If we controlled television, then we control America.

R: What would it mean if we had one station? We could, like the German SDS, make a demand for TV time. And then escalate our demand to a whole channel. What would happen if we got a channel?

B: We got to get them all. As soon as we get them all, we control this whole stupid middle class. We've got America.

R: You think the war is going to be fought out among the middle class and not among the poor?

B: Yes. Of course there is a way of eliminating the whole stupid middle class.

R: Yah, you know, you saw Daley's program. They talked about how there were plans to even put LSD in the water supply. Of course that's unworkable because LSD is an acid and a base neutralizes it, so it never could go through the water system. But let's say something like LSD could be put into a water supply of a city, what do you think it would do?

B: Well, I'm all for eliminating the whole stupid bourgeois middle class. I think the whole strata should be eliminated.

R: Do you think as human beings they are even alive?

B: They're not alive. They're talking tape recorders. It's not a question of eliminating human beings, it's a question of eliminating walking tape recorders.

R: Their children are realizing that too. That's one reason long hair scares them. So, their own children are throwing it up, saying, "Your lives are nothing. Your lives are dead plastic existences."

B: Yeah. It's not a question of eliminating human beings, it is a question of turning off tape recorders.

R: Do you think the poor are less tape recorders?

B: Much less. They've been up against something. They have to be alive to survive.

R: And the middle class person has to be dead to survive. Because if he's alive, he gets kicked out. He gets squashed in the system, like a bug among the gears. If the guy in the office shows any streak of originality, of individuality, then he's crushed. Because his boss can't stand that. If he questions why should I push these papers around, Bamm, he's crushed.

B: Those alive in this system are the people on the bottom.

R: How about the people on the top? Is Mayor Daley alive or is he cut off from all human emotions? What is he like?

B: Well, Mayor Daley is alive so long as the system is alive. He is a completely evil Irish toad.

R: Do you see Johnson or Daley as more evil?

B: It's hard to say. Daley is right out in the open, 100% establishment. A completely evil Irish toad. There he is. WOW! Johnson isn't very subtle though. He shows his scar on television.

R: Do you think there is a real difference—Kennedy, both Kennedy's—they seemed alive. They projected some kind of vitality. Do you think that's true?

B: They did. That's why they killed them. They had something the others wanted.

R: Do you think that Sirhan acted as an individual in killing Robert Kennedy?

B: Oh what bullshit. Now look. He killed Kennedy because Kennedy said he supported Israel. Well, both Nixon and Humphrey have come out supporting Israel. It's bullshit.

R: Who do you think was behind it, CIA?
B: No idea, no idea at all.

R: Nobody believes that Jack was shot by Oswald, or Oswald acted alone anyway.

B: There's no question of that. Oswald acted alone. That thing reeked to high heaven.

R: They can't force too many lies on people though. There's a certain point when people begin to realize that it's not true, that the whole thing is a fucking lie.

B: What is that point?

R: It's coming soon. You begin to look at it . . .
B: I hope so.

R: . . . Sixty percent didn't believe the official version which was in all the newspapers of Kennedy's death. That's the majority. That's a lot of 'em.

B: That thing just reeked to high heaven. It was so raw. It just reeked to high heaven. . . . It seems to me that the most important point of student revolt should be a demand that all research—the results of all research—be made public with specific reference to so-called top-secret government projects.

R: If that's critical to maintain the present order, then we're as likely to get that demand as the Communists in the '30s, were to get nationalization of industries.

B: Certainly, but there is also the point of confrontation. And as soon as you focus a real beam of attention there, then there are going to be professors working on those projects who will reveal what is going on; there are going to be leaks and so on. But if you allow the administrators to divert your attention from this area, then such research will continue and such research will be used for monopolistic, authoritarian ends. And the more attention that is focused, the more possibility there is of a breakdown in security.

R: You think that we can mobilize people around that issue?

B: Undoubtedly you can. I mean, there have been many instances of this already—of professors working on these projects that had scruples about what they were doing, and some of them said they didn't see why it should be top secret. There's been quite a bit of questioning in the area.

R: And yet people who do that research are integrated into the values and comforts of the establishment; they feel that they really need that $20,000 a year salary; they need the equipment to maintain their research, etc.

B: Undoubtedly, that's just why you have to put all the pressure on them you can. Those are the places to picket.

R: Why do you say picket, rather than . . .

B: Attack? Disrupt, attack, use any tactics necessary with the demand that we want to know what's going on. Because, see, it's often easy—once you get any idea of the nature of the research—it's often easy for someone who knows anything about it to figure out what's going on there.

R: How does your life as a writer fit into that situation? How do you see your role in making that kind of an attack?

B: Well, my role has always been to guess what's going on in these research centers. And I think I have made some fairly good guesses. Because many of them have been substantiated. Guesses that I made ten years ago are being substantiated now as to precisely what they can do in the way of thought control, for instance.

R: Sometimes you get offers from universities to be a resident fellow or something of that sort.

B: Never have had such an offer.

R: Is that true? That's quite an honor in itself.

B: No, never attained one cent or any offers.

R: That's a great honor. Because that means they don't think you're safe enough.

B: No, I imagine not.

R: And so, really, maybe we shouldn't be buoyed by a place like Chicago. Because Chicago was fighting it all out in the old tactics. The nineteenth century ones.

B: Those have their place. Without that, you have no apparatus for disruption. But the point is to concentrate on important targets. No, I think a great deal was accomplished in Chicago. Particularly in showing what could be done through the mass media. But now I think the emphasis should be secret research taking place in universities.

William Burroughs: *Penthouse* Interview

Graham Masterton and Andrew Rossabi / 1972

From *Penthouse* (March 1972), 44, 46, 52, 122. Reprinted by permission of *Penthouse,* General Media Communications, Inc.

With the same analytical facility that led his grandfather to build the world's first effective adding machine, William Seward Burroughs is intent on shaping what he believes will be the greatest step forward in human thought for centuries. His philosophies have their foundation in his legendary novel of drugs, violence, and homosexuality, *The Naked Lunch*—which despite its violent sensationalism was a serious study of how one man can exert control over another. Burroughs, now 57, is convinced that mankind's cerebral future lies in electronic manipulation of the brain—a science still in its earliest infancy, but with limitless (and frightening) potential. His latest ideas, though a natural extension of his former work, show that Burroughs is ideologically a moving target. Past attempts by the beats and the hippies to embrace him as the mysterious Father of the Underground have failed simply because Burroughs *belongs* to no-one: he considers himself a citizen of the whole world, if not the universe. His novels talk with bland familiarity about entire planets and endless galaxies. In this exclusive *Penthouse* interview conducted in Burroughs' London apartment by Graham Masterton and Andrew Rossabi, he discusses the mental engineering which can make or break mankind.

Penthouse: It's nearly ten years since you gave a satirical but graphic description of totalitarian control in *The Naked Lunch.* Do you think your visions of a decade ago are any nearer reality?

Burroughs: *The Naked Lunch* was a science-fiction idea but is now absolute fact, mainly because of the development of electrodes which can control the brain. If anyone has these electrodes planted in him—and there may be many ways to do this, not necessitating an actual surgical operation—he can be made to think, feel, or even experience, anything that the manipulator of the electrodes wants. He can be made to make involuntary movements: to pick something up against his will. Also to feel fear, or sexuality, or any other emotion. Where such control is possible, the question arises of who is

39

to exercise it. Once someone has the control box he is in complete control of anyone fitted with electrodes.

Penthouse: But a would-be dictator would need to overcome the practical problem of implanting such electrodes.

Burroughs: One can imagine all sorts of scandalous ways of doing it. "Doctor had 100 Love Slaves" . . . he would lure young girls in for minor operations, plant electrodes in their brains and that would be it. Or an equivalent to electrodes could be produced possibly by a virus, by microwaves or by an electro-magnetic field. We also know that certain chemicals stimulate particular brain areas, such as apomorphine which stimulates the back brain, the hypothalamus. These brain areas haven't been carefully plotted but of course they can be on an encephelographic machine.

Penthouse: How much are we herded already without electrical means?

Burroughs: There is always psychological influence, there's nothing new about that. All governments, all religions have used it throughout history. The point is that now the means of control are much more efficient. We have computers. We have populations exposed to exactly the same images and words, millions of people every day. So the opportunities to control are much more potent now than they have ever been. The same development started with the industrial revolution, the same thing has happened with weapons— they've become more and more efficient, which of course has brought a whole new, almost a biological mutation, into revolutionary tactics. Anyone can go down into his basement and make a spear or a club—but they can't make automatic weapons, they can't make tanks, they can't make dive bombers. So while the methods of psychological control are much more effective, so are the methods of physical control. Since the people in control hold heavy weapons, 1% could keep down 99% if it came to that. This was all implicit in the industrial revolution: first, that we'd have larger and larger populations, which means more and more control. Just take the job of feeding all these people in London—think of the technical job of doing that and the number of people involved in it. When Jerry Rubin and people like that talk about dropping out and doing their thing—my God, how many people could live on what England could produce? As you have larger and larger populations, more and more elaborate apparatus is needed to give them even the necessities. The bigger the thing gets, the more control you need just to run it, just to keep it moving, just to keep it from foundering completely. The nature of control is also hierarchical. You can't really get anything done unless someone does it, unless someone gives the orders. So I don't think it's too far-fetched to say that the orders now are given by fewer and fewer people.

Penthouse: So society would be even more hierarchical if electrode control were to reach a high degree of refinement?

Burroughs: Who's going to use it, and how, is an absolutely open question. I cannot think of any existing society in whose hands I would like this power to fall. Suppose the people in the Pentagon could condition people to believe in what they believed in—or what they pretend to believe in, at least—and turn everyone into decent Americans. That would be *horrible.* This control would be more than just a case of pressing this button here and this button there, this could be a whole computer program. Scientists have already wired up an ape's brain to a computer. Now the ape's brain can give orders to the computer, and initiate action in the computer; then the computer can chew this over and shoot it back. In other words it's a feed-back between the computer and the brain. The computer can be programmed to erase past conditioning—this has been done with apes—or to accentuate any particular aspect of conditioning. You would have a computer program that would determine a person's entire actions and feelings, and the person would be physiologically incapable of doing anything about it. But the fact that this knowledge is all out in the open is encouraging, because these developments need not be used for control at all.

Penthouse: Are there other potentialities in electrodes?

Burroughs: Yes, you could attach yourself to a computer and have all its advantages: it would figure out, for example, everything you owe, accounts receivable, bam, bam, bam, and give you an answer. Say two businessmen are doing a deal; one would tune into his computer and say: "No, it's no deal unless you up 55 percent. I've just been through the whole thing with my little computer here."

Penthouse: Wouldn't such facilities make us too reliant on automation? Surely there are still many capabilities within the human mind itself to be explored and developed?

Burroughs: Yes, but the way to explore them is to assume control of them. People can now do in a few hours what a yogi took 20 years to learn, that is to control their brainwaves, and learn to implement them at will. This facility of course would offer you protection from mental intrusion—you would know immediately whether any tampering was going on—so automation need not necessarily lead to a control situation. There are several centers for autonomic shaping, as it's called—Joe Kamiya in San Francisco and about three or four others. It seems to me that this is one of the most important developments in recent years. You see, you can cut your learning time for anything immeasurably by a feedback with autonomic shaping. You might be able to learn to become 12 dan in judo in just a few hours instead of 40 years. The use of this knowledge for learning processes hasn't even been gone into yet.

Penthouse: Autonomic shaping sounds a good deal more accurate in its effect than hallucinogens.

Burroughs: I've frequently noted a regrettable vagueness in most accounts of hallucinogenic drugs. People feel they are part of everything, all that sort of thing, vague pantheistic feelings. Huxley said a lot of it in *The Doors of Perception,* that hallucinogenic drugs simply make you more aware, on all levels. But over a period of time I think they can lead to another area of non-awareness, to a sort of hermetic, dreamland state which is not what they are there for, as Huxley expresses it in *The Doors of Perception.*

Penthouse: So does the use of autonomic shaping supersede hallucinogenic drugs?

Burroughs: Not only that, it supersedes any form of psychotherapy—any form of psychiatry at all. We can find the actual brainwave of any obsession and locate it accurately, so there's no need to fool around with any kind of verbal investigation. Autonomic shaping can teach people how to control and produce at will different brainwaves which correspond to different emotional states. They can also teach them to control digestion, blood pressure, rate of heart beat. These things are of course symptoms of anxiety. Remove all the physical symptoms, and anxiety cannot persist in the absence of all its physical manifestations, muscular tension, and so on.

Penthouse: Is this the beginning of genuine telepathy?

Burroughs: Immediately. Immediately, because two people could stimulate the same brain areas, and be in instant communication. But remember that mental communication of a sort is in operation all the time. I don't know if you've ever watched two horse-dealers. I happened to be present at one of these transactions. You could just see the figure in someone's mind. I would say, well, I know now what figure he's going to quote and what figure he will accept. That was the whole point of all this feeling over the horse and chat back and forth, to find those things out. And of course all gamblers pride themselves on the intuitive faculties and also on being able to shut out other people's mental feelers. That's the poker face of course, the block. So I think basic communication is very much an accomplished fact and a part of every-day life. Another thing: I think your ability to read other people's thoughts is dependent on your ability to suspend your own, to suspend any preoccupations you might have. In other words, it's simply a matter of giving your full attention. This ties in with hallucinogenic drugs. I think that insofar as they help people to keep their eyes open or open their eyes, they're valuable. But if people made a habit of keeping their eyes open at all times, then many of the phenomena of hallucinogenic drugs would be produced simply by extending their own awareness, simply by seeing what is going on when they walk down the street. The reason why most people do not see what is there when they're walking down the street is that they've just got a sound-track turned on, so they're walking along in their own haze of world images.

Penthouse: You've studied Egyptian hieroglyphs and pictorial forms of communication. Would these be the language of telepathy instead of normal words?

Burroughs: Yes, though Joe Kamiya is talking about developing a whole new language which would not only be a pictorial but a symbol language. This has been in existence for a long while in mathematical physical sciences and computers, but would now be developed as the language of telepathy.

Penthouse: This is obviously going to bring people into much closer mental contact than at any time in history. Will this lead to any kind of cultural shock?

Burroughs: There's a book by an anthropologist called Carlos Castaneda, and it has become a sort of underground hippie classic. Anyway, it tells how an old medicine man had some far-out hallucinogenic drugs. One was so powerful, and removed all covers, and a young man took it and was terrified and he asked the medicine man: "What did I look like?" The medicine man said: "I didn't look at you." He said: "No two people can take the little smoke and look at each other and live." What he is saying there is that no two people can *really* look at each other and live, and remain people. We can of course biologically defend ourselves against something which we cannot assimilate. But when they'd taken a drug, as in this case, there's no way in which they could defend themselves against the knowledge of what they were and what they represented: they can't look at each other and they can't look in a mirror.

Penthouse: Won't this effect hamper the progress of mental training?

Burroughs: I don't think so. Allegedly what everyone wants is to be closer to other people. If people sometimes seem to want to get further and further apart, it's because contact is unpleasant. It's not a question of contact going too far; perhaps it doesn't go far enough, and perhaps it goes in all the wrong directions.

Penthouse: Could autonomic shaping be used to cure drug addiction?

Burroughs: It could certainly be used to implement any cure, we don't know to what extent. For example, withdrawal symptoms are undoubtedly accompanied by certain brainwaves. To what extent these brainwaves could be tuned out and relieved by autonomic shaping or by direct electric brain stimulation, we don't yet know. Sleep can be induced by passing a light electric current through the brain in what the Russian scientists who are working on it call "electrosleep." This is not as precise as either electric brain stimulation or autonomic shaping because the sleep centers are not being directly stimulated. I would say that electric brain stimulation would be much more the answer to drug addiction, though you might be able to isolate some alpha waves and get the addict to control them, but by and large when someone is in that disturbed a state it's not a time for *teaching* him something.

Penthouse: Do you think that governments are making serious enough attempts to end addiction?

Burroughs: Certainly not in America. It's too big an industry. It's beneficial to the government because it greatly increases their range of control. That is, if they can make millions of people criminals by Act of Congress then they are brought under police surveillance. You've heard about this theft of FBI files; well only about 1% of those files had to do with serious crime.

Penthouse: On that basis you would expect official resistance to an effective electrical method of curing addiction?

Burroughs: When something like that gets going it isn't too easy to stop it. The time to stop it would have been before they obtained money for their research and published their results. And of course we don't yet know whether electrical stimulation *is* the answer.

Penthouse: What is the best available cure you know for drug addiction?

Burroughs: Apomorphine. But, you see, apomorphine causes certain brainwaves, and these can be isolated. The brainwaves of any drug could be isolated, and presumably you could simulate the effects of any drug electrically. You could do this particularly with apomorphine since it has distinctive brainwaves because it stimulates the back brain. The effects of barbiturates could be most easily stimulated; they are only sedatives working on the front brain.

Penthouse: Does this mean we could end pain electrically?

Burroughs: Yes. Theoretically, all a drug does is make certain changes, and those changes are electrical and they are chemical as well. Any electrical change has its chemical and metabolic correlants.

Penthouse: Are the means for autonomic shaping within the grasp of ordinary people?

Burroughs: The equipment is not all that expensive, depending on how elaborate it is, but you could set up a pretty good unit for about £12,000. There are also little machines that just isolate alpha waves, called Alphaphones—they're selling for $175 in the States and hippies are buying them. But you have to remember there are innumerable brainwaves, and the difficulty is in finding them, isolating them and learning to control them. This is the means, though, of making the first detailed map of the brain.

Penthouse: There are obviously large areas of the brain which are not used or have no apparent function. Will autonomic shaping allow us to develop them?

Burroughs: According to the methods we have now, we can only reproduce brainwaves that are actually being emitted, and if the area was totally disused you might not have access to it. If it were occasionally used, then you would. But undoubtedly learning to recognize brainwaves and emit those you have would bring others into range. That is, if you learn what is on top of this disused area, probably more and more that area would come into use.

Penthouse: Do you believe that any time in our history man was capable of using more of his brain?

Burroughs: There is no evidence in what we call written history, but remember that what we call history only dates back 7–8,000 years. The human species, according to anthropological evidence, was in existence in its present form from between 500,000 and a million years, so what in hell were they doing the rest of the time? It would be unwise to assume that they had no artifacts, nor made artifacts of a different substance. We know about the

Ice Age, and the fact that there was much more plentiful vegetation and that people might have been entirely vegetarian—in fact the appendix is a residual organ of an entirely vegetarian period. A completely vegetarian society might not have had artifacts, or they might have been made totally of wood, or been destroyed in the Ice Age.

Penthouse: Do you give any credence to the *Chariots of the Gods* theories that man's mental development was helped along in prehistory by visitors from other planets?

Burroughs: I've never seen a flying saucer. I think people's lives are very grey, and they like to imagine things like this. Also there's the dangerous myth of the "wise saviour who comes from without." That was the myth that undermined the Incas in the face of the Spaniards, the Great White Gods. They thought these people had come to do them some great favour, but they hadn't come to do any favours, they'd just come to do *them*. Should anyone arrive from outer space under such auspices, I think we would do well to be on our guard, as the Incas would have done to be on their guard when the Great White Gods started cutting off their hands to find out where the gold was.

Penthouse: Do you consider that our own space travel has helped our mental progress?

Burroughs: I think it was worth any amount of money that might have been spent to leave the earth and realize that there is another context, that we can actually leave the context of this planet. Of course, in its present form, the thing is not a great adventure offered to youth because so few people can participate and it's so terribly expensive. It isn't like, say, the great days when they started discovering America, when anyone could get together and outfit a ship and try his luck. This is way beyond even the largest private fortune.

Penthouse: What effects do you think space travel will have on astronauts? Will they become completely dissociated from earth, both physically and mentally?

Burroughs: No conditioning can maintain its force in the total absence of the stimuli that produce it. There is no doubt that leaving the earth for any period will give you an entirely different viewpoint simply because the whole context that was keeping your present viewpoint in operation would no longer be working on you.

Penthouse: Not many of the present astronauts seem to have noted this effect.

Burroughs: That's because they send up people with very limited perceptions. I think it's deliberate. They don't want anybody to get up there who would really be aware of what was happening. The pick very normal, very conventional human beings indeed—both the Russians and the Americans. But they've still let out some rather strange things at one time or another. One of them had the feeling that while he was, I forget how many miles, above the earth he could see what was going on in someone's back yard: that he had kind of telescopic vision as it were. He dismissed that as an hallucination. It would be interesting if they discovered any new principles of space travel so that more people could take part—like in the early days of aviation, with people building spaceships in their backyards. That would be an interesting scene. I mean, we are doing it in the most cumbersome way possible at the moment, lifting these tremendous weights from one place to another and then walking around in an aqualung.

Penthouse: Is it conceivable that autonomics could train our minds enough for us to levitate spaceships by the power of thought alone?

Burroughs: I think it is a fundamental confusion to think of mental force as exerting any influence or pressure on matter seen and conceived as matter. If I saw this cup in front of me as no more real than what goes on in my mind, then I *could* move it, or at least I could move the *image* of it, but I would not be moving the *matter* of it. That's the contradiction. Science is always being hampered by idealized concepts like this.

Penthouse: How quickly do you expect electrode control to be in general use? Or might it be held up by such old-fashioned concepts of scientific development?

Burroughs: It will be held up by the Christian attitude to sex.

Penthouse: Why?

Burroughs: Because this attitude prevents investigation. It shuts out any really objective study on the subject. Wilhelm Reich started studies with electrodes attached to the penis, and found that actual electrical impulses were given off and that these could be graphed, and that a pleasurable orgasm would show a different graph from an unpleasurable one. His experiments were totally disregarded and he was persecuted on account of them. A statistical approach like Kinsey's simply tells us the *incidence*; it doesn't tell us anything about the *phenomena*. But we are now in a position to investigate everyone's sex life through the study of brainwaves and autonomic shaping. There is no reason why everyone's sex life shouldn't be completely satisfactory—as satisfactory as they potentially can make it.

Penthouse: Do you foresee that the whole process of sexual intercourse could change in methodology?

Burroughs: It may well be. We don't know what sex is, so the process it represents may be doing something that you don't think it's doing at all. We'll find out.

Penthouse: How could electrodes improve sex?

Burroughs: Well, socially, first of all. Here's one person over here and another person over here, and they want something sexually but they can't get together and society will see that they don't. That's why the law persecuted magazines carrying advertisements for sex partners. But advertisements are a crude method; the whole process could be done on a computer. People could be brought together on terms of having reciprocal brainwaves. Everyone could be provided through the computer with someone else who was completely sexually compatible. But it's more important than this. If the human species is going to mutate in any way, then the mutations must come through sex—how else could they? And sooner or later a species must mutate or it dies out.

Penthouse: What would be the most desirable mutation that autonomic shaping could bring about?

Burroughs: Simply removing any past conditioning that has a subconscious effect on our behaviour would tremendously increase human efficiency. I don't mean that people would be emotionless, but they would not experience emotions which they felt to be alien to them. They would be able to identify and control the sources of their emotions.

Penthouse: So you think the principal mutation will be in the brain rather than in the body?

Burroughs: A mutation in the brain could rapidly bring about a mutation in the body. It is my theory that evolutionary changes do not take place gradually over a period of years or millions of years by natural selection. They take place quite suddenly in a few generations. Darwin came in with these theories and postulated long periods of time in which changes could occur. But geographical features like the Himalayas do not arise gradually;

they occur very suddenly indeed. There have been mammoths found frozen with their food undigested in their stomachs. They were frozen solid in a matter of seconds.

Penthouse: How much change can we withstand within our present social system?

Burroughs: It seems to me that once a formula on this planet gets started, gets firmly established, it's very hard to change or replace it. And the more mechanized and overpopulated the world is, the more difficult it becomes. Overpopulation is the problem which makes all the other problems insoluble. There just isn't enough to go round. There is no solution except to cut down the population. You can expand productive capacity, you can accommodate more people in South America—that's the only underpopulated country. But what then? There's the idea of moving into the sea. But according to Cousteau, the sea is already 40% destroyed by pollution. The more people you have, the more pollution you have and the fewer resources as a result. That really is an insoluble situation unless they get together on a world-wide population control. What is the purpose of all these millions and millions of people? England could comfortably support about 20 million and they've got 50 million. Another absolute, another cul-de-sac that the whole world is in, is that the creaky social systems would not support any basic discovery. So instead of discoveries being immediately exploited they're covering them up. Did you read *The Biological Time Bomb*? Well, that's his great point. He says these things aren't 300 years from now—they're 10, 15, and 20 years. Genetic control, prolonging life—whose life is going to be prolonged? We've got so many people now that we'll have to stack them up like cordwood if they all live to be 135. But what government could decide? In other words, the social system which dates back, my God, to the 18th century at least, could not support discoveries that are here or will be here in a few years.

Penthouse: We're being deprived, then, of useful and labour-saving inventions?

Burroughs: Oh, my God, yes. I was brought up to believe in the tradition that the good product would always find a market. But it's not in industry's interest to put out a pair of socks that won't wear out. The original nylon socks would not wear out. I wore one pair through South America, walking through jungles and water. Now they wear out in a week just like any other socks. It's not to manufacturers' advantage to produce good products. It's not to their advantage to produce houses that won't wear out or anything else that won't wear out. Industry and government don't want these products because they would disrupt a very creaky social system. In other words, scientists are producing new inventions much quicker than the social system can possibly absorb them without great disruption.

Penthouse: Do you feel then that our present society has outlived itself?

Burroughs: What we see is a whole series of practically insoluble problems and the simple fact is that there isn't a single politician who can get up and say the whole thing is basically wrong. They can't say that it won't work. We see world-wide inflation which could jump suddenly geometrically and have millions of people out in the street overnight . . . pollution . . . radiation—we don't know how far that's going, they're all lying about it . . . and of course there is a war which seems to be getting worse. Animals usually die out because the conditions that make their life possible cease to exist—a change of climate and whatever kind of food they have disappears. Control of our minds, our society and our environment may be the answer. I think the human species has reached a point where it's going to have to take some form of forward step or we're just not going to make it.

Penthouse: Mr. Burroughs, thank you.

William Burroughs: *Rolling Stone* Interview

Robert Palmer / 1972

William Burroughs lives in a sparsely-furnished flat near Piccadilly, in London. The neighborhood is comfortable, but Burroughs works and lives with a minimum of encumbrances: typewriter, table, plain chairs, bed, books, a cassette machine. Brion Gysin, Burroughs's friend and long-time collaborator, lives upstairs in surroundings that include Moroccan rugs, a few of Brion's paintings of Marrakesh and the desert, a stereo, two Uhers, and an extensive library of sounds which Brion recorded in Morocco. It's a quiet place for a man who has made some of the biggest waves in contemporary literature: from the early autobiographical *Junkie* through the influential *Naked Lunch* and early experimentation with psychedelics, lightshows, and the surreal cut-up writing technique.

The interview took place in Brion's flat, which he recently occupied after an extended residence in Tangier. Tapes of trance music, Fifties rock and roll, Sun Ra, and Coltrane, furnished by Brion, Charlie Gillett, and myself played in the background and various young people, many of whom Burroughs met while teaching at the University of the New World in Switzerland, were in and out.

The first question I asked Burroughs concerned infrasound, air vibrations that oscillate at less than ten Hertz, or ten vibrations a second, below the range of human hearing. Professor Vladimir Gavreau of Marseilles has developed and patented a "Death Ray" using these inaudible sounds, but Burroughs has suggested other uses for them. He gave me, as explanation, a clipping from the *National Observer*; he had underlined the following passages:

". . . the team built a giant whistle, hooked to a compressed air hose. Then they turned on the air.

" 'That first test nearly cost us our lives,' Professor Gavreau says. 'Luckily, we were able to turn it off fast. All of us were sick for hours. Everything in us was vibrating—stomach, heart, lungs. All the people in the other laboratories were sick too.' "

You've mentioned the possibility of using this infrasound in music. Could you expand on that?

The point is that here it has been developed as a weapon. Now there are possibilities, say at the borderline of infrasound, experimenting with very slow sounds, that you could produce rhythmic vibrations that would not necessarily be fatal or unpleasant; they might be quite the contrary. In other words, it would be another step toward producing—as all music, all writing, all art is really attempting to do—is to produce very definite psycho-physiological effects in the audience, reader, viewer, as the case may be. Of course they've never been completely successful in that. If they had they would have taken over years ago. But if they were successful, presumably you could kill a whole Shea Stadium full of people in their seats.

There's been a great deal of work done recently in autonomic shaping and brain waves—people now being able to reproduce brain waves and to learn to control heartbeats, etc. That is, people can now learn in ten hours what it takes a yogi 20 years to learn, if they want to. They have a battery now that they can plug people into which records brain waves, blood pressure, heart beat, resistance, tension, etc. As far as I know, no experiments have been done along these lines while listening to certain music to see what the actual physiological and psychological correlates of that music are and what happens when someone listens to it.

So I wanted to suggest the possibility of very precise musical experiments.

How would that relate to Moroccan music? How precise do you think Moroccan trance music is at producing definite states?

Certainly Brion knows a good deal more about that than I do, but I would suggest the same experiments be carried out. If you knew what a state of trance was, what the brain waves, blood pressure, heart beat and so forth was, then you'd have some idea as to how to go about producing it, and also you'd know when you are producing it and when you're getting close.

What about your experiments with projections?

I've said quite a lot about that in *The Job*. Anthony Balch and I did an experiment with his face projected onto mine and mine onto his. Now if your face is projected onto someone else's in color, it looks like the other person. You can't tell the difference; it's a real mask of light. Brion was the first to do this at the rue Dragon in Paris, and no one would believe how it was done. They thought it was all a film.

Jan Herman was here with his little video camera outfit and we did quite a precise experiment, which was: Anthony brought up the Bill and Tony film, I sat there, and he projected it onto my face, which was rephotographed on the video camera, but that faded in and out so that it would be that face, then fade back to the now face, so that you got a real time section. We wanted to project it onto the television screen from the camera, but we couldn't because the cycles were different; Antony and Jan Herman were fooling around and they managed to fuck up the television. But even seeing it on a little view screen, it was something quite extraordinary.

Another experiment that Antony and I did was to take the two faces and alternate them 24 frames per second, but it's such a hassle to cut those and resplice them, even to put one minute of alternations of 24 frames per second on a screen, but it is quite extraordinary. An experiment I always wanted to make was to record and photograph very friendly and very unfriendly faces and words and then alternate them 24 frames per second. That should have quite an upsetting effect, I think; you don't know until you actually do it.

What about your story in The Job *about the Buful Peoples projecting baby faces on their audiences and making them run out and shit in the streets? Is that your idea of what the effects of such an experiment might be?*

They could be. It's a question of getting a sufficient degree of precision. If I really knew how to write, I could write something that someone would read and it would kill them. The same way with music, or any effect you want could be produced if you were precise enough in your knowledge or technique.

How would that work with writing?

Exactly the same way. What is a writer trying to do? He's trying to reproduce in the reader's mind a certain experience, and if he were completely successful in that, the reproduction of the experience would be complete. Perhaps fortunately, they're not that successful.

Can words actually be that successful?

I think so. I think words possibly above all.

Back to music: do you feel that a pop group's dependence on costly equipment and establishment media makes it difficult for these groups to disseminate an anti-establishment, anti-control message?

I think the dividing line between establishment and non-establishment is breaking down. People tend to say that if an underground paper succeeds and makes money, that it is now part of the establishment, or if pop singers make a lot of money and their records make a great deal of money for big companies that they are now part of the establishment, but the underground or any

movement is not going to succeed by not succeeding. If you publish an underground paper that nobody reads or produce music that nobody listens to,
there's no point. And if people do read your paper or listen to your music,
then you are subject to make money.

*Do you think the force and amplitude of rock can make it a force for libera-
tion, regardless of the lyric content?*
   I would say so, very definitely. And potentially a tremendous force, in
view of the experiments that I have suggested.

It's hard to say how much it has to do with the words and the lyrics.
   Very difficult to say. I usually can't hear the words.

*Well, some groups, like the Rolling Stones, purposely mix the words down in
the track.*
   [Alfred] Korzybski [the semanticist] pointed out that one of the basic errors
of Western thought is the either/or proposition, which is implicit in our language. "Are they broadcasting an anti-establishment message or are
they . . ." Well, they might be doing both at the same time quite well. Or all
sorts of variations. Really it's not an either/or proposition.

And it might affect each listener differently.
   Right. But the mere fact of the number of people reached and the fact that
these people are young people and therefore the most subject to revolutionary
ideas makes them a terrific force.

*Do you think a group that's operating its own record company has a freer
hand than a group that must operate through a conglomerate?*
   I do not know enough about the music business to answer that question,
but a similar question: Do you think that writers would have more effect if
they published their own work? Definitely no. Because the publisher is set
up to distribute just as the record company is. If you're going to try to do all
that yourself—for one thing it's going to take up all your time, and you're
not going to do it as well. If you regard a record company simply as a means
of distributing or selling your records, as I regard a publishing company . . .
now that doesn't mean that record companies and publishing companies may
not have all sorts of establishment preconceptions about what they distribute,
and how hard they push it, but the question of taking over their function, for,
say, pop stars to do all that themselves, they wouldn't have time. Any more
than writers should take over publishing, although they've talked about it,
but nothing has ever come of it.

The media are really accessible to everyone. People talk about establishment media, but the establishment itself would like to suppress the media altogether. There was a program on television the other night where they came right out and said that showing wars and riots on television can produce wars and riots. There's never been a comparable situation, where whatever is happening anywhere people can switch on their televisions and see it. I recall in Chicago, the riot pictures were shown in the convention hall live as they were happening, and then all sorts of similar incidents broke out in the convention hall. Cops blackjacked delegates . . .

You'd say, then, that pop music is not a part of what you've called "the control machine"?

No; it might overlap with it, but it's not a part of it.

Bob Dylan has mentioned his interest in and indebtedness to your work, and several of your phrases have popped up in Rolling Stones songs—like in "Memo From Turner" from 'Performance.' Have they been into your work from reading, or from talking with you?

In both cases, definitely from reading. I have only met Bob Dylan on one occasion, and Mick Jagger about four or five times, occasions when there were other people around. There was no discussion of the books. So it must be from reading.

Do you have anything to say about the music of Soft Machine and the Insect Trust, groups which took their names from your work?

Not really. I've listened to the music. It's interesting. It's certainly very fancy music, very sophisticated music.

Do you think their music relates to your work in any way?

It's my feeling, none whatever, and I can say that with a clear conscience because they have never underlined the connection. I mean many people don't know that *The Soft Machine* is actually one of my titles, and they haven't mentioned it in their interviews.

What about the many references to popular songs in your books, especially some of the sequences in The Soft Machine *which are made up of song titles and lines?*

In writing, I see it as a whole set. It's got a script, it's got pictures, and it has a sound track. And very often the sound track is musical. I've used quite a bit of these techniques actually—that is, a sentence to be sung to a certain tune.

Do remembered tunes call up stronger and more specific associations than images that aren't related to tunes?

Very definitely, yes. That's what tunes are all about. I think it's pretty well established pragmatically that music is more precise in evoking a scene, particularly a past scene, than, shall we say, a neutral sound tack of words. But I notice that they are tending, at least in the Joujouka record [*Brian Jones Presents The Pipes of Pan at Joujouka,* Rolling Stones Records], toward deliberately using some of the background noise: shouts, dogs barking in Joujouka, the chauffeur snoring in another reference. That's something I think that has to be done with a very precise hand. In practice, the music is played on a location so that there will be background noise as well.

Would you like eventually to put out books with accompanying records? Moving the musical and sound references along with the writing?

I had not thought of that. I think that is a very brilliant idea, because people have put out books with a record. I even did that, but the record simply consisted of a spoken tape of the book, which in this case was a short book. But to me spoken tapes, you can just take so much. It's a different operation than reading. The idea of spoken books is completely unworkable. But I hadn't thought of a sound track, which could actually be quite carefully prepared, have some of the dialogue, etc., but be principally musical. Or some of the sound effects that people haven't heard, for example, like howler monkeys, the noise that howler monkeys make. It's like wind in the trees, but not quite, because there's nothing quite like it. And listening to it for a few seconds is much more precise than talking about it.

You wrote in The Job, *"It is now possible to decondition man from the whole punishment—reward cycle."*

I simply mean that if we had sufficient knowledge we could—any neurosis, any hangup resulting from past conditioning must express itself in actual physiological reaction patterns. Now recent experiments have indicated the possibility of simply reprogramming reaction patterns, as you would reprogram a computer. Scientists have attached an ape's brain to a computer, so that the electrical impulses from the ape's brain were giving orders to the computer—that is, setting programs which could then be fed back the other way. Now undoubtedly they could get to the point of simply reprogramming, and they might be able to do that in a matter of hours. We don't know because it has never occurred in history what a completely deconditioned human being would look like, or act like.

Or whether he would exist at all.

Right. But as Korzybski always used to say, I don't know, let's see.

What about the giant black centipede the deanxietized man turned into in Naked Lunch?

I have no reason to think that the result would be . . . of that nature. [Laughter] And if it is, what the hell, I mean we're all black centipedes at heart, so why worry about it.

Isn't it going to be very dangerous if, as seems likely, the people who control these techniques are the people most opposed to deconditioning?

That argument is always raised with any new discovery or any piece of equipment, but this equipment is not all that expensive, or difficult. Anybody can do it. It is simply a very small electrical charge in a certain brain area. Now scientology processing on the E-Meter—the E-Meter passes about a half a volt through the brain and body—is really sort of a sloppy form of electrical brain stimulation, because it consists of repetitive questions like, "What are you willing to talk to me about? What would you like to tell me about that? Repeat it and repeat it and repeat it." So the current is going through there, and they are directing that current toward a certain area. It seems to me that the best insurance that the discovery is not used for control purposes is people knowing about it. The more people that know about it, the less chance there is to monopolize it, particularly such very simple techniques as these, which consist simply of electrodes in certain areas, which anyone can learn.

Now the E-meter is in fact a lie-detector and a mind-reading machine. You can read anyone's mind with it—but not the content, only the reactions. But if I ask a specific question, say if I ask someone, "Did you fuck your mother? Did you ever fuck your mother?" I'll get a read. That's a protest read, maybe dreams, fantasies. But if after going through all that, it still reads, by God, he did. I mean there's no reading a lie detector on a direct question like that.

How does the machine read the subject's reactions?

It is a read on the needle. Takes quite a while to know how to work it, because you have all sorts of reads. You have protest reads. All sorts of things that can happen. You can have a stuck needle—very rare—where the needle doesn't move at all—that usually means you have a mental defective or something wrong with the apparatus.

Now there are many actions that you can get on this needle, but the commonest is a fall, which indicates a read, which indicates a reaction. A fall is only one reaction, there are others. There's a rise, which means boredom, inattention. There's also a floating needle, which is a point of release, which the scientology processing aims for. The needle floats back and forth, quite free.

What kind of effect is achieved on a personal level after you've learned to get a floating needle on very high-charged questions?

It's a very handy thing. If you've got a business associate and you get a strong read on his name, you're much more suspicious of him than you may realize, and usually with good reason. Any incident that disturbs you, if you run it to a floating needle, it sort of evaporates. I use it sometimes for that, not very much any more, but it works, very well. If some disturbing incident has just happened, you run it on there until you get a floating needle. It may take varying lengths of time, usually not more than ten or 15 minutes at the most. A floating needle means that it's gone for now. It may come back; it may disturb you tomorrow.

Now there's every evidence that a floating needle here would correspond to alpha waves. Joe Kamiya in San Francisco has done an awful lot of work with this autonomic shaping. He found that the way to inhibit alpha waves is to make anything very solid in your mind. All you have to do is to get a very clear picture of something, and that knocks out the alpha waves, which exactly corresponds to what happens here, there's something solid in your mind. So this could be cross-checked with those machines.

Aside from the value of the E-Meter, are your feelings on scientology pretty much what they were when you wrote The Job?

No. I've written another little article since then where I criticize the reactionary policies. And some of the old scientologists have defected and set up a new organization, protesting what they consider the fascist policies of Hubbard and his organization.

You've talked about hieroglyphic or picture writing. Do you feel that we're living out the end of the age of literacy, that people are going to be reading more and more picture books?

Well, that is not at all certain, because the actual picture magazines are all going out of business, *Life, Newsweek,* and all of them. There are ideas that I had which have not been borne out. Like when I said in the Academy Series, "recommend that the daily press be discontinued." Remember that the Acad-

emy Series was all predicated as occurring in 1899, and it was my feeling
that if certain measures had been taken then, the present mess might have
been avoided, that being an arbitrary date when it might have been possible.
But that is 1899, and this is 1972. I would certainly not recommend it now.

You're working on a comic book?
Yes. It is a comic book in that it has whole sequences of action in pictures.
But there are also about 60 pages of text, so it's something between a comic
book and an illustrated book.

Malcolm MacNeil is doing the art work. It is most closely similar to the
actual format of the Mayan Codices, which was an early comic book. There'll
be pictures in the Codices, and sometimes there'll be three pages of text in
writing that we can't read. We can read some of it, and we can read the dates.
A great deal of it was dates. The story concerns someone who has discovered
the control secrets of the Mayan books.

*Is the fact that the Mayan books were a control system, able to control the
people very precisely by having the calendar dates and knowing what stimuli
were going to be applied on any one day, your main interest in the Mayan
civilization?*
Yes. It was a control system that required no police, working on psychological controls. The priests were only about one percent of the population.
Priests and artisans would certainly not come out to more than five percent.
And how did they keep them working?

A good question.
Yes, come to think about it. [Laughter]

Any ideas how the might have done it?
Oh, very precise ideas, which I developed in the books.

Have you looked at the Mayan books here in London?
I've seen them all, but there were only three. You see, Bishop Landa burned
a stack of them as big as that rug. Somebody who was there grabbed three
out of the fire. They're burned around the edges. Those were the Dresden,
the Paris, and the Madrid Codices, named for the places where they now are,
in the respective museums. These turned up, I think, in the 17th century, in
some old bookshop somewhere. There are copies of those available. They
have them over there at the British Museum, and I went over and looked at
the copies with Malcolm, and then we had photostats made, but of course
those are not colored, and the originals are colored.

So there's no way of knowing what the others consisted of. I mean a whole civilization there went up in flames. It's as if you piled all our physics books, Shakespeare, and everything else into a pile and burnt the whole lot, and there was nothing left. We don't know what *is* left, you understand. The books that we now have, we assume, but perhaps not with good reason, were of a similar nature to the others.

Are you using any of the simplified hieroglyphic script which you gave samples and explanations of in The Job *in this new book?*
No. This is something that will have to be worked out, because there are all sorts of problems. I started trying to learn how to use Egyptian hieroglyphs, but picture writing at a certain point becomes incredibly cumbersome. The grammar is very complicated. To get around this and get something people could write, the scribes must have started at a very early age, I suppose like the Chinese, and I presume they each had a different style.

So you don't feel, as McLuhan does, that print is on the way out?
Well, no. What does he think is going to take its place? We know that physics and mathematics have whole non-verbal communication systems.

Apparently, he thought electronic media, spoken words, and pictures were going to take the place of print.
Well, you still have the problem of the actual prose. Now I see that in this book I'm doing with Malcolm, there are lots of sections which go just like film. But the text is really still essential. There are 60 pages of text; we're already having problems with translating that into images—not the problem that we can't do it, but the problem that it would take 300 pages to do it all. If we took every sentence and translated it into pictures, we'd have a huge book that would be way out of our budget. And there are things really that there's no point in translating into pictures, since they are much clearer in prose. There's another point where a page of prose can't do what a picture can.

Well, when you said, "Rub out the word," was that another way of saying, "Learn to use words instead of being used by them"?
That's one I will have to think about, because I've been thinking about a whole field theory of words. I don't think when I said that I had any clear idea as to what it would involve, or even what words were. I have a much clearer idea now, as to what would be involved, but it's something pretty

drastic. Of course it was Brion's suggestion originally. . . . Let's us say you would have to first have some idea of what the word is and how it operates.

I predicate that the word is an actual virus, and a virus that has achieved equilibrium with the host, and therefore is not recognized as a virus. I have a number of technical books on that subject, and there are other viruses that have achieved this. That is, they replicate themselves within the cells but they don't harm the cells.

Are you thinking of something like the proliferation of responses to Mailer's one article about Women's Lib?

Not precisely. I mean that a phrase can replicate itself and jump all over the world. It usually is a pretty simple formula. An example: years ago I found out that a cure for the common cold was Vitamin A in massive doses. I've used it for years, and it definitely does work. Well, someone seems to have a vested interest in the common cold, because Vitamin A was completely ignored and they started this Vitamin C bit. And Vitamin C is absolutely worthless for a cold. Now time and time again I've told people about Vitamin A and they immediately say, in exactly the same tone, "You mean Vitamin C." No, I don't mean Vitamin C, I mean Vitamin A. I got exactly the same tone of voice from a number of people that I spoke to about this Vitamin A. It's a turn-off on Vitamin A.

Where do you think that turn-off originated? Has it been implanted by some of these vested interests you spoke of?

I would say so, yes. Because at the time I made this discovery, I was working for an advertising agency in New York, and I said, "We'll put it on the market as a patent medicine, put a little something else in it." Absolutely, the company didn't want to know, and they said, quite frankly, because it might work. They said, "The AMA is very down on self-medications." They don't care if you take a little pill with quinine and this and that in it that doesn't do a thing, but if you take something that actually does something, so that you wouldn't need them . . . for years the doctors have been afraid of any really effective panacea, or effective medicines that anyone could use, which are also harmless, and so that they wouldn't have any necessity for a doctor's prescription.

Is this similar to the fear of apomorphine?

Yes, I would say so, because apomorphine and the possibility of synthetic derivatives which would have a much stronger action—and they could probably eliminate the nausea altogether—could be just such a general panacea against conditions of anxiety and intoxication: a metabolic regulator. Well, a drug with such general application is something that they would regard with considerable misgivings. It is not a dangerous drug actually, and if it were widely used, that would become apparent; there really isn't any necessity for a prescription.

Do you have any information on the introduction of weight heroin into Harlem and into the ghettos during the Forties, which seems to have been the beginning of the current problem?

I don't. You see, I was there in the late Forties and early Fifties, and the agents then were just beginning to bother addicts. Before that they'd been more interested in pushers.

Why did they start bothering addicts rather than pushers?

In order to spread it. That kept the pushers continually looking for new markets.

Do you see that as a very conscious attempt to spread it for certain, say political ends, or as a tendency of bureaucracies to perpetuate themselves?

Both. The tendency of bureaucracies is to increase personnel, of course. If you've got one person who isn't doing anything, then he gets five or six subordinates in, and so it goes. They tend to make themselves necessary.

Well, they're really cracking down on grass and psychedelics now, and causing lots of kids to turn to downers. They called last year the year of the downers, and none of my friends who used to take acid, say, once or twice a week, have had any in the last year and a half.

Brion Gysin: Did you get uncomfortable physical side effects from acid?

No. Some uncomfortable psychological effects occasionally, but never a bad trip or anything like that.

Well, I had two bad trips, and I would never touch it again. So really my considerations on acid are pretty personal. I think it's horrible stuff.

Why do you think it's horrible stuff?

So far as I'm concerned, it has absolutely nightmare reactions—symptoms of an extreme and depressing nature. I felt as if I was on fire. Maybe someone didn't get all the ergot out of it. But I just don't want to know about acid.

Do you think it can have value for some people?

It seems to, but then it's very dubious, because lots of people that take it all the time, *they* think they're benefiting, but I don't as an observer.

Gysin: Oh, but I think everybody should have taken it at least once. I don't think that anybody has to take it more, in fact. Essentially very square people have taken it just once, and it's made an astounding difference in their lives and their outlook.

Burroughs: But couldn't they have done the same with majoun [a preparation of hashish]?

Gysin: I don't think so. It doesn't take you quite as far out.

Burroughs: Not quite as far, but at least there I'm in an area that I can control . . .

Gysin: No, but the experience is to get into an area that you can't control and realize that you can go there and come back again.

Burroughs: I find both mescaline and yage, which has never been circulated, though it could be—it's just a question of chemical analysis—much more interesting. Peyote made me terribly sick, so sick I couldn't get any enjoyment out of it.

Do you have any ideas why many of the popular rock groups today are those that put out a wall of noise for people who come in with a wine and seconal head?

I don't know. I'm not really in touch with the situation in the States at all. I was there two years ago for six weeks, and before that I left in 1965. So since '65, I have only been back for the Chicago Convention and a brief stay in New York . . . it seems that alcohol is on the increase, as opposed to pot. I hear that from a number of sources.

"Ripple and reds . . ."

Oh my God, that is absolutely terrible. You really get some terrible effects from that. I've always hated barbiturates. I hate the sensation, and the most unpleasant hangover in the world is the barbiturate hangover. Worse than alcohol, and of course in combination . . . Also it's very dangerous. You know, alcohol ups the toxicity by about 30 percent.

Of the drugs people take to get high say, barbiturates, speed, cannabis, psychedelics—which ones do you think have some value?

Cannabis, I think, has the most value. Amphetamines, absolutely none. Barbiturates, absolutely none. I just can't see anything that could possibly result from either barbiturates or amphetamines that could be considered desirable from any point of view.

How about for going to sleep?

The worst thing possible, because all you're doing is further interfering

with the cycle of sleep and waking. OK, you take one nembutal and you go
to sleep. Before a week is out, you're going to need two. And also, you're
not going to sleep without them. But you'll sleep when you're ready to sleep.
I think barbiturates are really the last indication, except in certain extreme
cases. But apomorphine is very good for insomnia. It's frequently prescribed
in France. No addictive properties at all, and you never have to increase the
dosage, or depend on it.

Do you think cannabis has any effect on sleep or keeping you awake?
  No, the only result that I have noticed from cannabis is that if you smoke
a lot of cannabis, you won't dream as much. Now there it's quite obvious
that you're doing your dreaming while you're awake, and therefore you don't
dream as much while you're asleep. Now if I've been smoking a lot of cannabis and not dreaming, and then I suddenly don't have any cannabis, I'll have
very vivid dreams, every night.

*Do you foresee a situation of cannabis being legalized in the West any time
in the near future?*
  I don't know. It would seem to me to be a concession that they could not
afford to make. "Grant too many concessions and they'll ask for more and
more and more." It seems doubtful that they could risk making that concession.

*Many State laws have been amended to make simple possession a misde-
meanor, and there's talk of decriminalizing it entirely.*
  Oh, there's no doubt about it. Lots of politicians have been talking about
it. I don't know if it might happen. If America legalized it, everyone would,
because all the pressure's coming from America.

Let's delve into the past a little. Where and what was the "Beat Hotel"?
  Gysin: The Beat Hotel was in Paris at 9 rue Git le Coeur, just off the Place
Saint Michel in the Latin Quarter. For a lot of young people in Paris it was
more than a home. That's where the Beat scene in Paris was born. A Dutch
painter turned Allen Ginsberg onto it in 1956, I am told. I didn't get there
myself until 1958 when I ran into Burroughs on the street, and he told me he
lived in Room 15.
  The hotel was run by a wonderful Frenchwoman named Madame Rachou,
who might have made herself rich and famous if she had laid away just a few
of the manuscripts of what was written under her roof or collected some of
the pictures painted in her hotel. She was a funny mixture of peasant shrewd-

ness and hardness along with the most disinterested generosity. She would
do anything to help anyone just coming out of jail, no matter who they were
or what they had been in for. She had her own ideas about who she wanted
in her so-called hotel and some people waited forever, buying drinks at her
little zinc-covered bar. I remember her telling an American that there would
be a room ready in ten minutes. From behind her bar, she could see the
municipal undertakers going up the stairs to take out a poor old French pau-
per who'd died in his rent controlled room. Americans pay more, even beat-
niks. On the other hand, the better-off anyone looked, the more likely she
was to turn them away, and she certainly preferred young people—even trou-
blesome young people—to old.

Were you working on the Naked Lunch *materials at that time?*
    I wasn't doing all that much at that time, actually. Girodias of Olympia
Press, the eventual publishers, had turned the manuscript down the first time,
around two years before that, and I just wasn't doing much work.

Had you written Naked Lunch *in Tangier, then?*
    Right.
    Gysin: In a hotel we called the Villa Delirium, which was another great
spot, near the beach in Tangier. It had a garden and . . .
    Burroughs: Another memorable Madame . . .
    Gysin: The lady from Saigon. The number of people who revolved through
those two hotels is really remarkable. All the Beats . . .
    Burroughs: . . . and so many people who have really gone places since
then. That young filmmaker, for example . . .
    Gysin: Oh, Mel Van Peebles.
    Burroughs: Terry Southern, Mason Hoffenberg . . .
    Gysin: The list is really endless. An enormous number of musicians. The
place was always bubbling with music, whether being produced on instruments or being played on tapes or records. Mezzrow's son lived there . . .
Mezz Mezzrow! My God, he was a fantastic cat. He was around the hotel
quite a lot. I remembered one day in winter. It was very, very cold, and I
opened the door, and here was this big, fat, black woman complaining about
something. She really put on such a scene that I just told her, "I don't know,
I don't know" and I slammed the door, and she went banging on the next
door, which was Gregory Corso's, across the hall. And I think it was Gregory
who cracked up and said, "But Mezz, what are you doing?" The old man
had got himself into drag, put some kind of makeup on his face and he went

through the entire hotel until somebody just said, "What is that you're doing?"

Was it during this time that you discovered the cut-up technique?

Gysin: I had a big table on which I worked very often with a Stanley blade, and I had cut up a number of newspapers accidentally. They had been underneath something else that I was cutting. The pieces sort of fell together, and I started matching them up, and I thought, Wo-o-o-ow, it's really very funny. And I took some of them and arranged them in a pattern which was visually pleasing to me and then typed up the results, and I have never laughed so heartily in my entire life.

The first time around, doing your own cut-ups and seeing the results, there's a sort of feeling of hilarity . . . But it doesn't happen again. It's a oner, a single sensation that happens just that one first time, it seems to me. But I was really socked by that. And it had exactly the same effect on him. But I must say that I had thought of it as a rather superior amusement, and was very impressed by William's immediate recognition that here was something extremely important to him, that he could put to use right away, and did.

With great excitement we put together a book, and the title was really pulled right out of the air. It seems to me we were standing in the doorway to my Room 25 when someone said, "Hurry, hurry, there's only minutes to go!" and I said wow, that's the title obviously.

What was it you saw in the cut-ups initially, after you stopped laughing?

Well, I saw the possibility of permutations, particularly of images, which is the area in which it has worked best over a period of time. A book of Rimbaud's poetry or any extremely visual text will cut up and give you new combinations that are quite valid new images. In other words, you are drawing a whole series of images out of this page of text.

Does this technique relate to 20th century painting?

Gysin: A whole lot. Look at it like this: 20th century painting ceased being representational, gave up story-telling, and became abstract. Today, only squares can stand in front of a work of art whining: "But what does it *mean?*" Confronted with a piece of writing, that is the only question that readers still do ask. Perhaps there could be abstract literature, as abstract as is what we call abstract painting. Why not? We wanted to see.

We began to find out a whole lot of things about the real nature of words and writing when we began to cut them up. What are words and what are they doing? Where are they going? The cut-up method treats words as the painter treats his paint, raw material with rules and reasons of its own. Representational painters fucked over their paint until they made it tell a tale. Abstract painters found that the real hero of the picture is the paint. Painters and writers of the kind I respect want to be heroes, challenging fate in their lives and in their art. What is fate? Fate is written: *"Mektoub,"* in the Arab world, where art has always been nothing but abstract. *"Mektoub"* means "It is written." So . . . if you want to challenge and change fate . . . cut up the words. Make them make a new world.

Within weeks of stumbling on the cut-ups, I came across the Divine Tautology in Huxley's *Heaven and Hell.* I AM THAT I AM. I took a long look at it and found that the design of the phrase did not please me at all. I decided to make it more symmetrical by displacing the words. The biggest block was THAT, so I decided to leave it in the middle. My first move was to put at each end the word I. It read: I AM THAT AM I. That sounded more like a question. What had been one of the most affirmative statements of all time had become a question, and a poignant one, simply by changing the word-order around.

As I began to run through some of the other one hundred and twenty simple permutations of these five words, I heard the words running away by themselves. THAT I AM I AM, AM I THAT I AM? etc. They went on asking and answering themselves like the links of a chain, jingling against each other as they fell apart and changed places musically. I heard them. I actually heard the words falling apart. I fell back on my bed in Room 25, hearing this strange distant ringing in my ears like Newton said he heard the music of the spheres when he stumbled on the laws of gravitation. I was as high as that. All that period in the Beat Hotel was one enormous intellectual high, wasn't it, William? I have a whole book of permutated poems I've never been able to get published. Ian Sommerville put them through the Computer for me. In 1960, I gave a program of them on the BBC and they have come out on records issued by Henri Chopin for his review, Ou.

William, would you encourage people to read Minutes to Go *before reading your subsequent books? Is it important for people who want to understand what you're doing?*

I think it's quite an important book, and it does give a much clearer indication as to what I'm doing and the whole theory and development of cut-ups.

Where do you feel you've used cut-ups to greatest advantage?

I would say in sections of *The Soft Machine, The Ticket That Exploded* and in *Nova Express* as well. In certain sections it has worked. I feel that in all those books there was too much rather undifferentiated cut-up material, which I eliminated in *The Wild Boys.* The cut-up technique has very specific uses.

Brion, what about your Dream Machine? You've both used it?

Gysin: Yes. It's a stroboscope, in one word. But regulated to produce interruptions of light at between eight and 13 flashes a second, complementing the alpha rhythms in the brain, or eventually bringing the two into phase, and at that moment, immediately, one begins with sensations of extraordinary, bright color and infinite pattern which is quickly elaborating itself into fields that appear at 180 degrees to begin with and eventually seem to be occurring around 360 degrees. There are several different areas of color, of intensity and changes of pattern, which follow each other in apparent random order, and then give way, at a certain point, to things recognized as dream images, imaginary events occurring at a certain speed, much like a speeded-up movie. But depending on one's own state, or the length of time one watches, they become like the most elaborate, highly structured sort of dreams. I've had science fiction dreams, I've imagined that I was swimming over what seemed to be an ocean bottom and that big molluscs at the bottom opened up and through them appeared swimmers in Leonardo da Vinci-type helmets, and a lot of dreams about fights between them, or flights of them.

There seems to be no end to it. I've watched for literally hundreds of hours, and things never repeat themselves. Patterns do. Apparently they can eventually be learned and recognized. Some of the people who've investigated them, including a group in Germany, have identified a great many of the elements of design all over the world, found in weaving or in pottery or in archaeological objects elements of these patterns. All of them have been related to the sort of visions that one has with the Dream Machine. But there just haven't been many of these machines around; it's never been possible to have them made. We struggled along for years and years to try to get someone to manufacture them, and nothing has ever come of it.

Did you say something about someone doing some of the first light shows during this Beat Hotel period?

Gysin: Yes, they were invented by us in the Beat Hotel, by Ian Sommerville and me. And with the very small amount of electricity we were allowed by Madame Rachou, who like all French hotel keepers rationed it out with a fuse box down in her bistro. If you started using too many watts, you'd blow out a fuse, so we used to sometimes have to hook up two or three rooms together to get things going. We put on shows that most of the people who later went into the thing as a business were turned on by—those shows we did in Paris with projections and tapes and sound poetry.

Are the technologically-equipped homosexual warrior packs of The Wild Boys *projections of yours, or a prediction? And are there things about the developments in* The Wild Boys *scenario that you would consider desirable?*

Is the book a projection? Yes. It's all simply a personal projection. A prediction? I hope so. Would I consider events similar to *The Wild Boys* scenario desirable? Yes, desirable to me.

Do you think things might get to the point of there being guerrilla armies of young people throughout the world, marching on the citadels of authority?

There is a presupposition in *The Wild Boys* book of some disaster or plague which has reduced the population of the world by about three-quarters. All these empty streets, etc. So they are in a set that is already quite depopulated. Of course, under the present circumstances, any such thing is impossible; there simply isn't room, there's no place to go. Well, South America.

You're assuming that this plague would've killed off mostly older people—that the younger people, being stronger, would have survived?

Yes, definitely. Bore down kinda heavy on the whites, too. I think it was 99 percent fatal in South Africa and the Bible Belt.

Brion has talked about a decay of services—canceled mail deliveries, unsafe streets—before the fall of the Roman Empire. In The Wild Boys *civilization is reduced to holding enclaves, and the suburbs are no-man's land. Were you thinking of historical parallels?*

Well, that is the set that I presupposed in *The Wild Boys* as already existing, which means that communications have broken down, there's very little gasoline, people are going back to signal drums or other primitive communications systems.

Why aren't women involved in these bands of wild boy guerrillas?

I have a number of things to say on that subject. . . . Because women are trouble. It is another organism with interests perhaps basically irreconcilable with the male interests—which has installed itself as indispensible. Well, they may be indispensible to some people, but they're not necessarily indispensible to me. So I was merely proposing this as one experimental line that I would be most interested to follow, in the direction of mutations from the present humanoid form. That is, boys who had never had contact with women would be quite a different animal. We can't imagine what they would be like. I certainly have no objection if lesbians would like to do the same . . .

Women who had never had contact with men would be a pretty different animal too.
Indeed they would. They could be given female babies to raise from birth.

Have you got any ideas on what that might lead to?
I don't know. They could mutate into birds, perhaps. But what I was proposing on an overall scale is that the present human product seems to have gotten itself into a real bind. And what we need is variety, in other words, mutations. Now, at one time there may have been many humanoids, but only one strain survived. Have you read *African Genesis*? Well, there was the aggressive southern ape, who survived because he was a killer, and has really in a sense forced his way of life on the whole species. There is only one game and that game is war.

Do you feel that that game is genetically built into the species as it exists now?
Yes.

Have you seen any signs of mutation such as you're looking for beginning to occur?
Well, occasionally you do see really quite extraordinary people that look like they might be mutating. I've seen rather more lately.

What kind of characteristics do they have that are different?
Well, I don't know whether a genetic mutation would be necessary for this, but, if people were simply actually in control over their bodies, they would appear superhuman. That is, if they never dropped anything, spilled anything, fumbled anything. Which, obviously, they're quite capable of doing. The only problem is that after thousands of years they've never learned to operate their own machine. It's a quite complicated machine, but still, they should learn over a period of time. They go on trying to do the same things that just don't work. And that's what no politician can ever admit. You can't get up there and say, "Boys, the whole thing just won't work."

Does the writing technique in The Wild Boys *differ from that of the previous four novels?*

Yes, I think that in *The Wild Boys* I was really quite deliberately returning to older styles of writing. Quite a bit of it is really 19th century. It's a different style of writing.

Did you use cut-ups in The Wild Boys*?*

Yes, but sparingly, and very carefully selecting the phrases from the cut-ups, sifting through them many, many times. I didn't use it to the extent it was used in *The Ticket That Exploded* and *The Soft Machine* and *Nova Express,* nowhere near.

Has there been a progression in your writing to using them more sparingly and with more precision and control?

Yes. And also there are literary situations in which they are useful, and others in which they are not. Now, in recreating a delirium, they're very good, because that is what is happening. In high fever the images cut in, quite arbitrarily. So I used that in the dream section where the Boy is dying in the jungle.

Is The Wild Boys *closely connected to your previous novels, or does it stand by itself?*

I think it stands by itself. There's no carry-over of characters as there are in the other books. *Naked Lunch, The Soft Machine,* and to some extent *The Ticket That Exploded* and *Nova Express* even, were all part of about a thousand pages of manuscript. And then I had to get together one book for Girodias in two weeks. And I did. That is how it happened. I thought, which chapter goes where is going to be very complicated, but it came back from the printers, and Sinclair Beilles took one look and said, "Why don't you leave it like this?" And we did. That's just pure chance, as the chapters were going in as we typed them out.

That was *Naked Lunch.* Then I had lots of material left over, and I started writing *The Soft Machine* after that, from this material. But there were no cut-ups as such used in *Naked Lunch* at all.

How far does that material go back?

The actual notes for *Naked Lunch* started, I think, around 1955, or '54. They piled up over a period of years, and I sent one version to Maurice Girodias, who didn't want it at that time. A few years later I was in Paris, and he sent Sinclair Beilles over to say that he wanted to publish it within two weeks. And a month later, a month from his saying that he wanted it, it was out on the bookstands.

Eric Mottram calls your first four novels "The Tetralogy." Is a similar grouping emerging from your new work?
Yes, everything I'm doing now is connected with *The Wild Boys*. The comic strip is using one of the same characters, as well as the other book . . .

What does this other book have to do with?
It concerns an incestuous family of father, mother, two brothers, and two sisters—completely interchangeable sexual combinations. And they succeed because they are incestuous, liberated from all their inhibitions.

Succeed at what?
Well, by selling short during the Depression, they're able to fill a swimming pool with gold dollars.

Is that the last or the next Depression?
The last one; it's set back. What they do, in a sense, is make capitalism work. That is, they buy up the dust bowl, so they keep people there on the land and turn them all into incestuous family groups in completely interchangeable sexual combinations. So not only are they happier, but they're much more efficient, and nobody could compete with these families.

So this is a very different scenario sexually from The Wild Boys, *but it's approached in the same way?*
Yes. I thought it might have more popular appeal . . . And that of course brings them into conflict with the sinister forces of Big Money; they're subverting the whole meaning of money.

We haven't talked about your teaching gig in Switzerland. Were you applying the deconditioning process we talked about earlier?
Hardly. My impression of the University of the New World was that while the general idea was good, there was not a clear enough concept as to what the education process was supposed to bring about. You must have some idea as to the product you wish to turn out before you can go about taking the necessary measures. And there didn't seem to be a clear enough idea in this case of what they were going to teach people to do. I was vaguely teaching "Creative Writing." There's a question in my mind as to whether writing can be taught. There are techniques of writing, but I don't think any writer has

ever lived long enough to really discover these, or cofidy them. I gave two talks, and I had 20 to 30 students in each talk.

I don't see how you could bring about any deconditioning in two talks. If I was running such a university, I would teach people very definite things, like how to make change, even in a street crap game, how to get service, and so on. How to do things. I would set up a number of dummy situations, and I think that would teach them to transport themselves, etc., efficiently, or as efficiently as possible. Of course I went into those ideas in *The Job* and in the Academy Series.

All of those things mentioned could be taught, and would be extremely beneficial. Now, by product I mean, for example, the English public schools were set up to turn out these old school ties, English gentlemen who ran the Empire when they had one. There's not much point in that now, but at least they knew what they were trying to do, so therefore they knew how to go about doing it. Now, the general proposition of all these free universities is they're to teach people to think for themselves, whatever that may mean. But it all has to be quite precise when it comes to actually giving courses. And I think that's where that university, and many others that were formulated on a similar basis, have broken down.

If you were running such a university, would you offer the synthesis of Eastern/mystical and Western/technological disciplines you proposed in the Academy Series?

Well, personally I've always drawn very much of a blank on yoga, and I feel that in view of electric brain stimulation and autonomic shaping, I would not be inclined to spend much time on the slower methods for accomplishing the same thing. It's questionable in my mind whether these Eastern disciplines do have very much to offer. I mean, after all these thousands of years, where is India? If we're thinking now in terms of possible new mutations into more efficient forms, certainly nothing of the sort is taking place in the East. In other words, their statistics are not all that good. If they were able, through yogic disciplines, to achieve the level of awareness that they claim they're able to achieve, it would seem odd that their area is in such a complete mess. They haven't come up with solutions to the overpopulation, soil exhaustion, etc.

You said at the end of The Job, *with particular reference to young people, "If you want the world you could have in terms of discoveries and resources*

*now in existence, be prepared to fight for that world. To fight for that world
in the streets." Would you still say that today?*

My ideas have undergone a number of changes since *The Job*. But certainly
the most important factor is the young, and who will be controlling in 25 or
30 years. It's questionable whether they can go on breeding their old forms,
stockbrokers and lawyers and whatever, in sufficient quantity. What I mean
is, suppose the young people are in power simply because they're the only
people left in 30 years, when the old reactionaries and that whole stratum has
died out. They're running things now, completely. And what are they going
to do?

*You've often pointed out attitudes and styles shared by young people all over
the world—they dress similarly, use cannibis and other consciousness-ex-
panding drugs, hear the same music. Are these generational ties more bind-
ing than national, cultural, family ties?*

Yes, I would say so, very definitely. And one reason that they are is of
course media.

*Do you foresee these ties eventually unifying the world's youth to the point
where they can destroy the control machine being perpetrated by their elders?*

Certainly. They will become their elders, and therefore make the changes.
Now in 20 or 30 years all the Wallace folks etc. will have died. Well, who's
going to take their place? Occupying all the positions that are now occupied
by their elders, either occupying all those positions or nullifying them, you're
bound to have a whole different picture. I mean, if they've got some cool,
pot-smoking cat as President, he's not going to make the same kind of decisions or impose the same policies. Now the question of whether the control
machine, as you said earlier, would impose certain necessities on anybody
that used it—that's another consideration, and to some extent it would. But
they certainly would be more willing to listen to the idea of basic alterations,
and perhaps change it.

The control machine is simply the machinery—police, education, etc.—
used by a group in power to keep itself in power and extend its power. For
example: in a hunting society, which can only number about 30, there's nothing that could be called a control machine in operation. They must function
effectively as a hunting party in order to survive, so leadership is casual and
you have no control machine. Now as soon as you get an agricultural society,
particularly in rich land, you will tend to get inequality. That is, the advantage

of slave labor then becomes apparent and you may have, as with the Mayans and Egyptians, workers and priests—in other words, stratification, repression, and you have a control machine. As I said, the ancient Mayans had almost a model control machine through which about one or two percent of the population controlled the others, without police, without heavy weapons. The workers all had such weapons as were available, stone axes, spears, etc. So it was pure psychological control.

Is the modern control machine's dependence on heavy weapons a sign that psychological control is breaking down?

Yes. Of course, the whole concept of revolution has undergone a basic change with the introduction of heavy weapons. Now anybody can go down into his basement and make a sword or a spear, and they can make some approximation of small arms. But they can't make automatic weapons, tanks, machine guns, planes, and so on. So with heavy weapons five percent can keep down 95 percent by just sheer force, if they have to. Of course no government has ever survived for any length of time anywhere by sheer force, because of the personnel that they would have to have. They would have to have constant surveillance, unless they used some form of psychological control like electric brain stimulation. But the problem that you see in all guerrilla warfare of occupying a territory where the governed are hostile, or even a good percentage of them, of course is terrific and ultimately insoluble. The French had to get out of Algeria; they'll all have to get out of Vietnam.

Now, as to the effectiveness of street fighting in a revolutionary context, you must remember that America is not in a state of revolution. It is not even in a state of pre-revolution, and any guerrilla movement, in order to survive, must have supplies from outside. The liberals in the Colombian civil war had seized an area that bordered on Venezuela, so they were getting their arms in through Venezuela. In Vietnam they're getting their arms from the North. Without something comparable to that, no guerrilla movement is ever going to be able to survive. They may talk about guerrilla movements in the large cities, but they're just not talking in realistic terms. In Algeria the rebels occupied the mountains, and therefore they could supply their guerrillas in the cities. And also an underground army must have popular support. They don't have the potential for much support in America.

So that would not seem to be a viable tactic at present. I don't take back what I said in *The Job,* that there should be more riots and more violence, because at that time—May, 1968—they were indicated. They accomplished something, there's no doubt about it. If there had been no riots, no violence, they wouldn't pay nearly as much attention to militants or their demands as they are paying now.

You also wrote in The Job, *"once a problem has reached the political-military stage, it is already insoluble."*

Yes, because it's not meant to be solved. This is a game universe. Basically there's only one game and that game is war, and we just have to keep it going, if we're to have political/military units at all.

But a new generation just might not be interested in such things. They've got all those countries on the west coast of South America, countries like Colombia and Peru—they all have armies and they all consider that Peruvians are bad people, or Ecuadorians are bad people. And that, of course, is kept going by the military and by the very wealthy people. Otherwise, there'd be no reason for their existence. Now if a generation took over that just wasn't interested in maintaining these states, there'd be no reason for these countries to have any boundaries, or armies, at all.

What would you say to young people who want to change things through street fighting?

The only context in which street fighting would become important would be in the wake of some catastrophe, possibly an atomic war. In the chaos following an atomic attack on America, street fighting is a very important factor. I've already pointed out that I don't think street fighting is at all a viable tactic, or a revolutionary tactic in the States. It is not in any country once it reaches a certain technological stage.

There are, of course, weapons that anyone can make in their basement, if they know how, and those are biological and chemical weapons. I have a reference, commenting on the discovery of the synthetic gene, from the science representative of one of America's major embassies: "This is the beginning of the end. Any small country with good biochemists can now make the virus for which there is no cure. Someone will do it." That means, of course, any small country or any private group with a good biochemist and a small laboratory. It could be done in a place as small as this room. If they can make life particles, they can make death particles. They can make a virus to order, a virus that will do what you want it to do.

But how do you protect yourself from it if there's no cure?

No cure for the attack. Usually they develop antitoxins at the same time. It would be quite possible, for example, to develop a plague that would attack only whites. And incidentally, any college physics major, with that much technical knowledge and about $300,000, can turn out a low-yield nuclear device and take out New York from Times Square to Central Park. Nothing big, you understand . . .

The thing about virus weapons is that they need not be recognized as such. It could just come on as a paralyzing depression. Everyone just feels a little worse and a little worse until they can't get out of bed, and the whole thing founders.

Do you think any particular dissatisfied group in the society might be most inclined to use this kind of weapon? Say, the right wing?

I think the right wing more than the left. The left is still back there with Che Guevara and barricades and bullets. But to hesitate to use them I think would definitely be foolish.

You and Brion have described your collaborations over the years as the products of a "third mind." What's the source of this concept?

Burroughs: A book called *Think and Grow Rich.*

Gysin: It says that when you put two minds together . . .

Burroughs: . . . there is always a third mind . . .

Gysin: . . . a third and superior mind . . .

Burroughs: . . . as an unseen collaborator.

Gysin: That is where we picked up the title. Our book *The Third Mind* is about all the cut-up materials. It's probably one of the saddest stories in publishing. It's taken so long to get nowhere. Since 1965 . . .

Burroughs: So much work has gone into the project . . .

Gysin: . . . not only ours but . . .

Burroughs: . . . the designer's at Grove Press . . .

Any ideas why it hasn't been published?

Gysin: Well, I think it's partly connected with Grove's troubles in general. And it has something to do with publishing itself. Obviously the whole problem of how to get text and image together is beyond them, except at really outrageous prices apparently, outrageous to them. And I suppose as Grove's troubles grew, they kept putting this thing off. They said they spent a great deal of time and money on it, which they presumably did, but that's neither here nor there when their legal position was that they had to either do it or hand us back the stuff, and they finally have handed it back, after years of yathering and great insistence on our part.

We're very sure that we'll have to sit down and look at it, maybe cut it differently. From the beginning it needed a stylist, something that they weren't willing to admit, somebody who could take the whole thing together and see it as a whole, like Robert Brownjohn did, and presumably Bob Cato does, because Tim Leary's *Jail Notes* has a credit at the beginning saying it was designed by Bob Cato, and it's a very handsome book, typographically. There are several different typefaces used, blending one into the other, contrasting. And that's the kind of thing we were after, and never got.

The book is a statement, in words and pictures, of what the two of you have achieved through your collaborations?
Yes, exactly that, from the very first cut-ups through elaboration into scrapbook layouts, cut texts and images.

Brion, what did you mean when you said "Rub out the word"?
Gysin: Rub out the word was essentially to do with the fact that all the religions of the "peoples of the book," that is the Jews, the Christians, and the Moslems, all these three religions are based on the idea that in the beginning was the word. Everything seems to be wrong with what was produced from those beginnings, and so let's rub out the word and start afresh and see what really is going on. The methods were first of all a disruption of the time sequence, as William said a few minutes ago, produced by the cut-ups, and one had the idea of rubbing out the word itself, not simply disrupting its sequential order, and finding out some other way. There are other ways of communication, so an attempt at finding them would begin by rubbing out the word. If the whole thing began with the word, well then, if we don't like what was produced, and we, don't, let's get right to the root of the matter and radically alter it.

Burroughs: Rubbing out the word would probably entail considerable physiological alterations in the whole structure. The reason apes can't talk is because their inner throat structure is not set up to do so. We can imagine that the word could have occasioned the alterations in the inner throat structure that then made the words possible, and that his alteration was then genetically conveyed. Now, rubbing out the word could make objective alterations in the actual physio-psychological structure. What these alterations would be we have no way of knowing.

What precisely is the desirability of not verbalizing?
Well, verbalization has got us precisely where we are: war is a word. The

whole war universe is a verbal universe, which means they've got us in an impasse. And in order to break out of that impasse it would seem desirable to explore alternative methods of communication.

How would you compare exploring these avenues to exploring more and more precise manipulation of words?

Well, it would certainly be a step in the same direction. The more precise your manipulation or use of words is, the more you know what you're actually dealing with, what the word actually is. And by knowing what it actually is, you can supersede it. Or use it when you want to use it. Most people never stop talking—"talking to themselves," as they call it. But who are they actually talking to, and why? Why can't they simply lapse into silence?

In my case, because I have just a couple more questions. I've seen the Naked Lunch *filmscript which Brion adapted from the book. What is the current state of your movie making project?*

Gysin: The shooting script is finalized and budgeted. All we need is half a million dollars to finance it. Have you got any ideas?

Ummm . . . just one more question: William, what are your thoughts on the future of writing?

The future of writing is to see how close you can come to making it happen.

The Last European Interview
Philippe Mikriammos / 1974

Originally appeared in *Review of Contemporary Fiction* 4:1 (Spring 1984): 12–18. Reprinted by permission.

What follows, being now nearly ten years old, is a document, not unprecedented material that will shed new light on William S. Burroughs. In any case, William Burroughs has pushed farther than other writers the art of always answering the same things to the same questions, so his answers are very well known to those who have sought them. But then again repetition has a particular purpose for him; it is part of his cultural and literary tactics.

This interview was conducted on 4 July 1974, the very day before William Burroughs left England for good and went back to live in America. I think he had already partly moved to New York the preceding year, but obviously he still had some business to attend to in London, where he was when I had called from Paris a few days earlier to ask if he could see me. Mr. Burroughs answered yes immediately, and I crossed the Channel as rapidly as possible.

I wanted the interview to conclude the book I had just finished on him, the first full-length book on Burroughs in French (published by Editions Seghers, 1975). Strangely, I was to find out later that, while I was an unknown, young author writing this book in Athens in 1973, William Burroughs came there to see Alan Ansen and get the manuscript of *The Naked Lunch,* which Mr. Ansen had. William Burroughs did not want the very precious manuscript to travel by post, and so he flew to Greece to collect it by hand. Of course we did not meet then; he did not know a young man was there writing a book on him, and in my complete isolation, how could I ever have heard that William Burroughs was in town?

Anyway, William Burroughs was then a complete legend. It may seem hard to believe it now, in America and elsewhere, but the man was really *el hombre invisible.* Quite a few thought he had died years before. Imagine what I felt when, dialing his London phone number and asking for Mr. Burroughs, I heard the famous sharp voice answer, "Speaking . . ."!

Since then, of course, I have met William Burroughs several times, in Geneva, Paris, and Brussels. I have learned to know him as an individual being, to the point of being able to perceive whether he enjoys the steak we

80

are having in a restaurant, or to know, simply by an almost imperceptible move of his head to the side, that he has spotted some handsome red-headed boy passing in the distance in a street. For I have always preferred, when in his company, to deal with the living man, not with an abstract author. I would have found it rather morbid to try to wheedle clues to his literary works out of him. Anyway, I am convinced that, in William Burroughs's case, the more relevant explanations to his works are to be found in his sensitive personality, his way of feeling.

PM: To what extent is the prologue to *Junky* autobiographical?
WB: Largely.

PM: Several people have mentioned a text of yours called *Queer,* which would be a continuation of your Mexican adventures and of *Junky.* What has become of these pages?
WB: It's in the archives. Now, the catalogue of the archives was published by the Covent Garden Bookshop. It took us five months to get all the manuscripts, letters, photographs, etc., from fifteen, twenty years. And the archives are in Vaduz, Liechtenstein. Whether they will let it be transferred to Columbia University in America, I don't know. But Roberto Altmann, who has the archives at the present time, has not made them available yet. He is setting up something called the International Center of Arts and Communication in Vaduz. But they had a landslide which destroyed part of the building, and they haven't opened it yet. The catalogue's a very long book; it's over three hundred pages. And I wrote about a hundred pages of introductory material to the different files, and where this was produced and so on and so forth. Literary periods, what I wrote, where, and all that, is in the catalogue, and the material itself, including this manuscript *Queer,* is in the archives.

PM: Did you use parts of the *Queer* material in other books?
WB: No, no. Frankly, I consider it a rather amateurish book and I did not want to republish it.

PM: In *The Subterraneans,* Kerouac spoke of "the accurate images I'd exchanged with Carmody in Mexico." Does this sentence refer to experiences in telepathy and non-verbal communication between you and him?
WB: Well, I think we did some elementary experiments, yes.

PM: Have you been influenced by Céline?
WB: Yes, very much so.

PM: Did you ever meet him?

WB: Yes, I did. Allen and I went out to meet him in Meudon shortly before his death. Well, it was not shortly before, but two or three years before.

PM: Would you agree to say that he was one of the very rare French novelists who wrote in association blocks?

WB: Only in part. I think that he is in a very old tradition, and I myself am in a very old tradition, namely, that of the picaresque novel. People complain that my novels have no plot. Well, a picaresque novel has no plot. It is simply a series of incidents. And that tradition dates back to the *Satyricon* of Petronius Arbiter, and to one of the very early novels, *The Unfortunate Traveler* by Thomas Nashe. And I think Céline belongs to this same tradition. But remember that what we call the "novel" is a highly artificial form, which came in the nineteenth century. It's quite as arbitrary as the sonnet. And that form had a beginning, a middle, and an end; it has a plot, and it has this chapter structure where you have one chapter, and then you try to leave the person in a state of suspense, and on to the next chapter, and people are wondering what happened to this person, and so forth. That nineteenth-century construction has become stylized as *the* novel, and anyone who writes anything different from that is accused of being unintelligible. That form has imposed itself to the present time.

PM: And it's not vanishing.

WB: Well, no, it's not vanishing. All the best-sellers are still old-fashioned novels, written precisely in that nineteenth-century format. And films of course are following suit.

PM: Would you say that Kerouac also belonged to the picaresque novel?

WB: I would not place Jack Kerouac in the picaresque tradition since he is dealing often with factual events not sufficiently transformed and exaggerated to be classified as picaresque.

PM: Isn't it a bit striking that a major verbal innovator like you has expressed admiration for writers who are not mainly verbal innovators themselves: Conrad, Genet, Beckett, Eliot?

WB: Well, excuse me, Eliot was quite a verbal innovator. *The Waste Land* is, in effect, a cut-up, since it's using all these bits and pieces of other writers in an associational matrix. Beckett I would say is in some sense a verbal innovator. Of course Genet is classical. Many of the writers I admire are not verbal innovators at all, as you pointed out. Among these I would mention

Genet and Conrad; I don't know if you can call Kafka a verbal innovator. I think Céline is, to some extent. Interesting about Céline, I find the same critical misconceptions put forth by critics with regard to his work are put forth to mine: they said it was a chronicle of despair, etc.; *I* thought it was very funny! I think he is primarily a humorous writer. And a picaresque novel should be very lively and very funny.

PM: What other writers have influenced you or what ones have you liked?

WB: Oh, lots of them: Fitzgerald, some of Hemingway; "The Snows of Kilimanjaro" was a great short story.

PM: Dashiell Hammett?

WB: Well . . . yes, I mean it's of course minor, but Dashiell Hammett and Raymond Chandler in that genre, which is a minor genre, and it's not realistic at all. I mean this idea that this is the hard-boiled, realistic style is completely mythologic. Raymond Chandler is a writer of myths, of criminal myths, not of reality at all. Nothing to do with reality.

PM: You have developed a personal type of writing called the "routine." What exactly is a routine?

WB: That phrase was really produced by Allen Ginsberg; it simply means a usually humorous, sustained tour de force, never more than three or four pages.

PM: You read a lot of science fiction, and have expressed admiration for *The Star Virus* by Barrington Bayley and *Three to Conquer* by Eric Frank Russell. Any other science fiction books that you have particularly liked?

WB: *Fury,* by Henry Kuttner. I don't know, there are so many of them. There's something by Poul Anderson, I forget what it was called, *Twilight World.* There are a lot of science fiction books that I have read, but I have forgotten the names of the writers. *Dune* I like quite well.

PM: There is no particular science-fiction author that has notably *influenced* you?

WB: No, various books from here and there. Now, H.G. Wells, yes, *The Time Machine,* and I think he has written some very good science fiction.

PM: What about the other Burroughs, Edgar Rice?

WB: Well, no. That's for children.

PM: In *The Ticket That Exploded* you write: "There is no real thing—Maya—Maya—It's all show business." Have Buddhism, Zen, and Oriental thinking in general exerted a strong influence on you?

WB: No. I am really not very well acquainted with the literature, still less with the practice of yoga and Zen. But on one point I am fully in agreement, that is, all is illusion.

PM: Has the use of apomorphine made any progress that you know of since you started recommending and advocating its use?

WB: No, on the contrary. Too bad, because it is effective.

PM: In a recent interview, you said that apomorphine combined with Lomotil and acupuncture was the remedy for withdrawal. What was wrong or insufficient with apomorphine to require the combination of two other elements?

WB: I found out about Lomotil in America some time ago, and then doctors have been using it here with pretty good results. The thing about apomorphine is that it requires pretty constant attendance. In other words, you've *got* to really have a day and a night nurse, and those injections have to be given every four hours. And it isn't everybody that's in a position to do that. But at least for the first four days, it requires rather intensive care. And it is quite unpleasant.

PM: And it's emetic . . .

WB: Well, no, there's no necessity; see, it's not an aversion therapy and there's no necessity for the person to be sick more than once or twice when they find the threshold dose. They find the maximum dose that can be administered without vomiting, and they stick with that dose. You'll get decreased tolerance; sometimes the threshold dose will go down. Usually, almost anyone will vomit on a tenth of a grain. So then they start reducing it, but as the treatment goes on, you may find that a twentieth of a grain or even less than a twentieth of a grain produces vomiting again. You may get decreased tolerance in the course of the treatment. So it's something that has to be done very precisely, and of course people must know exactly what they're doing. It's very elastic, because some people will take large doses without vomiting, and some people will vomit on very small doses. Continual adjustments have to be made.

PM: And acupuncture?

WB: Well, I thought immediately when I saw these accounts, as well as a television presentation of operations with acupuncture, that anything that relieves intense pain will necessarily relieve withdrawal symptoms. Then they started using it for withdrawal symptoms, apparently with very good results, and are using it here, I think.

PM: Most of your books definitely have a cinematographic touch. *The Last Words of Dutch Schultz* actually is a film script, and *The Wild Boys* and *Exterminator!* are full of cinematographic details and indications.

WB: That's true, yes.

PM: Why haven't we seen any film made from one of your books?

WB: Well, we've tried to get financing on the *Dutch Schultz* script, but so far it hasn't developed. Very, very hard to get people to put up money for a film.

PM: What films have you liked recently?

WB: I like them when I go, when I see them, but it's rather hard to get myself out to see a film. I haven't seen many films lately. I saw *A Clockwork Orange;* I thought it was competent and fun, well done, though I don't think I could bear to see it again.

PM: Do you write every day?

WB: I used to. I haven't been doing anything lately because I gave a course in New York, and that took up all my time; then I was moving into a new flat there, so that during the last five months, I haven't really been doing much writing.

PM: When you write, how long is it each day?

WB: Well, I used to write . . . it depends . . . up to three, four hours, sometimes more, depending on how it's going.

PM: What is the proportion of cut-up in your recent books, *The Wild Boys* and *Exterminator!?*

WB: Small. Small. Not more than five percent, if that.

PM: Parts of *Exterminator!* look like poems. How do you react to the words poem, poetry, poet?

WB: Well, as soon as you get away from actual poetic forms, rhyme, meter, etc., there is no line between prose and poetry. From my way of thinking, many poets are simply lazy prose writers. I can take a page of descriptive prose and break it into lines, as I've done in *Exterminator!,* and then you've got a poem. Call it a poem.

PM: Memory and remembrances of your youth tend to have a larger and larger place in your recent books.

WB: Yes, yes. True.

PM: How do you explain it?

WB: Well, after all, youthful memories I think are one of the main literary sources. And while in *Junky,* and to a lesser extent in *Naked Lunch,* I was dealing with more or less recent experiences, I've been going back more and more to experiences of childhood and adolescence.

PM: Parts of *Exterminator!* sound like *The Wild Boys* continued. We find again Audrey Carson, and other things. Did you conceive it that way, as a continuation of *Wild Boys,* or is it just a matter of recurrent themes?

WB: Any book that I write, there will be probably . . . say if I have a book of approximately two hundred pages . . . you can assume that there were six hundred. So, there's always an overflow into the next book. In other words, my selection of materials is often rather arbitrary. Sometimes things that should have gone in, didn't go in, and sometimes what was selected for publication is not as good as what was left out. In a sense, it's all one book. All my books are all one book. So that was overflow; some of it was overflow material from *The Wild Boys,* what didn't go into *The Wild Boys* for one reason or another. There are sections of course in *The Wild Boys* that should have gone into *Exterminator!,* like the first section, which doesn't belong with the rest of the book at all; it would have been much better in *Exterminator!,* the Tio Maté section. There's no relation really between that and the rest of the book.

PM: There was the Egyptian Book of the Dead, and the Tibetan Book of the Dead, and then *The Wild Boys,* subtitled "A Book of the Dead." Am I stupid in seeing a connection between them?

WB: Oh no, the connection I think is very clear: everyone in the book is dead. Remember that Audrey is killed in the beginning of the book, in an auto accident.

PM: Did you inspire yourself from the old books of the Dead?

WB: To some extent, yes. I've read them both; not all of the Egyptian one, my God, or all of the Tibetan one, but I looked through them. In other words, the same concepts are there between birth and death, or between death and birth.

PM: You have kept an unchanged point of view about the origins of humanity's troubles. In *The Naked Lunch* you wrote: "The Evil is waiting out there, in the land. Larval entities waiting for a live one," and in *Exterminator!*, "The white settlers contracted a virus," and this virus is the word. But who put the word there in the first place?

WB: Well, the whole white race, which has proved to be a perfect curse on the planet, have been largely conditioned by their cave experience, by their living in caves. And they may actually have contracted some form of virus there, which has made them what they've been, a real menace to life on the planet.

PM: So the Evil always comes from outside, from without?

WB: I don't think there's any distinction, within/without. A virus comes from the outside, but it can't harm anyone until it gets inside. It is extraneous in origin at some point, but once it's inside, then of course it is within.

PM: Speaking of coming in and out, as you were arriving in London for a visit late in 1964, you were allowed only fourteen days by the authorities, without explanations. Have you had to suffer from a lot of harassment from authorities?

WB: Very little. That was straightened out by the Arts Council and was of course prompted by the American Narcotics Department. Allen Ginsberg had the same difficulties. The American Narcotics Department would pass the word along to other authorities. Well, I got that immediately straightened out through the Arts Council; I've never had any trouble since.

PM: May I ask the reasons for why you are moving to New York?

WB: Well, I like it better. New York is very much more lively than London, and actually cheaper now. I find it a much more satisfactory place to live. New York has changed; New York is better than it was; London is worse than it was.

PM: You have always described the System as matriarchal. Do you still have the same opinion?

WB: Well, the situation has changed radically, say from what it was in the 1920s when I was a child; you could describe that as a pretty hard-core matriarchal society. Now, the picture is much more complicated with the pill and the sexual revolution and Women's Lib, which allegedly is undermining the matriarchal system. That is, at least that's what they say they're doing, that they want women to be treated like everyone else and not have special prerogatives simply because they're women. So, I don't know exactly how you would describe the situation now. It's certainly not a patriarchal society—I am speaking of America now—but I don't think you could describe it as an archetypal or uniform matriarchal society either, except for the southern part of the United States. You see, the southern part of the United States was always the stronghold of matriarchy, the concept of the "Southern belle" and the Southern woman. And that is still in existence, but it's on the way out, undoubtedly.

PM: You call for a mutation as the only way out of the present mess. Right now, what positive signs, factors, or forces do you see working toward such a mutation?

WB: Well, there are all sorts of factors. Actually, if you read a book like *The Biologic Time Bomb* by Taylor, you'll see that such mutations are well within the range of modern biology, that these things can be done, right now. We don't have to wait three hundred years. But what he points out is that the discoveries of modern biology could not be absorbed by our creaky social systems. Even such a simple thing as prolonging life: *whose* life is going to be prolonged? Who is to decide whether certain people's lives are going to be prolonged and certain other people's are not? Certainly politicians are not competent to make these decisions.

PM: You hate politicians, right?

WB: No, I don't hate politicians at all. I'm not interested in politicians. I find the type of mind, the completely extraverted, image-oriented, power-oriented thinking of the politicians dull. In other words, I'm bored by politicians; I don't hate them. It's just not a type of person that interests me.

PM: What are your methods of writing at present?

WB: Methods? I don't know. I just sit down and write! I write in short sections; in other words, I write a section, maybe of narrative, and then I reach into that, but if it doesn't continue, I'll write something else, and then try to piece them together. *The Wild Boys* was written over a period of time; some of it was written in Marrakech, some of it was written in Tangiers, and a good deal was written in London. I always write on the typewriter, never in longhand.

PM: What is, in *The Wild Boys,* the meaning of sentences like "A pyramid coming in . . . two . . . three . . . four pyramids coming in . . ."?

WB: That is an exercise of visualizing geometric figures which I have run across in various psychic writings.

PM: Would you be interested in testing psychotronic generators too?

WB: Yes, the various devices described in *Psychic Discoveries Behind the Iron Curtain.* They have now come out with another book called *A Handbook of PSI Discoveries,* which is a how-to book telling just how to do Kirlian photography, how to build all these machines and generators and so on. I'm very interested in experimenting with those if I have the opportunity, time, and money.

PM: In the mid-seventies, you write that you wanted to create a new myth for the Space Age. Is it what you are still trying to do, and do you use the word myth in a particular sense?

WB: I feel that I am still working along the line of a myth for the Space Age and that all my books are essentially one book. I use myth in the conventional meaning.

Talking with William S. Burroughs

William Bates / 1974

Originally appeared in *The Daily Californian: Arts and Entertainment,*
November 15, 1974: 11, 20. Copyright 1974, The Daily Californian.
Reprinted by permission.

This has been "Burroughs week" in Berkeley. William S. Burroughs, now
60, was there to read from his novels one weeks ago Thursday; last Wednes-
day, he presented several experimental films and a short lecture on time and
space in Wheeler Auditorium. . . . Burroughs's humor, which is exceedingly
dry, comes through in every medium in which he works, including the interview. Using what is perhaps the inverse of the cut-up technique, I have
grouped random questions and answers into sequences that deal with his life,
the cut-up technique, drugs, and other issues.

Q: You're related to the adding-machine Burroughs, aren't you?
Burroughs: Yes. My grandfather invented the adding machine, or rather
he invented the device that made it practical.

Q: Did this make your family wealthy?
Burroughs: No. He died at a relatively early age, and a lot of people who
had put up money for his experiments held the bulk of the stock in Burroughs
Corporation. The holdings my family had were rather small, and they were
persuaded to sell out. The executors said that the adding machine wasn't
practical and wasn't ever going to come to anything. So we were out of that
before I was born.

Q: You were born in St. Louis in 1914. What did your father do there?
Burroughs: He ran a glass factory.

Q: How did you first get turned on to heroin?
Burroughs: Just exposure. Being around people who took it.

Q: About how old were you then?
Burroughs: Thirty.

Q: You were already in New York. When did you become aware of your
homosexual inclinations?

90

Burroughs: Oh, early puberty. I was aware of it, of course, but it was very much taboo in those days.

Q: What type of school did you go to before Harvard?

Burroughs: I went to a day school called John Burroughs School in St. Louis, and then I went to Los Alamos Ranch School. That's where they later made the atom bomb. It was taken over during the war.

Q: What year did you go to Harvard, and when did you graduate?

Burroughs: I went there in 1936, and graduated four years later.

Q: You've been accused of excluding women from your fictional universe. At the same time, you're very interested in questions of "mind control" and so forth. Do you think the women's movement has provided any new possibilities for breaking down authority and control?

Burroughs: Yes, if the women's liberationists really mean what they say. They say they want to be treated equally, like everybody else, and give up their special prerogatives as women. I was brought up in a very matriarchal society, where women insisted on their prerogatives. I'm certainly in agreement with the aims of women's liberation.

Q: What do you mean you were brought up in a matriarchal society?

Burroughs: I mean women ran it.

Q: Indirectly?

Burroughs: Yes, indirectly. But they were, it would seem to me, the real controllers, not men. M-o-t-h-e-r-k-n-o-w-s-b-e-s-t. Mother knows best.

Q: Did you try writing before 1949?

Burroughs: Yes, I made several attempts. Kerouac and I wrote a book before then. It wasn't very good. *Junkie* was written when I was thirty-five. Before that, I hadn't really much ambition.

Q: Did you have any difficulty getting *Junkie* published?

Burroughs: Allen Ginsberg was largely instrumental in getting *Junkie* published. Someone named Kurt Solomon was working for Ace Books, and Ginsberg got to Carl Solomon, who managed to interest his uncle in publishing the book. There wasn't much interest at that time in the subject of drug addiction.

Q: This is your second trip to California. How do you like Berkeley?

Burroughs: I like it very much. I like Berkeley's weather, the beautiful surroundings, the sunsets, etc.—I'm very favorably impressed.

Q: Have you been given a tour? What's your opinion—as the author of *Junkie*—of let's say, Telegraph Avenue?
Burroughs: I was very pleased. I also like to see all of this interest in the occult.

Q: What do you think of the aesthetic of spontaneity worked out by Ginsberg, Kerouac and some of the other beat writers?
Burroughs: It may work for Kerouac and, say, Wolfe. It doesn't work for me at all.

Q: Do you revise much?
Burroughs: A great deal. I usually have at least three revisions, and for any novel I publish, there will usually be three or four hundred pages that I don't use.

Q: Do you try to use them again later?
Burroughs: Yes, very often. It may be that they don't fit in one particular novel but will fit in somewhere else. Sometimes I find that the material that I rejected is better than what went in.

Q: Let's talk about the cut-up technique. It's made you rather notorious among the academics.
Burroughs: I don't see why. Eliot does cut-ups. *The Wasteland* is a cut-up.

Q: Is the cut-up your own form of spontaneity?
Burroughs: You can select and edit, once you have made your cut-up. With the cut-up technique you get new sentences, passages, words, and meanings, some of which may be useful, and some not. There's no necessity of using it all.

Q: Are you interested in experiments with computer-generated prose?
Burroughs: I have seen some randomly generated sentences that were produced by computers. Not much seems to come out of it. I think it has to be done by a person. I've never seen anything very interesting come out of a computer in the way of writing.

Q: So the cut-ups are designed to give you a new view of things?
Burroughs: Yes. Actually, of course, cut-ups simply make explicit a process that goes on all the time. When you walk down the street, that's a cut-up—because your stream of consciousness is constantly being cut by random

events. Life is a cut-up, by its nature. Every time you look outside the window, you're cutting up.

Q: Do you see the cut-up technique as getting to some ultimate atoms of perception?

Burroughs: I'd say it gets us closer. I wouldn't say ultimate. Cut-ups, like the collage method in painting, are closer to the actual facts of perception than sequential narrative or representative painting. Those aren't the way things happen.

Q: Do you think drugs enhance creativity?

Burroughs: Yes, I think there is some effect of some of the hallucinogenic drugs.

Q: Have you tried writing while you were stoned?

Burroughs: Oh yes.

Q: And what was the result?

Burroughs: Well, as far as cannabis goes, I wrote nearly the whole of *Naked Lunch* on cannabis. I think it stimulates the associational process, and visualization. Which is not to say that just by smoking cannabis, you can necessarily write.

Q: Do you use any drugs regularly at the moment?

Burroughs: Not really. Well, alcohol.

Q: You've been quoted as saying that Eastern techniques of meditation are "primitive" and soon will be superseded by scientific techniques, and that therefore you're basically opposed to Ginsberg's and Gary Snyder's "back to nature" trip. Is that a fair assessment of your views?

Burroughs: I would say yes, because yogi is superseded by autonomic shaping, electric brain stimulation, things like that. Things that it can take a yogi twenty years to do can be done quite quickly now.

Q: Do you think these techniques will lead to more pleasant forms of control?

Burroughs: Well, with electric brain stimulation, the possibilities are certainly there. Have you read *Physical Control of the Brain* [*Mind*]? There's no limit to what they can do. They can induce fear, anxiety, sexual excitement by push-button control or push-button choice, depending on who's pushing the button.

Q: Are junkies controlled, or in control?
Burroughs: Well, they're controlled by their need for junk.

Q: Would you legalize heroin?
Burroughs: No, I wouldn't want it legalized and sold over the counter. No, I wouldn't go that far.

Q: Under doctor's supervision?
Burroughs: Under doctor's supervision, yes. If someone is an addict, they might as well get their supply legally. They're doing that with methadone already. There's not much difference between methadone and junk.

(Questions by William Bates, David Reid, and others.)

An Interview with William S. Burroughs

J. E. Rivers / 1976

From *Resources for American Literary Study*, 1980, pp. 154–66. Copyright 1980 by The Pennsylvania State University. Reproduced by permission of The Pennsylvania State University Press.

William S. Burroughs is a writer who inspires extreme reactions—both lavish praise and fiery denunciation. Many readers and critics find his central themes—homosexuality, drug addiction, mind control—distasteful. Others hail him as a major writer and compare him to Poe and Joyce. Whatever else he may be, Burroughs is unique in the world of contemporary letters. Simultaneously aristocratic and vulgar, intellectual and anti-intellectual, innovative and imitative, he is likely to remain a puzzle to critics and literary historians for some time to come.

Burroughs approaches interviews with wariness and reserve: he seems afraid of oversimplifying in conversation the multifaceted vision he delineates in his works. This, combined with his laconic manner, makes him a difficult, though cordial, subject.

The following interview was done in late 1976, while Burroughs was teaching at the Naropa Institute in Boulder, Colorado. Founded in 1974, the Naropa Institute offers a curriculum based on Buddhist teachings. The creative writing program—the Jack Kerouac School of Disembodied Poetics—has as regular faculty members Michael Brownstein, Dick Gallup, Allen Ginsberg, and Anne Waldman. Recurrent visiting faculty include John Ashbery, Gregory Corso, Philip Whalen, and William S. Burroughs.

Interviewer: What made you decide to start teaching literature and creative writing?
Burroughs: Money.

Interviewer: Did you have an offer?
Burroughs: Yes. I was in England and was looking for a way to get out of

there. I was offered a job at New York City College for a semester. So I took it.

Interviewer: Was that last year?
Burroughs: 1973, I think. Three years ago.

Interviewer: Are the City College and the Naropa Institute the only places you've taught?
Burroughs: The only places I've taught for any length of time. I've given a couple of lectures or a couple of classes at various universities, usually with a reading. Sort of a package deal—two classes and a reading, something like that.

Interviewer: Do you enjoy teaching?
Burroughs: No. I don't like it on a long-term basis at all. It's a lot of work, and it's very time-consuming. I don't know how anyone can think about writing if he's teaching. You really have to give all your time to it. I find it impossible to do any writing while I'm teaching.

Interviewer: When you were at Harvard, you studied under George Lyman Kittredge and John Livingston Lowes. Do you think they, or any of the other teachers you had at Harvard, influenced your own teaching methods?
Burroughs: No. That was strictly the academic lecture. Same lecture for twenty years, same jokes for twenty years. Kittredge always had the same jokes.

Interviewer: Did you study Shakespeare with Kittredge?
Burroughs: No. I didn't take that course. But I did take John Livingston Lowes's course on the Romantic poets. He *was* a great lecturer. His book *The Road to Xanadu* is certainly a very important piece of scholarship.

Interviewer: Did he talk at all about opium and the Romantics? Coleridge's use of opium, for instance?
Burroughs: Yes. But he was more interested in finding the sources of Coleridge's material in Coleridge's reading.

Interviewer: The other night in class you mentioned *The Road to Xanadu* in connection with your own book *The Last Words of Dutch Schultz,* where you speculate on the origin and meaning of Schultz's last words. Did Lowes's detective work with Coleridge's reading give you the idea for *The Last Words of Dutch Schultz?*

Burroughs: No, not at all. The parallel occurred to me later, much later. You see, you take a phrase and ask, "Now *this phrase,* where did it come from?" With Coleridge, of course, Lowes was tracing literary sources. I was looking through the actual events in a man's life and trying to find out what his last words referred to in his experience. But the method is basically the same.

Interviewer: I remember you said in your *Paris Review* interview [1965] that you were planning a novel about the American West and a gunfighter. What ever came of those plans? Have you gone any further with them?

Burroughs: No. That's one of those things I shouldn't have discussed. It was based on the consideration that a good western has yet to be written. But I don't think it's going to be written by me. Oh, I had lots of ideas for gunfighters—Zen gunfighters, blind gunfighters.

Interviewer: You seem to have a keen interest in guns.

Burroughs: Well, it is no special or noteworthy interest, because in the 1920s everybody was brought up with guns. It was a very widespread thing. I read all the outdoor magazines; it was a sort of hunting and fishing culture. That's no longer true, at least not to the same extent. It was sort of a convention.

Interviewer: What do you think about the current movement toward gun control? Do you think it's a good idea, a bad idea, irrelevant, or what?

Burroughs: I think it's an irrelevant idea on both sides. The gun control people attribute all the murders to the fact that people can get guns; but of course murderers can use other instruments. And then the riflemen scream that gun control is disarming the citizen, as if that were a factor anymore. Do they think we are back in the minutemen days, or that we need an army of citizens armed with sporting rifles? I think it's an irrelevant idea from both sides.

Interviewer: Have you looked at the recent book *Naked Angels: The Lives and Literature of the Beat Generation* by John Tytell [New York: McGraw-Hill, 1976]?

Burroughs: Yes.

Interviewer: What do you think of his treatment of you in there?

Burroughs: I've taken that up with him. It's riddled with factual errors. You see, he didn't show it to me before it was published, so my rectification of these errors never got in. He says I was provided for by a trust fund. Well, I never had a trust fund. All this stuff came from Jack Kerouac, and Jack Kerouac was writing fiction.

Interviewer: You're referring to the Old Bull Lee material in *On the Road*—the character supposedly modelled on you.

Burroughs: Yes. Tytell's material just isn't true. The trust fund isn't true. The whole biography he's given me is not true. He talks as though we were the *crème de la crème* in St. Louis, which is absolute nonsense. My parents were in fairly good circumstances, but they were not at all in the millionaire class. Money means everything in the class system of a middle-western town like that, and we were very much outsiders as far as the really big money in St. Louis was concerned. And there are lots of other errors. As a matter of fact, my parents were working in a gift and art store they owned called Cobblestone Gardens, which they had in St. Louis and later in Palm Beach, Florida. With the money they made there they sent me an allowance of two hundred dollars a month for many years, until in the early '60s I began making enough money and told them I could look after myself. There was no trust fund. I noticed all these errors, and I called them to Tytell's attention.

Interviewer: What did he say?

Burroughs: Oh, nothing. Really nothing very much.

Interviewer: What do you think of his criticism of your work? He thinks very highly of it, as you know.

Burroughs: Yes. That was certainly better. Not that I don't think it's a valuable book. It certainly seems to have established the Beats.

Interviewer: You once underwent psychoanalysis in New York City. Did you gain anything from the procedure?

Burroughs: No. I think it is an absolute and utter waste of time and money. The whole of Western psychiatry has been sidetracked from the way it should have gone. It should have gone along the lines of Pavlov and the conditioned reflex. Instead, it was sidetracked into all this mystical nonsense of egos and superegos and ids floating around in some kind of vacuum. What exact reference do these concepts have to the human nervous system? Where is this wondrous id? I mean, precisely where is it in the human nervous system? Instead of getting closer and closer to answering that question, Freudianism got farther and farther away from answering any actual questions. Simple conditioned reflex therapy is now coming back into vogue, and it's so much more effective than Freudianism. There is just no comparison. It's as simple as the neurotic rat cowering in a corner. He won't go over there to get the food, even though the maze is gone. The conditioning situation is gone, but still the rat can't go over there, because the maze has damaged his nervous system. So, you then take the food and put it nearer to him. Then the rat will pick it up. They have done exactly the same thing with people who were afraid of flying, afraid of cats, afraid to go out of their houses, and that sort of thing. They just get them to do it by very small steps. Freudians can spend years asking where the problem came from. That's not the point. The point is an actual—I think probably physical—disturbance of the whole nervous system.

Interviewer: You said in class that approximately forty per cent of your material derives from your dreams. Do you think Freud oversimplified dreams by interpreting them as sexual wish-fulfillments?

Burroughs: Freud was dealing with extremely inhibited people. These people in the nineteenth century were incredibly inhibited, from their training.

Interviewer: So you think Freud's emphasis on sexual symbolism in dreams was a function of the sexually deprived patients he interviewed?

Burroughs: Oh, of course. Of course it was. You see, he was extrapolating from these fucked-up middle-class Viennese to make general rules about dreams and dreaming, which I don't think are valid at all.

Interviewer: Was your psychoanalysis of the classic sort? Reclining on a couch, a bearded doctor with a German accent, that sort of thing?

Burroughs: *[Laughs].* Some of them had German accents, and some didn't. I went to about three. But I really think it's a terrible fraud perpetrated on the public. Even things like est seem to offer a lot more than psychoanalysis. At least est might involve a few memory exercises you could *use.* It doesn't take much time and doesn't cost a lot of money.

Interviewer: In the transcript of the *Naked Lunch* obscenity trial reprinted in the paperback edition of the novel, Allen Ginsberg discusses the various kinds of addiction depicted in *Naked Lunch.* He mentions homosexuality and says that "Burroughs [considers homosexuality] also a sort of addiction." Would you say this is an accurate description of your view of homosexuality?

Burroughs: No. I think that really stretches the whole concept of addiction. If you get it too broad, it loses all precision. Something you're addicted to is something that, when it is withdrawn, causes rather acute withdrawal symptoms.

Interviewer: During the trial Ginsberg was asked about the Sender, the Divisionist who plans to flood the world with replicas of himself. Ginsberg said that "the Divisionist is a parody of a homosexual situation. . . . Burroughs *is* attacking the homosexuals in this book also." Do you agree with that observation?

Burroughs: Well, no, I don't agree with it. I think that attacking is never implicit in a novel, or in a fictional scene.

Interviewer: What about the idea that the Divisionist is a parody of a homosexual situation? Do you go along with the Freudian notion that homosexual people are looking for a narcissistic double of themselves?

Burroughs: Yes, that certainly is one aspect of homosexuality. But it isn't always the case. Very often homosexuals are looking for something the *opposite* of themselves. Some people are interested only in Negroes, or in people of other races. But that certainly is one aspect.

Interviewer: You once wrote a book about homosexuality called *Queer,* which was never published. Do you have any plans for publishing it now?

Burroughs: No, I have no plans for publishing it. It was a very amateurish book written after *Junkie.* It is presently in the [Burroughs] Archives, which are in Vaduz in Liechtenstein. No, I have no intention of publishing it.

Interviewer: What kind of book was it? Was it non-fiction?

Burroughs: It was fiction and non-fiction, more or less based on actual experiences, like *Junkie.*

Interviewer: How do you feel about the goals and achievements of the Gay Liberation movement? Do you feel sympathy for that movement?

Burroughs: Yes. I feel sympathy for all these liberation movements, and I think they've accomplished a lot toward greater tolerance for minorities. You see, the mere fact that blacks have had these riots means that a cop thinks twice now before roughing up a black or a Puerto Rican. Well, they sure didn't in the 1920s or the 1930s. People had no comeback at all. Now they do, and I think that's a very positive social gain.

Interviewer: I see you have a book there on the couch called *How to Give Up Smoking* [by Herbert Brean]. Are you trying to give up smoking?

Burroughs: Well, I read the book.

Interviewer: What kind of method does it recommend? Will power? Tapering off?

Burroughs: There is no such thing as will power. That's something to remember in trying to stop any habit.

Interviewer: You once said the same thing about your addiction to drugs. You said a cure has to be physiological, that one has to reach a state in which one doesn't need or care about the addictive substance. I believe you were talking about the apomorphine cure you successfully underwent for heroin addiction.

Burroughs: It's true of drugs, alcohol, anything. The idea of will power is a fetish, a myth.

Interviewer: What does the book on smoking recommend?

Burroughs: It's very, very good. It says first just to think about stopping. Just think about it without any grim resolve or determination. No will power. Just think about it. And now write down everything you don't like about smoking, and carry the list around with you. That's very interesting, the concept of making it happen by writing it and thinking about it. It's like the Buddhist technique I recommended to the writing class—looking at a set of data and simply allowing it to arrange itself in the mind. The book about smoking says the same thing. Look at your data, and a solution will present itself.

Interviewer: You've often spoken of your admiration for Jean Genet. Have you ever met him?

Burroughs: I met Genet at the Democratic Convention in Chicago in 1968.

Interviewer: That's when you were covering the convention for *Esquire?*

Burroughs: I was covering it for *Esquire.* Genet and Terry Southern were also covering it for *Esquire.*

Interviewer: How did you get along with Genet?

Burroughs: Very, very well. He's almost exactly as you would expect him to be. He looks like a saintly convict. He has this extraordinary direct presence. He doesn't speak much English, or hardly any English at all. And my French is pretty bad. But I never had the usual difficulty of communication that I have with a French-speaking person. He's very intuitive and very easy to communicate with. There's a story about him. He was being chased by the police at one point in Chicago. So he took refuge in an apartment building and knocked on a door at random. Someone said, "Who is it?" and he said, "C'est Monsieur Genet!" And it so happened that the guy in the apartment was writing a thesis about him! And then he had a big beef with *Esquire*. He got the money and then refused to give them the story for a while. The editor called him a thief. He said, "Mais bien entendu, Monsieur."

Interviewer: Had he read your books in 1968?
Burroughs: Yes, he had. He had indeed.

Interviewer: Did he comment on them?
Burroughs: Yes. He was very complimentary. Of course, I had read all of his books as well.

Interviewer: Which of your books did he speak about in particular?
Burroughs: *Naked Lunch,* which was very well translated into French.

Interviewer: Has Genet completely abandoned writing? Is he not doing anything at all anymore?
Burroughs: I think almost nothing. He told me, "I've done it."

Interviewer: He feels that he's gone as far as he can go in literature?
Burroughs: I guess that's it. He's fairly well fixed for money. You see, his publisher Gallimard set him up something like a trust fund. He gets about three thousand dollars a month, or something like that. And he can live where he wants to. The last thing he wrote was, I think, his play *The Screens.* And that was twenty years ago. He's done a few articles since. And that's about all. It's odd, but he seems to feel that he's done it.

Interviewer: Does he still live from hotel to hotel?
Burroughs: Yes. In Hiltons. He really digs the Hiltons.

Interviewer: You called a section of *The Wild Boys* "The Miracle of the Rose." Is that an allusion to Genet's novel of the same name?
Burroughs: Yes. I thought *The Miracle of the Rose* was a great book. All of Genet's books are great.

Interviewer: In *Naked Angels* John Tytell calls Jack Kerouac "even now our most misunderstood and underestimated writer." Would you agree?
Burroughs: No. I've never felt that. I think he's received a *great* deal of attention. He's very, very widely read and has a worldwide influence. If you go to other countries—France, Holland—you'll find that Kerouac is usually

the *first* thing they've read. So I don't think he's either underestimated or misunderstood.

Interviewer: I've heard you say several times that the portrait of Old Bull Lee in *On the Road* is an example of how Kerouac flavored what he did with a great deal of fiction and was not just a reporter. What are the salient divergences in that portrait from the way things actually were?

Burroughs: Well, there is no way things actually were. But he has me marrying a Russian countess. There wasn't any Russian countess. He's got all kinds of things in there that weren't there. It's his fictional portrait, and that's a writer's privilege. But it should certainly be recognized as fiction.

Interviewer: Can you recognize yourself in the portrait?

Burroughs: I recognize that it may have been the way Kerouac saw me.

Interviewer: I know that Jack Kerouac suggested the title *Naked Lunch* to you. Do you know where Kerouac got the title?

Burroughs: That I don't know. I don't know where he got it.

Interviewer: When Norman Mailer testified in the *Naked Lunch* obscenity trial, he said, "There is no doubt as to [Burroughs's] talent; while it was, perhaps, excited and inflamed by drug addiction, it was also hurt. This man might have been one of the greatest geniuses of the English language if he had never been an addict." It seems to me, however, that your writing is inseparable from your experience with drugs. Do you think the drug experience helped or hindered your talent?

Burroughs: I really disagree very much with Mailer there. I think it was a very important experience, and it really got me started on writing. I don't know what I would have written without it. I must disagree.

Interviewer: What do you think of Mailer's statement, in the same trial, that "William Burroughs is in my opinion—whatever his conscious intention may be—a religious writer"?

Burroughs: I don't know what he meant by "religious writer."

Interviewer: He was talking about what he took to be a vision of Hell, a kind of nightmarish, Hieronymus Bosch-like landscape in *Naked Lunch.*

Burroughs: Well, I don't see that that would necessarily be religious. Would a vision of a nuclear holocaust constitute religious writing? It's really a pretty vague term.

Interviewer: I gather it's a term you wouldn't apply to yourself.

Burroughs: Well, no, I certainly don't subscribe to anything that calls itself a religion.

Interviewer: During the course of the same trial the defense attorney read a letter from you in which you stated that "a doctor is not criticized for describing the manifestations and symptoms of an illness, even though the symptoms may be disgusting. I feel that a writer has the right to the same freedom." I recall that you studied medicine in Vienna for about six months after you left Harvard. Do you think your medical study had a bearing on your writing? Are you describing the symptoms of an illness—the illness of society perhaps—in your books?

Burroughs: That's an aspect, certainly, of all writing. It describes all kinds of illnesses. Yes. And I also have—not as a result of my medical studies but as a part of the impetus that took me to medical studies in the first place—a great interest in medicine. I considered being a doctor, and medicine has been a sort of life-long hobby. I read a lot of medical literature. If there is anything new in the field, I want to hear about it.

Interviewer: At another point in the obscenity trial Allen Ginsberg spoke of *Naked Lunch* as a confession of "what was going on inside [Burroughs's] head." Ginsberg went on to say that "he really confessed completely, put everything down so that anybody could see it." Do you regard your writing in general, and *Naked Lunch* in particular, as confessional?

Burroughs: I don't really think of it as confessional. Obviously, any serious writer puts a great deal of himself into his work—take Genet, for example, or Beckett, or Joyce. But I wouldn't use the word "confessional" at all.

Interviewer: It's been suggested that these lines from *The Wild Boys* represent your personal view of love: "There is a word love that means nothing to me at all. It is just a feeling between the legs, a sort of tingle." How do you feel about that?

Burroughs: I don't know why critics would say that necessarily represents my position. I was talking about a very, very particular sort of character there, a rather withdrawn, schizophrenic character.

Interviewer: So the passage can't be lifted out of context and viewed as your personal opinion?

Burroughs: Of course it can't.

Interviewer: In class you have often mentioned picaresque novels such as Petronius' *Satyricon* and Thomas Nash's *The Unfortunate Traveler,* and you seem to think very highly of the picaresque tradition. Do you see your own writing as a part of that tradition?

Burroughs: Oh, very definitely. It's almost classical picaresque. A picaresque novel is very simple. It may take the form of a journey, like *The Unfortunate Traveler;* but it's really a series of misadventures, many of a horrific and often humorous nature, that the protagonist encounters. Céline's *Journey to the End of Night* is an example.

Interviewer: So even a novel like *Naked Lunch* could fall into the picaresque genre.

Burroughs: Oh, it's very definitely in that genre.

Interviewer: Your work has often been praised for its satirical power. Do you think of yourself as a satirist?

Burroughs: I think satire is certainly an element in all my books. Satire, parody, are forms I use repeatedly. Parody, really, more than satire.

Interviewer: You're speaking of sequences such as the "County Clerk" section of *Naked Lunch*—the parody of Southern redneck customs and speech patterns?

Burroughs: Yes. And the Dr. Benway sequences.

Interviewer: In the Introduction to *Naked Lunch* you mention Swift and say that the book contains satire of capital punishment done in the manner of Swift's *Modest Proposal.* Do you admire Swift as a satirist?

Burroughs: I admire him, yes. I haven't read him in a long time.

Interviewer: John Tytell says in *Naked Angels* that "the Yahoos of *Gulliver's Travels* become the perfect model for Burroughs's view of man." Do you agree?

Burroughs: I really think that's an oversimplification.

Interviewer: Has film been a significant influence on your writing?

Burroughs: I think that writing *is* a transcription of a film. And so I've used a lot of film techniques. I see something, and I say, "Well, this is a film, so this is take so-and-so, and we see it from this viewpoint." That is one way of presenting material.

Interviewer: You mean by transcribing a kind of film in the mind?

Burroughs: Yes.

Interviewer: Do you go to the movies very often?

Burroughs: Not very much. I don't get around to it, as a rule. But I usually enjoy them, when I go. I don't go to something unless I'm fairly sure I'm going to enjoy it and get something out of it.

Interviewer: Do you have favorite directors? Do you like Fellini, for instance?

Burroughs: Yes. And I like—who was it who did *The Damned?*

Interviewer: Visconti.

Burroughs: Yes, Visconti. He's very good on sets. And John Huston has made some good pictures—*The Treasure of the Sierra Madre.*

Interviewer: Do you ever use devices such as tape recorders and cameras as aids to your writing?

Burroughs: Those devices have nothing to do with writing. I use them purely experimentally. I never dictate into a tape recorder. I have made some experimental cut-ups on a tape recorder that are in *The Third Mind,* a book I did with Brion Gysin which is now out in France but has not yet been published in English. It includes some experimental tape-recorder cut-ups that have been transcribed. But, by and large, I don't use the tape recorder directly in writing. I pay a lot of attention to photographs because of characters. I'll say, "Well, that picture looks something like one of my characters," and I'll build up a composite picture of what a character looks like.

Interviewer: Do you photograph people and file them away for future reference as characters?

Burroughs: I photograph a lot of people. And I may eventually use them as characters.

Interviewer: Do you read reviews of your work?

Burroughs: Yes, I read the reviews.

Interviewer: How do you react to unfavorable reviews?

Burroughs: The whole technique for dealing with unfavorable reviews is not to react. As Raymond Chandler said, never answer a critic. You usually find that an unfavorable or very unfair review is written in violation of all the tenets of criticism. The proper questions are: What is the writer trying to do? How well does he succeed in doing it? Fair criticism is an assessment of what the writer is trying to do rather than simply a display of the personal opinions and prejudices of the critic. An unfavorable review might be based on the critic's distaste for the subject matter. Well, that's not the point at all. It's what's *done* to the subject matter that's important.

Interviewer: The orgasm of the hanged man is a recurrent image in your work. Why does it fascinate you so?

Burroughs: It's a very old image. You find it in the whole concept of the *Liebestod.* It is very much a Nordic image. You find the actual practice of sacrificial hanging described in *The Bog People* by Professor Glob. I believe that was his name.

Interviewer: *The Bog People* by Glob? That sounds like an invented work.

Burroughs: No, no. I think the name is accurate. He talks about people they dug up out of the peat bog up in Denmark somewhere.

Interviewer: And they had been ritually hanged?

Burroughs: They had been ritually hanged at a spring festival, apparently to insure good crops.

Interviewer: So you intend the image of hanging in your work to have similar ritualistic overtones?

Burroughs: Yes. It definitely has ritualistic overtones.

Interviewer: At the end of your *Paris Review* interview you said that in your books you are "creating an imaginary . . . world in which I would like to live." Is that literally true? Would you like to inhabit the vision of *Naked Lunch?* Would you like to step into those pages and live out your life there?

Burroughs: It's not that simple. In the process of constructing a universe you might want to live in, you will find, if you look at the problem realistically, that there are all sorts of disadvantages and dangers incumbent on such a universe, which perhaps must be accepted. My work is really a series of exploratory universes.

Interviewer: What is the ideal reaction of a reader to *Naked Lunch* or to your work as a whole? What are you trying to reach in your readers?

Burroughs: Well, like any writer, or any painter, you see something and you put it down in such a way that—you hope—someone else will be able to see it. And that's it.

Interviewer: In other words, you try to make the reader see through your eyes, see things the way you see them?

Burroughs: Yes. That's always the attempt of art, I think.

Inside the William Burroughs Bunker

Laura Delp / 1977

Originally published in *Weekly Soho News,* vol. 4, #25, March 24–30, 1977, p. 8.

When I was in college I lived in the shadow of a group of painters who spent a good deal of time talking about the "ugly"—it was their way of outlining what they thought would be a successful attack on the existing abstract establishment. Their paintings were, of course, hopelessly tasteful. Their literary hero was William S. Burroughs, who seemed to embody the rude disregard for novelistic tradition that they saw in themselves for, say, stripe paintings. I found reading Burroughs too difficult, and put the books down with a profound sense of personal inadequacy.

So maybe this is one of those quintessential New York stories. It's about how ten years later I was still frightened by Burroughs. How three days of sitting in bed surrounded by almost the entirety of his works did little to assure me that I was capable of interviewing him. I was, after all, becoming absorbed in the literature of a man who had judged women to be one of Creation's major mistakes. This seemed to be a bad recommendation for an interviewer. I felt like a sinner petitioning for an audience with the Pope. But then, I had decided Burroughs was more diabolical than papal. Clearly, this was not an assignment, but a dare.

I tried watching television all night, but nonetheless the day dawned and I did not oversleep. I packed up my tape recorder and headed for Phebe's, where I was to meet Burroughs's secretary James Grauerholz. This was to be, I had no doubt, the pre-interview screening. In the taxi I noticed that I was whistling, "We're off to see the wizard . . ." I fervently hoped I would fail the Grauerholz test so that I could go home and take a nap. Someone had told me that Grauerholz was, well, "difficult."

This proved to be untrue, and after an hour's worth of chattering we ventured out onto the Bowery and clucked over the thin spring sun. Two neatly and rather elegantly dressed older women approached us and demanded directions to electric oven stores. Grauerholz patiently inquired after their objective, which proved to be a toaster-oven. His suggestion of Macy's was rejected. The ladies wanted a *Bowery* oven. I wondered what they thought the Bowery was and if they knew William S. Burroughs lived there.

"A *toaster*," Grauerholz moaned as we continued down the Bowery, then, "There it is. That's where William lives," he said reverently, pointing across the street. The dingy building was suddenly transmogrified by his gesture. "William lives in the back. He doesn't have any windows. People call it the Bunker. You're about to enter the Bunker."

I abandoned my last chance to bolt and run.

"William, are you here?" Grauerholz called into the bowels of the Bunker.

"Yes," came back the disembodied voice, managing to sound neutral and resigned at the same time.

Burroughs was prowling around the strange bare space. He was quite formally attired in a suit, tie neatly tied, a very business-like pair of shoes. Everything but the hat. Totally lit by artificial light and almost devoid of furniture, the Bunker had a way of echoing. It seemed completely timeless.

Grauerholz put the kettle on and disappeared. Burroughs watched in a detached, but not unkind way as I bumbled about with tape recorder and jabbed myself in the eye with my finger. I sat down and scooted the chair closer to him, tipping dangerously as one of the chair-legs dove into a hole in the floor. We smiled. Burroughs lifted himself from his chair and did a geriatric shuffle toward the kettle that I instantly recognized as the same shuffle my father affected when he thought I was going to ask him for money. Not one to be fooled by this kind of diversionary tactic, I determined to be firm, and probing. But I was outclassed.

Maybe years of addiction have given Burroughs that sense of other-worldly perception. He speaks with the clarity of overview, not as one caught up in the struggle of deciphering day-to-day existence. So our conversation was more reflective than specific, and I was quite moved by a strain of optimism that appeared in his views.

We touched very briefly on the Carter administration.

"There seems to be a possibility," he said, "that Carter will do *some*thing. Of that much I'm positive. He's much more likely to do something about national health, which to me is one of the great problems. There are two great problems. One is national health. I never went on a tax strike against the Vietnam war, but I *would* go on a tax strike for national health, because we're paying for something we don't get. In the case of the Vietnam war, we were paying for something we didn't *approve* of, but in the case of national health, we're paying for something we're *supposed* to get, and don't. The other problem is nuclear war. And Carter takes a positively negative attitude to *any* nuclear power. I don't know if you read that article in *Playgirl,* but it says that if they go on with any nuclear power, they're going to wind this scene up in fifty years."

Burroughs is not in favor of gun-control laws, and he dismissed the issue as "minor." As for revolutionary groups, like the SLA: "Well, I think it's ridiculous. It's unrealistic for any small group to make any political changes, except for the worst. The days of old-fashioned terrorism and barricades are over. A revolution is not feasible in any industrialized country, even a country industrialized to the point of Mexico. It's simply because of the weapons. The heavy weapons are in the hands of the country."

We talked about some of the political statements he had made in *The Job.* Burroughs laughed when I reminded him he had said that in lieu of living in nation-states people should be divided up according to their own social interests. "That *would* have been feasible a hundred years ago. Then there was more diversity. It's not possible now that this is the norm. There's not very much we can do to get rid of the nation-state. But, remember when that book was written, things were much worse than they are now. America is now the freest country in the world. I'm sure it wasn't at that time."

I asked him about his past disastrous pronouncements on women. "Well," he said slowly, "it was really more of a philosophical concept than anything else. The concept being that the dualisms between man and woman, black and white, etc., are to a large extent, almost *entirely* a sociological creation. I was speaking from the viewpoint of a matriarchal society, like that in the South, which also tends to be racist."

As for the women's movement. "Well, they are opposed to the matriarchal society. They don't want to be treated as women. I certainly have no objection to any of their objectives. They say they want job equality, and to be treated the same way as men. The difference between the sexes is certainly more sociological than biological. Like the Southern belle who was put on a pedestal."

Junky was Burroughs's first published novel, but in 1938 Burroughs wrote a piece introducing the character, Dr. Benway. "I didn't get regular rejection slips; I got particularly nasty notes, saying that they didn't publish anything of this sort. I didn't do much writing until after *Junky* was written, and that was when I was 35. But then I was compulsive writer. When I couldn't get the bit about Dr. Benway published in 1938 I kind of lost interest.

"*Junky* is a very straightforward account of my experiences with junk and the people I met. I didn't attempt too much."

I told him that I found his descriptions of addiction in *Naked Lunch* quite a bit more evocative than those in *Junky*.

"Well, *Junky* is almost journalistic. And I was still addicted. When I wrote *Naked Lunch* I wasn't addicted, and that gives it a different perspective.

"There are far worse things you can be than a drug addict," he said flatly. "So far as the health damage goes—on morphine, and heroin, for that matter—it is very slight. Addicts live about as long as anybody. Or they would, if they could afford their habits. It's the opposite of alcohol—an alcoholic loses his job when he drinks. A junky loses his job when he can't get heroin. In England bank clerks and doctors are addicts. As long as it is illegal, there's an economic pressure on the addict. There should be a legal system in which prescriptions would be given to addicts. When I was in London, they had such a program, before the Americans went over there with their missionary work and started messing around. And they only had 300 people on the whole program!"

I wondered if in these years his convictions still held with apomorphine, a drug with which he had been treated, and cured of addiction, in England. It is not used in the United States.

"Oh yes," he said, gaining enthusiasm for the first time. "I still think it's by far and away the best system for treating addicts—drug addicts *and* alcoholics. In fact, just recently there's been renewed interest in it in Europe. They've been using it in conjunction with a similar drug called *L-dopa,* which has been used in treatment of Parkinson's Disease. It's most encouraging.

"In the United States, they use opium antagonists, that get all the heroin out of the addict's system and bring on withdrawal symptoms. All these drugs are in themselves somewhat addictive, and they are painful. Some of them are used on maintenance programs. They neutralize the effect of heroin. Methadone doesn't do that at all. If you're full of methadone, you're not going to get much from the heroin. All these drugs are addicting, probably to the extent to which they're worse.

"Acupuncture has been used with considerable success in curing addiction. You see, anything that relieves intense pain works. And since they give operations with acupuncture, it stands to reason it would work, and in fact it does."

Alcoholism is abhorrent to Burroughs. "It's a terrible, terrible thing," he shuddered slightly. "Worse than drug addiction. Health goes, and just the whole character. It degrades a person . . . I drink in moderation. Because, in the first place, a hangover is the most horrible thing in the world."

I was faintly surprised when Grauerholz appeared. We had been talking for over two hours, and it seemed minutes. I had become quite fond of Burroughs, and I wanted to go home and look at his work again now that I knew there was no malevolent spirit behind it.

The three of us straggled out of the Bunker, and I was half-way down the stairs when Burroughs wheeled around. There was something very essential missing.

"I forgot my hat," he observed.

An Interview with William S. Burroughs

Jennie Skerl / 1980

Originally appeared in *Modern Language Studies* 12:3 (Summer 1982): 3–17. Reprinted by permission.

This interview took place in Burroughs's loft apartment located on the fringe of the Soho district, where skid row and the new bohemia meet. The date was Good Friday, April 4, 1980; the weather was gloomy; and the city was in the midst of a massive public transit strike. The day seemed an ominous one for a talk with a man who has written of the dying gods and the collapse of the city of man. In the loft, however, we were closed off from the outside world in a large, interior room with no windows and a few basic, utilitarian furnishings (a large conference table with eight chairs, a couple of small tables bearing books and magazines on the sides of the room, and a kitchen area at one end). Burroughs was wearing an informal jacket and tie, not the business suit noted by previous interviewers. His manner was reserved, but he was generous with his time. The interview lasted almost two hours, and the following conversation has been condensed from a sixty-page transcript. In editing the transcript, I discovered that Burroughs's oral remarks translate well into print (in contrast to my own), and that he was most expansive on subjects that inform his work rather than the works themselves. Indeed, a Burroughs interview is something of an art form, with Burroughs picking up and improvising on themes that interest him the most.

JS: I'd like to start with some questions about what you've been doing since you returned to the United States in 1974. Why did you decide to return to the United States?

WSB: Well, I was one of many who decided to return to the United States. The tide was now running from Europe to America instead of the other way. No one wants to live in Europe anymore. New York is now a great deal cheaper than London and Paris or anywhere in Europe. I was living in London at the time and it was getting less and less satisfactory and more and more expensive—you were paying more and more for less and less. I was very glad to get out of there. I was never so glad to leave anyplace in my life as I was to leave London.

JS: What differences do you see in the social climate in the United States now as compared to when you left, which was about 1949 or so?

WSB: The difference is unrecognizable, and America is vastly more liberal and easy to live in than it was at that time. A lot of that, of course, is since Watergate. So, I think that there are a number of people now who are coming back here for the same reasons that they left. They left to find a more liberal climate and cheaper prices. Now they're coming back here because these things are found here and not in Europe.

JS: Have you been giving a lot of readings in this country during the past several years?

WSB: Well, yes, ever since I got back to the States, I've been doing readings, whereas, I never gave any readings when I was in England. They didn't pay anything. Ten pounds or some such nonsense. I didn't do it there, but since I came back here in 1973 I've done a great deal of readings.

JS: Is this mostly on college campuses?
WSB: Mostly—universities, but not exclusively.

JS: I know that you taught a course at CCNY.
WSB: I taught one course when I first got back here. That was the immediate precipitating factor. Allen got me a job at New York City College to teach a semester, and I did that when I first came back.

JS: Have you done any other teaching since then?
WSB: No, I didn't like it. I wouldn't do it again if I could possibly avoid it. I have taught, but just very briefly, at Naropa in the summertime. I give three lectures [at Naropa], but giving a whole semester, twice a week—that's quite wearing.

JS: Was that a creative writing class or a literature course?
WSB: Yes, it was a creative writing class—whatever that means! I had grave doubts as to whether anything was being taught. Or whether writing can be taught or if the technology of writing can be taught. At any rate, I certainly am not anxious to accept a regular teaching job again.

JS: I understand that recently you were taking part in a film that is to be a documentary about your own life.

WSB: Yes, Howard Brookner is doing a documentary. He's been working on it for about a year. He took a lot of footage during the Nova Convention. He took some footage in Colorado when I was there, and he's done some footage here.

JS: And is this film going to be on your life, as I understand, or your works?

WSB: Well, yes, it's a documentary.

JS: Haven't you been involved in a number of other films?

WSB: No, I did some short films with a friend of mine named Anthony Balch. That was years ago—in 1965—when those were done. Some of the work was done in Paris, London, Tangiers, and some of it was done here in New York. Most of them were short films. One was called *Towers Open Fire,* one was called *Cut-Ups,* and then there were some fragmentary films which were experimental, purely experimental. And that was in 1965.

JS: And, were these films based on your own work?

WSB: No—no, they were experimental films—I wrote some of the continuity for them.

JS: Did you appear in the films?

WSB: Oh, yes, yes, I appeared in the films, and I was the main character in the films actually. In both films, myself, Brion Gysin, and Ian Sommerville were the main people who appeared in the films.

JS: Weren't there some plans to make a film of *Naked Lunch?*

WSB: There were, but they never came to anything. The financing never jelled.

JS: I noticed that a couple of your recent works are called film scripts or movies. *Dutch Schultz* was a film script.

WSB: It was written in a film script form—yes.

JS: Was it intended to be an actual script?

WSB: Yes, that project went on for seven years. . . . It was originally conceived as a film, yes.

JS: What about *Blade Runner?* That's called a movie.

WSB: Well, that is just a form. It is not a practical movie, but someone named Diego Cortez is trying to do something about putting it into a film. I don't know whether it will come together or not.

JS: You mentioned a book by Nourse called *The Blade Runner.* What is that?

WSB: Well, it's a science fiction book on which this was very loosely based. The idea of the underground medicine was in the book, and I got the idea from that. Then I got in touch with Nourse and he said he would be glad to have the name used because he considered it good publicity for his book.

JS: On the other hand, *Exterminator!* was called a novel and *The Wild Boys* was called a book of the dead. I'm just wondering about the categories in which you place your books.

WSB: No, they're not categories. I would never call *Exterminator!* a novel.

JS: It's not a novel?

WSB: No, it's not a novel at all. I don't know why they have to call it a novel because it really was a collection of related short pieces.

JS: The stories do seem to have a thematic unity, though.

WSB: They may, but I don't see you have to call it anything—that's my feeling. It is what it is. By calling it a novel you simply lay yourself open to criticism. People could say it's not a novel. And, of course, by the novel they mean the purely arbitrary nineteenth century form which has a beginning, a middle, and end, and chapter structure. And it certainly doesn't conform to that. So there's no reason to call it anything, really.

JS: So, when you write your fictions you really don't think of them as falling into any particular category?

WSB: No, no. There's no need to categorize like that or to call something a novel. On the other hand, calling *The Wild Boys* a book of the dead was merely accurate.

JS: Was that your own subtitle?

WSB: Yes, that was mine. It's because everyone is dead.

JS: Yes, I know that you have said that before. If everyone in it is dead, is this then a picture of the afterlife?

WSB: No, it's a picture of the period between death and rebirth—if rebirth occurs. It's modeled on the Tibetan Book of the Dead. In the Tibetan Book there is a period in which the person doesn't know that he's dead and undergoes all sorts of adventures and difficulties and then is reborn or not reborn as the case may be. So, it is definitely modeled on the Book of the Dead and it can be called a book of the dead.

JS: I have noticed that in some of your more recent works—in *The Wild Boys* and *Exterminator!, Cobblestone Gardens*—you seem to be drawing upon memories from your childhood and your St. Louis background more so than in the previous books. I wondered what you were doing with this material, whether you were trying to break control lines again, in a sense.

WSB: No, no, not at all. It's material that was to hand. You see, some of the material that went into *Cobblestone Gardens* was from the original material from which *Naked Lunch* was drawn. *Naked Lunch* was an arbitrary selection from about six or seven hundred pages of manuscript that I had at that time which had accumulated over the years. Also then derived from that [manuscript] were *The Soft Machine, The Ticket That Exploded,* and *Nova Express.* But there was quite a bit left over, and some of that material is in *Cobblestone Gardens,* and in *Exterminator!* and the other books.

JS: I'm surprised to hear you say that. I knew that *Naked Lunch, Soft Machine, The Ticket That Exploded,* and *Nova Express* had all come out of the same materials, but I thought that after that you were drawing upon new material.

WSB: Well, I was drawing upon new material, but also some of the old material was still there, and I did use some of that.

JS: You know, there is a line in *Blade Runner* that explains what the book is about and which I thought was a comment on all your books: "For man *has* no future unless he can throw off the dead past and absorb the underground of his own being." Could you comment on that?

WSB: A man has to get beyond his conditioning, or his future is going to be a repetition, word-for-word repetition. I would say that for a great percentage of people, all they do is repeat their past. They really don't have a future at all. And it's only by a sort of break with the past that anything new and different will emerge—which is very rare—a very rare occurrence.

JS: What about "the underground of his own being?"

WSB: Well, that would be what he's really doing. His real or his actual purposes are as opposed to his ostensible purposes. . . . It needs to be remembered that few if any people know what their purposes are.

JS: Are you thinking of the unconscious?

WSB: Well, that would vary tremendously with the individual but someone may be convinced, perfectly convinced, that he is doing one thing when he is doing quite another in actuality. Someone recently wrote me who was writing a book on what makes people tick, and what their purposes are, and I wrote back that nobody knows what their purposes are. If they knew what made them tick, they'd stop ticking. But in point of fact, no one is allowed to know what their real purposes are. If they knew, there'd be no point. It would be like seeing a film for the second time. And only occasionally does someone glimpse their purposes with what the psychoanalysts call 'surprise"—a recognition of "Yes, this is what I'm really doing." But that only occurs when they're actually doing it. If you ask somebody what their basic purpose is, you're going to hear a lot of nonsense unless they know enough to say that they don't know.

JS: Isn't it the purpose of a lot of your writing, though, to reveal that underlying purpose—the surprise?

WSB: Well, yes, that is a factor of writing, but as soon as you reveal that, then that particular purpose is, in a sense, neutralized.

JS: What are you working on right now?

WSB: I'm not doing any particular project at the moment. I'm working with Vic Bockris on a book of essays and some editorial work. I just finished a long book. I just finished editing *The Cities of the Red Night* which is the longest book I've ever done to date. It should be out in January of next year.

JS: And this is another work of fiction?

WSB: Oh, yes, it's fiction.

JS: Does it introduce any new characters or themes?

WSB: Well, some of the same characters are there, but it's certainly the most near approximation to what is called a novel than what I have written before. That is, it does have plot or a number of plots; a beginning, a middle, and an end, and is pretty much straight conventional narrative style. So in that sense it would be a not much of an innovation.

JS: What are you reading right now? Are you reading any current authors that you find interesting?

WSB: I don't do much serious reading in that I read a great deal of thrillers, horror stories, and that sort of thing.

JS: Science fiction, too?

WSB: Well, sometimes. There's very little science fiction I find that I can read.

JS: Really? That's surprising because of the science fiction motifs in your books.

WSB: Well, no, I mean I've gone through a whole wall of science fiction actually, but I find few books I can read because it's a very difficult form. Very rarely does the author manage to convince you that it ever could have happened anywhere.

JS: I just read Eric Frank Russell's *Sentinels from Space.*

WSB: Eric Frank Russell is one of the best. He's dead. *Free to Conquer*—out of print—is a very good book by Eric Frank Russell. But really I can just name the few good science fiction books that I have read—there are not very many. There's something by Sidney McKay Charnos called *A Walk to the End of the World*—Eric Frank Russell—Allen D. Foster does a good one every once in a while. Some of them are at least entertaining. But by and large I read what are called, come under the heading of mystery, I suppose.

JS: Which mystery writers do you like?

WSB: I hardly even know their names. Just the titles. I read a lot of ghost stories. A few of those are good. Let's see, I read a very interesting book called *The Contaminant* about a plot by the CIA to put cancer-producing agents in food they exported to Russia. Just a whole category of stories along those lines. I read all plague and epidemic stories. I've read *The Coma.*

JS: Do you read best sellers?

WSB: It's very rarely that I find a best seller that I can read—I read *Jaws* and I read *The Godfather.* The best writer of best sellers that I can think of is Forsyth—he's quite good.

JS: Are there any younger writers—more literary writers—whom you find interesting?

WSB: Can't think of a one.

JS: I did some research on your family background, and I wanted to ask you some questions about that if you don't mind. I wonder if you could describe what your parents were like.

WSB: Well, they didn't really fit into any category. People are always trying to fit them into a category. In that book, *Naked Angels,* he was trying to fit them into some sort of a category where they didn't belong at all. They were never wealthy people. He said that they were wealthy. They were never what would be called wealthy. They kept to themselves; they weren't very socially active.

JS: But, they were both from rather prominent families, weren't they?

WSB: No, I wouldn't say that. Well, of course, my father's father invented the adding machine, but that doesn't mean a thing because he sold his stock way back in the early 1920's or even before then. So he had nothing to do with the company. So there was no connection. Belonging to a prominent family doesn't mean a thing unless the money's still there.

JS: So, there's really no connection between your family and the company any more?

WSB: No, none whatever. Hasn't been for about 50 years, more than 50 years, 60 years or so.

JS: But, didn't you at one time have an income from a trust fund?

WSB: Never! There was never a trust fund. This is some nonsense that Kerouac put out.

JS: Really?

WSB: There never *was* a trust fund. It's impossible to get out from under Kerouac's fabrications. There never was a trust fund. My family in their latter years ran a gift and arts shop called "Cobblestone Gardens." It started in St. Louis, then moved to Palm Beach, and they sent me an allowance of $100 out of the money they earned. It was not a trust fund. I never had a trust fund. There never was one.

JS: So, you would not call yourself a scion?

WSB: Certainly not. No connection with Burroughs Adding Machine at all. That was Kerouac's doing. He said somewhere I had a trust fund, and it's just been repeated and repeated. I can't get it through to people that there just never was a trust fund.

JS: Your mother's family, though, must have been fairly prominent. Her father was a well-known minister, and they claimed to be descended from Robert E. Lee.

WSB: Oh my God, everyone south of the Mason-Dixon line is descended from Robert E. Lee. It's the commonest name in the whole South. There's no reason to think there was anything to it. Well, he was a circuit-riding Methodist minister with 13 children, and then he got this rather fashionable parish in St. Louis. I knew him very slightly—he died when I was 6 years old. He was a man of great charm, and he made quite a name for himself in St. Louis. His family—the 13 children—some of them did quite well. Ivy

Lee was one of them. Wideman Lee married quite a wealthy woman and he did quite well, although they lost their money in the depression. But he still had great charm and belonged to a lot of clubs and did quite well in New York. And Louis Lee was in advertising—the youngest son, I believe.

JS: You mentioned Tytell's book. It seems to me he got a lot of that information about your parents from your son's article in *Esquire.*
WSB: Well, he may have, but he didn't consult me. He also has me owning a hundred acres in Algiers. In Louisiana, I'd be a millionaire if I owned a hundred acres in Algiers. It's city property. Actually, I owned about a quarter of an acre.

JS: What did your parents think of your books?
WSB: They didn't read them.

JS: Because they didn't want to read them, or?
WSB: They didn't want to.

JS: Why was that?
WSB: Why they just didn't. They were, in a way, very conventional people.

JS: Did you write very much as a child? Were you interested in writing then?
WSB: Not very much. I wrote a little.

JS: Did you actually write something called "Autobiography of a Wolf?"
WSB: Yes I did. That was after reading Aristotle Seton's *The Biography of a Grizzly,* which someone found for me recently. It's the story of a grizzly bear. So that was the inspiration.

JS: One of the things that comes through in some of the later books that involve the childhood memories about St. Louis and even way back in *Junky*—in the prefatory part of *Junky*—is the theme of intense boredom during your early years and an idea that boredom is an evil—not just a nuisance—but an evil. Do you feel that conventional life in the Midwest was intensely boring?
WSB: Well, it was—yes—quite factually was—not just for me but for a lot of other people. You see at that time usually people who lived in provincial towns like St. Louis, Cincinnati, etc., all wanted to get out and go to New York or Paris or somewhere like that, just as people who live in provincial

towns in France want to go to Paris. But that tendency to some extent has
been reversed now. It isn't necessary to have come from New York anymore
and people are going the other way now. Going to live in Eugene, Oregon,
and Boulder, Colorado, and Berkeley, and Santa Cruz, and places like that
which aren't quite as interesting as New York, but where there's as much
opportunity for people with an irregular life-style as in New York. So that
tendency is now being reversed, at least in this country. I don't know whether
that's occurring in France or in England, but it is occurring here.

JS: Another thing that comes through about the St. Louis of the past in the
later books is the theme of racism. Were you very conscious of that at the
time?

WSB: Well, no, I wouldn't say that I was conscious of it. It was just a part
of what everyone took for granted.

JS: You expressed some admiration in *Exterminator!* for a black man
called "Davy Jones" who stood up to a judge.

WSB: Well, yes, but I mean the whole society of St. Louis was completely
racist. I wouldn't say that I agreed with them, but that was taken for granted.
When you read someone like Fitzgerald you don't think of Fitzgerald as
being a racist. Yet you try to find the black man—you don't find the black
man there. And it was almost the air that you breathe in a city like St. Louis.

JS: It seems that over the years you maintained a lot of contacts with old
friends from St. Louis. I'm thinking of Kells Elvins and Lucien Carr.

WSB: Well—those two, absolutely. Kells is dead. He died in 1960, I think.
Lucien Carr lives here. He is the head of the UP—the night office of the
UP. . . .
I had lots of contact with Kells. We raised cotton together in the Rio
Grande Valley in 1947–48, around in there. I saw him in Tangiers, and I think
he went to live in Europe and I saw him from time to time there. I saw him
in Tangiers; I saw him in Denmark, and so we had considerable contact.

JS: I'd like to ask you some general questions about your work as a whole.
It seems that, earlier in *Naked Lunch* and in the trilogy of books that followed,
you were taking an attitude that was anti-literary and anti-word. Then later
on you seemed to change that attitude somewhat. At one point you said in an
interview that there wasn't really anything to replace literature with as a
form. I wonder what your thinking on that is now?

WSB: I would say the same thing. There's no book, say in literature, comparable to the way that painting has developed. There's no such thing as minimalism, impressionism, or any of those developments. You just can't do those things with words. Well, you could, but it would be meaningless to anybody who would read it. So, so far as writing goes, you can't get away from a narrative style altogether because they won't read it. Nor does it, in my opinion, convey very much. When you get all these concrete poetry experiments of making arrangements on the page, well you're getting close there to painting or something else.

JS: Why do you think that there has to be that basic narrative structure in literature?

WSB: I just don't think there's any substitute for it. I mean—people want some sort of story in there. Otherwise they don't read it. What are they going to read? That's the point.

JS: Is it just a convention that they're use to?

WSB: No, it's what they read *for.* You see, in painting, the whole representational position in painting was completely undermined. They had the whole thing knocked from under them by photography—and photography can do it better. But there is no comparable invention so far as writing goes, that is to say, that is to writing what photography was to painting. And then, of course, you have montage, which is what I was doing in cut-ups, and so on and on and on. As to where painting is now, I don't really know.

JS: In the late sixties an awful lot of people thought that reading was going to be replaced by TV and movies and other electronic media. Would you say that they've turned out to be wrong?

WSB: Very simply, they have not taken the place of reading, and reading and bookselling are very much a going concern.

JS: But, is there some danger that there are going to be fewer and fewer readers simply because people have these other media to turn to?

WSB: No, not necessarily because they don't do the same things. Not at all. I find, for example, that I can read quite a lot of trashy material because I can get some of the ideas and content out of it all, whereas to see that on television makes me very impatient, indeed. I just don't see much in television. I have a set that someone gave me. I just turn it off. I rarely use it. That is, I can read the equivalent of Star-Trek and stuff like that, but I can't watch it.

JS: I would have thought you would be somewhat interested in watching TV just for the popular culture that comes across—the popular images that appear in your work. You do seem to have an interest in popular culture.

WSB: Well, that's kind of a vague term. I think I'd be at a loss to define or describe popular culture.

JS: Oh, I guess I mean images and words from advertising, from popular fiction such as you mentioned, like science fiction, mysteries, thrillers. Are you pointing out to me that in order to call something popular you have to be making a distinction between low and high culture?

WSB: Yes, I don't know what the distinction is.

JS: You don't really make the distinction yourself?

WSB: No.

JS: Do you see your work then, in terms of drawing material or images from your immediate environment?

WSB: Well, that's it, yes, it's total input. Naturally, I read papers. I read magazines. I single out reading, input in the immediate environment—conversations.

JS: Can you give your definition of art?

WSB: Well, I have given various definitions. I would say that the function of art or, in fact, of any creative thought is to make people aware of what they know and don't know. For example, in the Middle Ages, the people living on the seacoast knew that the earth was round, but they believed the earth was flat. It took Galileo to come and tell them what they knew already—that the earth was round. When Cézanne first exhibited his canvasses, people were so incensed they attacked the canvasses physically in some cases because it was something they weren't used to seeing. They didn't realize that this was a pear—just seen from a different angle, in different light. OK, then after the furor died down, then everybody accepts it. There's been an advance in awareness. People now know that the earth is round because they couldn't navigate without knowing it. Any child will now recognize the objects in a Cézanne painting—no one is even bothered by that. James Joyce made them aware of their own stream of consciousness, and was accused of being unintelligible, but I don't think very many people would find it very unintelligible now, certainly not *Ulysses*. So that is my working definition of the function of art.

JS: It's to increase awareness?

WSB: To make people aware of what they know and don't know—you can't tell anybody anything he doesn't know already. Take someone on the seacoast and tell him the earth is round, and they see it a hell of a lot better than someone who has never seen the sea. They have to have some idea of what you're telling them. They may not know it, but they know it on some level. If they don't know it on any level, they won't see it.

JS: So, in that sense there's always some kind of avant garde—a cutting edge of artists who are always increasing our awareness.

WSB: Well, I would say artists and any sort of creative thought—that would be physicists, scientists, film makers, economists—anyone who is really doing anything in the way of original avant garde thinking.

JS: Are you interested in what scientists are doing nowadays? Do you read about current scientific research and that sort of thing?

WSB: Oh, yes, yes, indeed, I keep up with that, particularly anything to do with drugs, psychiatry, the new discoveries about brain stimulation, etc., yes.

JS: What's your current thinking on drugs?

WSB: Well, very, very simple, I mean so far as my recommendations. I recently attended a drug conference in Grossinger's in upstate New York. Number one, any addict should be able to have maintenance if he wants it and should be able to have treatment if he wants it. That was the recommendation that our Task Force put forward. . . .

The clash, you see, is with the maintenance people—the methadone maintenance people. I'm saying if you're going to allow methadone you might as well allow heroin because it's the same thing anyway. And the therapeutic communities who are just Anslinger coming around the other way say that you should be completely free of drugs. Well, I say that that is someone's own business and shouldn't be compulsory, but they feel it should.

JS: Do you still think that the apomorphine cure is the best?

WSB: Yes, the apomorphine cure is very effective. There has recently been corroboration of that. They've seen that apomorphine stimulates the production of endorphin just as acupuncture does. Of course, sooner or later, they will synthesize endorphin and then, who knows, that may be the answer. And they'll just maintain people on endorphin like insulin. Seems likely.

JS: You mentioned that you're also interested in psychiatry. What are some current developments that you are interested in?

WSB: Well, there are the latest developments in the area of electric brain stimulation and biofeedback. There's a book by Professor Delgado called *Physical Control of the Mind,* which shows the potential of electric brain stimulation. There's a lost of new research on sleep and dreams. The fact that cold-blooded animals do not dream is interesting.

JS: How do we know that?

WSB: By the brainwaves. All warm-blooded animals, including birds, do dream. Not only do they dream, but—this is something that is relatively new—it's a biological necessity. In other words, they would die; if deprived of REM sleep they would eventually die.

JS: What do you think is the function of dreams?

WSB: Nobody knows, but we know it's a biological necessity. We know that if people don't dream they would eventually die, but as to what the function actually is—. The fact that cold-blooded animals don't dream, well what is the difference between cold-blooded and warm-blooded animals? Well, one very important difference is that the neuro-tissue of cold-blooded animals renews itself and ours does not. You cut a nerve—it will not grow back. You cut a nerve in a cold-blooded animal—it will. If you make an incision in the brain, it will heal just like plasterboard with a cold-blooded animal. Now, there is a section of the human brain that does have this facility. This is called pons, which is a very primitive part of the brain. Removal of the pons in cats causes them to act out their dreams. The pons immobilizes people during their sleep for the most part. Of course, there are occasions of sleepwalking as cats dream in their sleep. But by and large, they don't get up and act out their dreams. If the pons was removed, undoubtedly it would be dangerous. But this is just data which doesn't add up to a theory as to the overall function of dreams. It may have something to do with the resting of neuro-tissue or with the fact that there are tissues that renew themselves in cold-blooded animals. But we just don't have enough data.

JS: What do you think about the Freudian theory of dreams?

WSB: Well, it just doesn't hold water in view of recent discoveries. He says that dreams are wishful thoughts, but it just doesn't stand up. I mean, in what sense for example are nightmares—battle nightmares—wish fulfillments? I don't think they're wish fulfillments at all. In fact, people who have been in stress—in battle—will have recurrent nightmares experiencing this, and this is no wish fulfillment. Of course, Freud had no idea that dreams were a biological necessity.

JS: He didn't?

WSB: No, no, that discovery has been made in the last 10 years. You see, he couldn't have had any idea about brain waves, and REM sleep, and all that. So his theory just doesn't fit in with what has been turned up by modern research about dreams and the unconscious. I attended a psychoanalytic conference in Milan fairly recently which was on the unconscious, and my point was that the unconscious really isn't unconscious at all. It's partially conscious. Freud has been really pretty well antiquated.

JS: Do you think that Wilheim Reich's theories hold up? I know that you have been interested in him ever since the thirties.

WSB: I think his cancer theories hold up better than anything else. I think that very definitely research into magnetism would be promising. In fact some doctors have said that cancer cannot exist in a strong magnetic field, but of course the whole matter of cancer—cancer research—is oriented toward spending as much money as possible. If you've got some simple cancer cure, no one wants to hear about it—unless it's expensive. So, it requires larger and larger appropriations. For example, megavitamin therapy for cancer gets very little in appropriations, because it's too simple.

JS: Do you think there is any one cure for cancer?

WSB: Probably not, probably it doesn't have the same cause. There are 200 different varieties of cancer, so it's doubtful that they can all have the same underlying cause. In fact, it's almost certain that they don't. I doubt if you would find one overall cure, although you might look at the number of the completely seemingly disparate illnesses that are successfully treated with antibiotics.

JS: Do you have interest in politics—what's going on in American politics?

WSB: Very little.

JS: You seemed to have been interested in political events that were going on in the late sixties, early seventies. You attended the Democratic convention in Chicago in 1968.

WSB: Oh, yes, I made some token appearances. Everyone was much more politically minded at that point. The whole point is that there has been a terrific *cultural* revolution in the past thirty or forty years which to me is the important thing because any cultural revolution involves political changes, but political changes do not necessarily involve cultural changes at all. You can have one dictator in South America, and another who will do the same thing.

JS: So your interest in the youth rebellion of the late sixties was more an interest in cultural revolution, rather than political revolution?

WSB: Well, I think that's what it was about. It never had a chance at being a political revolution actually. They may have thought that they were going to take over France, but they never had a possibility of doing that.

JS: In a sense it seems to me that *The Wild Boys* is sort of about that—about the youth rebellion that was going at the time.

WSB: To some extent. *The Wild Boys* was actually predicated on some disaster—the plague or something that reduced the population very drastically. So there's something that's happened between *The Wild Boys* and any actual political context that we know.

JS: Speaking of politics, I want to ask your opinion about a current political drama. It seems to me there are some parallels between Ayatollah Khomeini and Hassan I Sabbah. Do you see a parallel yourself?

WSB: None whatever! . . .

In the first place, Hassan I Sabbah never made any attempt to extend power. He kept what he had—one or two fortresses. And he certainly was not a puritanical man. Puritanical about some things, but—no, I guess I wouldn't make a comparison. . . .

Very little is actually known about Hassan I Sabbah. But it was a unique phenomenon—his ability to assassinate at a distance, and the fact that he did that as a sort of a particular sort of chess that he was playing. He was an Ishmaili, a member of the Ishmailian cult, which is still represented by the Aga Khan, although their lineage, their descent from Hassan I Sabbah is somewhat shaky, but it's supported by the English for political reasons. But, there's no writing. Hassan I Sabbah didn't leave any written text. Although there was supposed to have been a library at Alamout, no books have ever turned up. I don't think there ever was one there. There couldn't have been more than a very few people in Alamout—not more than a hundred.

JS: And he selected individuals to assassinate?
WSB: Yes.

JS: That story about the gardener killing the general he worked for all those years—that's a true story?

WSB: Well, yes, according to the scholars of Hassan I Sabbah, that's a true story. That's the way he worked. He got somebody ready long before trouble. And then, at a given signal, the assassination would take place.

JS: Brion Gysin did a lot of research on him, I understand.

WSB: Yes. Brion went to Alamout and said that very few people could have stayed there. There was certainly no place for the library that was supposed to have been there. I think the library is a myth. Alamout was taken by the Mongols—about 200 years after the death of Hassan I Sabbah, and if there were any books there I'm sure they would have turned up somewhere. There's no evidence of any books. Of course, Alamout was one of a number of such fortresses in what is now Iran and occupied by Ishmailians or sympathizers, so it's not just Alamout. There are several others.

JS: In your books, then, Hassan I Sabbah seems to be a kind of model for a man who rebels against the control system—sets up his own counterforce.

WSB: Yes, because most of his assassinations were of the conventional Moslems at that time. I don't know what particular Moslems were ruling Iran at that time, but he was in conflict with them. You see, the Ishmailians were considered heretics and they were very much persecuted. It was a vast secret society because of persecution.

JS: You lived in France for a while, and your work has been well-received in France. Do you know any French critics personally?

WSB: Well, I've gotten very good criticism in France. Some of the more intelligent criticism has been there. And naturally, I've known a lot of French critics personally. One of my translators could certainly rank as a French critic—Gérard Lemaire, and yes, certainly, I have had contact with French literary critics. Their approach seems to be more intellectual than Americans.

JS: Do you think that the most intelligent criticism has come from France?

WSB: Some of it has, yes. I would say that by and large it's been more intelligent—although I've gotten, of course, some very good perceptive reviews in America and England.

JS: Do you read the reviews very much?
WSB: Well, yes.

JS: Do you ever think about your readers?
WSB: Well, yes, certainly. But until I came to America and started giving

readings, I didn't have so much contact with them. Now I go out and give readings and I am in contact with people who read my books. That's why they come to the readings, and that's been very interesting and very rewarding.

JS: Oh, so you do like to talk to people and find out what their reactions are?
WSB: Yes.

JS: Who do you think your readers are?
WSB: Well, statistically, for the most part they are young people, but by no means all. But I'm mostly reading at universities.

JS: Quite a few books have started to come out lately about the Beats, Kerouac, bibliographies of your work.
WSB: There are a lot of Kerouac books, about five of them.

JS: Yes, I have been noticing that too. Have you read the books?
WSB: No, I read most of the Ann Charters biography which was pretty good, but I haven't read all of them.

JS: You always said that Kerouac was the one who had the most influence on you as a writer, that he encouraged you to write.
WSB: I said he had influence in encouraging me to write—not any influence on what I wrote. He was the one who thought of the title, "Naked Lunch." Yes, that is very true, but actually so far as our style of work and content, we couldn't be more opposite. He always said that the first draft was the best. I said, "Well, that may work for you, Jack, but it doesn't work for me." I'm used to writing and rewriting things at least three times. It's just a completely different way of working, that's all.

JS: How would you compare your work to Ginsberg's?
WSB: I wouldn't.

JS: Not at all?
WSB: Not at all. In the first place, I'm a prose writer and Allen is a poet. So there aren't really many points of comparison, or any points of comparison, really.

JS: It seems to me there are some general similarities, though.
WSB: General similarities, yes. I think we're both oriented towards freedom. I mean we have some shared objectives—like the breakdown of censor-

ship, sexual freedom, legalization of marijuana, a more liberal attitude toward drugs in general—but literarily, there's not as much of a comparison.

JS: You have indicated in the past that you really don't like to be identified as a Beat.

WSB: Well, no, I didn't object to being identified with them, since it's a loose designation, although as Allen pointed out we have shared a number of objectives over the years, and there are reasons to classify these as a movement. We were trying to get a breakdown of censorship—that is, that the words that people actually use would be used on the printed page, and that was very important at the time. Of course, now it's taken for granted.

This Is Not a Mammal: A Visit with William Burroughs

Edmund White / 1981

Originally published in *Weekly Soho News,* Feb. 18, 1981, pp. 10–11.

"Let me demonstrate," William Burroughs said. He stuffed the dart in one end of the plastic blowgun, stood back six paces and exhaled the dart into a bull's-eye emblazoned with Chinese characters. "I ordered it through the mail," he said with dry satisfaction. He put the weapon aside in a graceful gesture. "You'd be surprised what you can get through the mail. Like this." He emptied the last bit of sugar from a box, tossed the box in the air and slashed it in half with a strange device I'd never seen before, a flexible metal rod compressed and held magnetically in a case until a flick of the wrist causes the rod to extend with murderous force and speed. "Here, follow me, I have some literature on it you'll want to consult."

There's a certain pale brown tinged with pink—a flesh color, really—that Burroughs likes to wear. Tonight his shirt is of that color, but only the collar shows under his argyle sweater and the plain tie and plainer gray jacket. When he sits and talks with you he has the cold immobility of a piece of sculpture. He seems imposing, carved, big. Only when he moves does he suddenly appear frail and birdlike—*discarnate,* to use his word. Very late at night, when he's stayed up past his usual bedtime of 9 or 10 and smoked a lot of joints and downed a few vodka and cokes, he can become quite animated. Then he orates a bit and emphasizes each point with a preacher's raised hand or sudden lunge over an imaginary pulpit (his grandfather was in fact a circuit-riding Methodist minister); his movements then can seem perilous, as though he were slowly going out of phase. Right now, however, he is lucid and hospitable, his usual mode. Somewhat detached and formal, the Martian who's learned to be patient and cordial in his dealings with mere earthlings.

He led me into his spare room, rooted around in a filing cabinet through pornography magazines with titles like *Teen Punks* and *Jock Scene* and finally fished out a six-page pamphlet by the inventor of the weapon. In another cabinet I saw stacks and stacks of sci-fi paperbacks. "Perhaps you'd like to look at my scrapbooks, too?"

132

I very much wanted to, since I was avid for any clue as to what has released
the imagination of one of the most puzzling and original writers America has
ever produced—to say which means something in a country that has spawned
such self-invented uniques as Melville *and* Henry James *and* Ezra Pound *and*
Wallace Stevens, beings who emerged out of nowhere and who stand in the
strongest possible contrast one to another.

I knew from conversations with other artists how inconsequential the first
stimulus behind a work of genius can be. Jasper Johns, for instance, had told
me that an outer wall of a Harlem store painted to resemble fieldstones, something he glimpsed from a car window once and could never find again, had
provided him with a motif for some of his recent paintings. Similarly, Burroughs is alert to any source of excitement, though he is far more systematic
about assembling and exploring his materials. He has kept dream journals,
he's experimented with exotic hallucinogens, he's worked at thinking in images without the intrusion of words, he's devised a means of traveling
through time in his imagination, as an actor he's impersonated the characters
he's writing about and he has invented literary techniques contrived to produce striking and unpredictable juxtapositions.

Starting with *Nova Express,* Burroughs began to rely on the cut-up and
fold-in techniques, methods of taking a text by another writer or from a
newspaper and rearranging the order of the words and then introducing them
into his own text. Subsequently he has played around with the tape recorder,
picking up random noises and mixing them with others recorded under other
circumstances. Burroughs has never been interested in random nonsense;
rather, he has drawn on the aleatory as a way of presenting himself with fresh
thoughts and images. He is a supremely *conscious* artist; he is also someone
who believes experimental writing must be readable. Since I had just finished
reading the highly readable *Cities of the Red Night,* his most ambitious book
since *Naked Lunch,* I was specially curious to know about the pendentives on
which he'd floated this vast new pleasure dome.

The novel is certainly obsessed with teenage boys, with beautiful, heartless
redheads covered with erotic sores, who hang one another to the point of
ejaculation and whose eyes light up as they come or die—a complex network
of boys who fade and cross-fade through time and inhabit other boys in other
centuries. "The subtlest assassins among them" Burroughs writes, "are the
Dream Killers or Bangutot Boys. They have the ability to invade the REM
sleep of the target, fashion themselves from the victim's erection and grow
from his sexual energy until they are solid enough to strangle him." All these

exotic homosexual (and heterosexual) couplings are quick, explosive, sometimes lethal but never romantic. As Burroughs once remarked, "I think that
what we call love is a fraud perpetrated by the female sex, and that the point
of sexual relations between men is nothing that we could call love, but rather
what we might call *recognition.*"

Now before me on a desk I had several large, black volumes into which
pictures of naked boys had been pasted. In his sketchy, hard-to-read hand-
writing Burroughs had scrawled notes to himself over the photographs. "One
of the Kraut kids," read one note. Another said, "Possibility for Noah
Blake?" a reference to a character in *Cities of the Red Night,* described as
"20, a tall red-haired youth with brown eyes, his face dusted with freckles."

I realized that for Burroughs writing is like mineral refining, many steps
to extract from tons of dross an ounce of the precious substance. If so, then
these scribbled-over pictures, these sleazoid sci-fi books, these files on weapons and epidemics, these *National Enquirer* stories on cancer and Com-
mies—these were the great slag heaps of his art. So pure is that art that no
matter how cruddy or recherche the things he assimilates may be (the orgone
accumulator, Scientology, Mayan control systems), they are eventually refined and transformed into his own stamped ingots.

We returned to the main room. How appropriate it seems that Burroughs
should live in the locker room of a former YMCA, for isn't he the author
who celebrates ancient memories of a vanished adolescence? In the new
novel someone buys a "Firsty Pop," which we learn is compounded of "the
hyacinth smell of young hard-ons, a whiff of school toilets, locker rooms and
jock straps, rectal mucus and summer feet, chigger lotion and carbolic soap—
whiffs you back to your first jackoff and leaves you sitting there on the toilet—if you don't keep flying speed. Never linger over a Firsty."

Burroughs tours me through the toilet—here are the old urinals, no longer
functioning, and here the stalls with their marble walls and 1920s graffiti, a
golliwog's head and a strangely bifurcated penis. The main room, which is
adjacent, has been cleared of lockers, of course, though metal fittings on the
ceiling attest to where they once stood. "The locker room holds the silence
of absent male voices," Burroughs writes somewhere in the new novel. The
floors are of painted concrete. There is only one window, and it is small and
frosted.

"I can never tell in here whether it's night or day, hot or cold outside,"

Burroughs says, giving his thin-lipped smile. "What's wonderful is the heat here. I have terrific heat. Come here. Feel this wall."

I put my hand on the hot cement and can even sense the hot water coursing through buried pipes. In describing a friend's apartment in Paris, where he's just paid a visit, Burroughs again praises the abundant heat. Something about this insistence on heat strikes me as reptilian. Someone who's known Burroughs since the 1950s remarked, "When you meet him you think, 'This is not a mammal.' " Or was I detecting the deep freeze of the ex-junky? Certainly Burroughs is the poet of decaying cities, of the cold cup of coffee nursed at the Automat during the wait for a connection, the sad froideur of rented rooms, of "dead fingers in smoke," of the "Street of Missing Men," of "loading sheds in ruins, roofs fallen in," the whole malaise of America that long ago in *Naked Lunch* was dubbed "the U.S. drag" ("And the U.S. drag closes around us like no other drag in the world").

"This is really the best place I've ever lived in," Burroughs tells me. "There are four locked doors between me and the street." The street is the Bowery with its streams of urine snaking out of doorways across sidewalks, its hobbling bands of beggars, its broken wine bottles, winter fires in metal drums and rag-wrapped feet—but even so, Burroughs's concern for personal security does seem idiosyncratic. He calls his place "the Bunker" and he does sometimes give the impression of being the mad, beleaguered leader of a defeated Reich. He always carries at least three weapons on his person—a cane, a spray gun of Mace and his steel cobra, say. "I would feel naked without my weapons," he tells me. In a recent issue of *Heavy Metal* Burroughs published an article about civilian defense. To be sure, he is 67 years old and dramatically thin but, as he puts it, "I don't look like a mark" nor has anyone ever mugged him. Then why this paranoia?

Burroughs defines paranoia as "having all the facts." Politically he takes the eschatological view; he recently delivered a talk at a Whole Earth Conference in Aix-en-Provence titled "The Four Horsemen of the Apocalypse" in which he spoke about such coming attractions as biologic warfare and "ethnic weapons" designed to destroy one race but not the others. With me he discussed the recurrence of an epidemic like smallpox that would produce a 50 to 60 percent mortality rate within 11 days.

"That would be a real Hollywood spectacular," he said. When Burroughs the stylistic purist uses such an expression one looks up for the ironic twinkle, the inverted commas crinkling beside his eyes, but his delivery of even the

most motheaten gangster slang of the 1930s is as impassive and impeccable
as Cagney's. We must remember that Burroughs is the man who once an-
nounced with a straight face that it's "time to look beyond this rundown
radioactive cop-rotten planet" and who begins one chapter of the new novel
with this memorable sentence: "And here I was with a pop-happy skipper in
an old leaky jinxed gallows-propelled space tramp with all the heaviest guns
of the planet trained on us . . ." He is both the dour sower and the grim
reaper, with a smile the juice of six lemons might have induced, a great
misanthropic humorist in the tradition of Céline and W.C. Fields (Mary Mc-
Carthy once called Burroughs a "soured utopian").

Not that I disagree with his politics. In fact Burroughs is a useful sort of
anarchist to have around, someone who despises bureaucratic states on the
right as well as the so-called left, who has called for the end of the nation
and the family and who has written in *The Job:* "The police have a vested
interest in criminality. The Narcotics Dept has a vested interest in addiction.
Politicians have a vested interest in nations. Army officers have a vested
interest in war. Vested interest, whether operating through private, capital or
official agencies, suppresses any discovery, product or way of thought that
threatens its area of monopoly. The cold war is used as a pretext by both
America and Russia to conceal and monopolize research confining knowledge to official agencies." Paranoia is having all the facts.

Nor can I disagree with his esthetics. He is against realistic novels, which
he dismisses as "journalism." He admires Beckett, Genet and Conrad; he
was consciously writing in Graham Greene's tone in the opening pages of
Cities of the Red Night ("Farnsworth, the District Health Officer, was a man
so grudging in what he asked of life that every win was a loss"). He is against
censorship of any sort. He is for the tradition of the picaresque novel. His
fictions draw on pop sources—carny humor, comic strips, science fiction, the
movies, newspapers, travel books, vaudeville ("May all your troubles be little
ones, as one child molester said to another"). Of the writers in the generation
to follow the great moderns (Joyce and Stein), Burroughs was the only one
in English to remain constant to their ideal of continuing experimentation.
Like them he has practiced the art of montage but not in a way that resembles
their versions of that technique. Joyce built up a dense palimpsest from over-
lapping layers of talk (barroom brogue and neural chatter) and cultural allu-
sions (mythology and a more diffuse philology). Stein, less "intellectual"
and more temperamental, created her surprises on the local level, sometimes
treating words as pure, abstract sound.

Burroughs, by contrast, devised the cut-up and fold-in technique with the painter Brion Gysin—a technique, I might add, he has rejected in *Cities* except for three or four short paragraphs. Less formally, less diligently and far more slyly, Burroughs has learned to relate narrative fragments one to another. In *Cities* three separate tales intertwine. One takes place in the present and follows a private eye as he attempts to get to the bottom of a gruesome murder. A second relates a tale (based on fact) of a pirate in the 18th century who sought to establish anarchist city states in the New World and thereby overturn the hegemony of Spanish colonialism and Christianity. A third narrative deals with six cities in the Gobi Desert in ancient times. At first Burroughs merely alternates his narratives, just as any Victorian novelist manipulating a plot and one or two subplots might have done. But soon Burroughs established strange links among the three tales. His characters travel through time, inhabit one another and thereby unify the work. What appeared to be farflung and disconnected tales merge by virtue of time travel. Montage in *Cities* is not a Steinian juxtaposition of words nor a Joycean counterpoint of different levels of discourse but rather a montage of narratives. This solution seems to me wonderfully—but need I say the obvious?—wonderfully suited to the genius of the novel, which prefers to verbal intricacies, no matter how splendid, such large fictional structures as suspense and mystery.

I asked Burroughs where he had come upon the notion of the six cities of the red night. We were in his main room at the large dinner table. A few friends and neighbors had gathered and begun preparations for dinner (such communal meals are a nightly affair). In the background played a tape of Moroccan music recorded by Brion Gysin and Paul Bowles. "Brion gave me the idea," Burroughs said. "He told me to repeat their names before going to sleep if I want the answer to a question to come to me in my dreams. The odd thing is that Brion can't remember where he learned the names—Temaghis, Ba'dan, Yass-Waddah, Waghdas, Naufana and Ghadis."

Burroughs then took me around to look at the paintings by Gysin he owns ("He's the greatest of living painters," Burroughs murmurs). "Now this one I picture as the outskirts of Marrakech," he remarks as we stop in front of a canvas that at first glance seems entirely abstract, even calligraphic, and is painted in muted tones. "The artist shows you the spectral street of your own past associations. For instance, when you cross a street you might half-remember that 10 years ago you saw a car just here—well, see the car? The ghostly motorcycle? I try to do something of the same sort." On to another nonfigurative painting, a third and a fourth. In each painting Burroughs finds "little scenes" of streams and meadows or of the desert that are by no means obvious. I can imagine him consulting these pictures time and again for visions of the red night. "Now this one—photographs of Mars look just like this one, which Brion painted before those photos were transmitted. You know they found stones on Mars that had the letters B and G on them?" They did? Burroughs and Gysin?

Burroughs tells me that he is already well into the sequel to *Cities,* a book that takes off from the section in *Cities* "I Can Take the Hut Set Anywhere" about the Wild West in the last century. He plans yet another book after that—"And that should about wrap it up."

"Are you a Buddhist?" I ask, knowing how much time he's spent at the Tibetan Buddhist Naropa Institute in Boulder and recognizing the extent to which the transmigration of souls in *Cities* is a concept derived from Buddhist theology. Burroughs scoffs at the question. "Buddhist? No. But I do believe in reincarnation, though like everything else it isn't something that comes easy. You've got to *work* at it." Burroughs pounds the table. "I also—" long draw on the joints, eyes become slits—"I also think it's—I *know* it's possible to live in a—"perfect steely diction—"a *discarnate* state. The one I prefer."

My mind flashes on his famous remark: "It is necessary to travel, it is not necessary to live."

William S. Burroughs Interview
Vale / 1982

Originally appeared in *RE/SEARCH* #4/5, pp. 21–27. Reprinted by permission.

Vale: You see Outer Space as the solution to this cop-ridden planet?

WSB: Yeah, it's the only place to go! If we ever get out alive . . . *if* we're lucky. But it isn't just *cop-ridden,* it's ridden with every sort of insanity. Of course, all these nuts make the cops necessary. In New York there was one guy who was going out and pushing people in front of subways. Another guy—the Mad Slasher—he had a meat cleaver, he carried it around in a little bag, and he suddenly started cutting people up. He cut a guy's ear off. They got *two* mad slashers, another with a knife—a big hunting one—he killed about three or four people.

Vale: In New York?

WSB: Just suddenly on the street, he started cutting up! Stabbing everybody in sight. Just like the *amok* in Southeast Asia, just exactly the same phenomenon. He just went around and killed people. He escaped. Usually, with the amok it was a form of suicide, and they were usually killed. Everybody starts yelling out, "Amok! Amok!" and rush up with whatever weapons they have and they finally kill the amok. But this one got away and may do it again . . . You know, just one thing like that after another . . .

Vale: Have you witnessed any altercations recently?

WSB: Well, yeah . . . very often you see somebody freaking out, on a subway. I saw this guy he had a wild look in his eye, he was sort of swinging from one strap to another—he'd start at one end of the car and go down to the other end. As soon as the subway stopped *everybody* got off! The last I saw there were about four cops on their way in to subdue him.

Vale: It seems this sort of thing is escalating. What role do the media play in this? Are they just passively reporting, or—

WSB: I don't know, because they don't have this problem in other places. They don't have this problem in Paris.

Vale: In Tokyo they have a huge population, overcrowding, yet—

WSB: I know. In Paris they've got poor people, they've got everything, but it doesn't seem to express itself in that way. Doesn't seem to make any sense. That's what you're *really* worried about, the people that are just nuts, that don't have any rationality.

Vale: Usually the solution is to "beef up the police"—

WSB: The police, my god, the police have taken such a beating since New Year's. Some guy got in an argument with a cop and took his gun away and killed him. Another guy beat a cop almost to death with his own nightstick. These things happen all the time! Maybe you read about it; you see, the cops pulled this van over and two guys in the van jumped out and started shooting with 9-millimeters, those 15-shot Brownings. Man, they just riddled the car, both cops had about 5 bullets in them. They were slow on the uptake! You see somebody jump out—you'd better jump out too in a hurry! But they didn't. One of them's dead (the other will recover). He was shot in the brain, he lived about five days. Finally had to pull the plug.

Vale: I think criminals are raising their aiming point since so many cops wear Second Chance (body armor) now.

WSB: These guys knew what they were doing—they weren't muggers and they weren't lunatics. They knew how to use the guns, they had the two-hand hold . . . were really pouring it in there.

Vale: Ever had a desire to go to the Cooper School, Gunsite (a progressive arms training school in Arizona)?

WSB: Well . . . yeah, you'll get some tips there, I think. By and large it's just getting out on the range and doing a little practicing. What I do is, I start as close as I need to get, in order to get 'em all in the black, then start moving back. Then see what's wrong, if you're shooting high or low (I'm shootin' a little to the left on my 9-millimeter). Then move on back to fifteen yards. It's not very practical to bother with anything beyond twenty-five yards—there's no point.

Vale: That's seventy-five feet—

WSB: Seventy-five feet, that's far enough . . . Most anything to do with self-defense is going to be not fifteen yards but *five* yards.

Vale: It seems like it's going to get worse . . .

WSB: Well, some company has a shock stick—it's supposed to give someone a paralyzing shock. But I've never seen one. They also have this thing— it's just like a flashlight—it develops a tremendously bright flash that will blind someone, particularly in the dark. See, if someone came on you in the dark straight, and you give them a flash of that, they're all completely blinded long enough for you to either run . . . or give them a kick or two!

Vale: How would you use your cane?

WSB: There's *all sorts of things* you can do with a cane—practically anything except *that* [demonstrates using it as a club]. That's only a feint. If you ever do that with a cane you go like *that.* When he puts his hand up, you slice down to the knee. That cane of mine's not very heavy. Of course, if a guy's got something in his hand then slap the hand. Jam it into his solar plexus or adam's apple, or anywhere.

S. Clay Wilson just gave me a spring steel unit. I wouldn't carry it because I want a cane with a hook on it. It's incredibly inconvenient to have a cane that doesn't have a hook on it. You want to buy something, the cane's always slipping down, hitting somebody . . .

Vale: Society seems to be trending toward new survival requirements . . . you once mentioned that you yourself have three lines of defense. That seems to be thought out for a reason.

WSB: Yeah. A mace gun, a cobra, and a cane are my three lines of defense. It's something new. This didn't used to be true, you know. I talked to people in Los Angeles who said they used to leave their doors open and not worry about it, and now they've all got security systems and all the rest of it. I draw the line at keeping a fuckin' dog! I don't like them anyway—particularly not vicious ones—'cause they're always biting other people. [A friend] has a dog in New Mexico, outside of town. Well the dog bit three people who were friends of his—finally it killed his cat. He had to get rid of it.

But . . . if you don't have a dog, everybody knows it. And they know, of course, when you're going to town—how long it's going to take you to get there and back—so you just get ripped off for everything you own. I don't know what you can do, what substitute there is. That's what dogs are for.

Another thing that they do: they alert you if anyone is coming. And they know about three hundred yards away. It's amazing. Two or three hundred yards, all the dogs start barking. They know somebody's coming long before you would have any knowledge. And *that's* what they're for.

Vale: It seems a general state of alertness would be the first condition of being out in the Bowery where you live.

WSB: The Bowery house base is so watched. The Bowery itself, there's nothing there, just old bums; they're harmless. That's a safe neighborhood—safer than the posh neighborhoods. The Upper West Side and the East Side—that's where they have the *real* trouble, where they got these big apartment houses, because the muggers feel they *can* get something there. Not in the Bowery; there's no muggers in the Bowery. But, when you go down in the subways, of course, well then anything can happen.

Vale: You stay away from them?

WSB: No, no! I travel on them practically every day. If I have to get uptown for my various reasons, it's the only way to travel. Oh yeah, I travel on subways all the time.

Vale: Have you taken any special precautions for your YMCA in New York? (WSB lives in a former YMCA)

WSB: That's quite secure, it has no windows. It has some windows that open on a shaft—we've got bars on them. And there are four doors between me and the street. And in the daytime there's a guy downstairs with a pistol guarding the furniture store there. And they check people that come in and out. If someone comes in and asks for me, they look him over. So that's pretty good. I haven't had any trouble with people breaking in.

Vale: Do you ever practice with an air pistol?

WSB: I've got one, yeah. A *Diana,* I believe. It's got a gas cylinder. I'd rather have one that didn't have a gas cylinder, you're always running out of them. And it doesn't work exactly, I've got to put some sort of a wad in it to make it engage. But it's all right. I practice with it a lot.

Vale: Just shooting at targets?

WSB: Yeah, I've got a loft, and the walls are three feet thick. So there's no hassle. Usually I put up a telephone book as a backing. It'll chew a telephone book to pieces in about . . . oh, several days shooting and the telephone book is in shreds! It's pretty powerful, it'll imbed itself in wood, soft pine . . . It's good practice.

Vale: Except you don't get the feel of recoil . . .

WSB: Somebody says that he solved the whole problem of recoil by balancing the forward movement and the backward movement so there's no recoil. I saw a picture of this in *Soldier Of Fortune*—that's all I know about it.

But of course, I'd like to see a smoothbore shotgun revolver . . . even in

.410. If it was good and heavy you could even have it up to 20-gauge. After all, they're shooting these Thompson Contenders with really high-powered rifle cartridges—why couldn't they do the same with a shotgun? In other words, a hand shotgun. Double-barreled perhaps, heavy enough to balance the recoil, so you'd have hand shotgun hunting just like they have handgun-pistol hunting.

The point is, they can sell all they make, so why should they change? It's like the internal combustion engine—so long as they can sell 'em they're not going to change the design.

Vale: What magazines do you subscribe to?

WSB: I subscribe to the *American Rifleman.* The others I can buy, but that's hard to buy and has the best information. There are a lot of interesting things in there, like the combustible cartridge. They've been working on that for years. It's the simple idea that the whole cartridge is made of gunpowder with some sort of glue or something, so there's no cartridge to eject. Well, in the early days there were a lot of inventions, a lot of very *strange* inventions, and they had a lot of attempts to do this. None of them quite worked. Well now they're coming back to the idea. There were a lot of little inventions that were dropped that they're now interested in again. Any way that you get rid of one step, like the ejection of the cartridge, you can get a whole new look.

And then there's something new called a rail gun. It's got two rails like this, a very strong magnetic field in there. A small explosive charge presses them together and shoots the pellet at ten times the velocity of any known rifle. Well there's an immediate problem there; at that velocity the pellet would disintegrate from air pressure as soon as it left the barrel. But all these things, like the sonic barrier, are technical details that can be ironed out in one way or another . . .

Vale: What do you think about the recent assassination attempts on Reagan, the Pope—

WSB: It looks like it's going to get very dangerous to be a pope or a president or a prime minister. The time may come when they can't get anybody to take the job!

Vale: It seems like they weren't totally serious. Using a .22 . . .

WSB: Well *he* was a nut, the other guy wasn't. The terrorist, I think he was really trying. If it had been a .45 I think it might have been *it.*

De Gaulle had real professionals after him for years and they didn't suc-

ceed, because his bodyguards knew what they were doing. That's the point—
they would never have let anyone get *that* close to *Le General.* But here was
this guy in the press circles, he had no press credentials. If they're going to
let people come around the president without even checking to see whether
they're who they say they are, it's just ridiculous. Not only should they have
checked the press credentials, but they should have put *all* the fucking reporters through one of those metal detectors. Because a nutty reporter could get
the idea of assassinating the president—same thing would happen. They
really should exercise some precautions—they always wait until it happens
before they do anything.

A bodyguard has to be *telepathic.* Oh, absolutely! He's got to be able to
see around corners. And another very important thing is—*looking up.* A lot
of people don't do that. The American Secret Service—*they don't have it!*
They're not alert like that.

Vale: How can we improve our telepathic abilities? Are they genetically
limited?

WSB: No, I think everybody has them. It's just a question of *pressure.*
Pressure! Those guys *had* to do that, or they'd find somebody that would. In
other words, if they were going to be bodyguards to De Gaulle, they had to
be *intuitive.* Not just telepathic, but intuitive—know something's wrong: I
don't like the looks of that guy . . . or, that window . . . or, that's a bad place
there . . .

Vale: I'm interested in turning points in history—like, in *Cities of the Red
Night* there's that story of Captain Mission, which presented an entirely different possibility for the Americas which didn't happen . . .

WSB: Well, there are lots of those turning points or dates; important,
crucial dates. One of them is certainly (although it isn't a clear-cut date like
a battle or something like that, but it's one of the great dates of history)
Systemic Antibiotics. Because before that—boy, you got an infection, you
were dead! It's nothing now to have an infection. And pneumonia was a *big*
killer. So, that's a very big date . . .

Vale: Why are bodyguards doing such a bad job these days?

WSB: They're just not paying attention to what they're doing, that's all.
They've never been up against real professionals. Well, they're not now—
Hinckley's not a professional. But De Gaulle's bodyguards were up against
army officers with money and weapons and knowing how to use them—not
.22 pistols! And they tried and they tried but they never got him . . .

The week before President Kennedy was assassinated, he was in New York. He stopped at a red light and some girl rushed up and photographed him from a distance of three feet. Someone said, "She could have assassinated the President!" That was a week before Dallas! But that didn't seem to inspire them to tighten their security. Of course, the protection from a rifle with a telescopic sight is not so easy. But De Gaulle's men—they covered all the buildings on the route . . .

That Ruby and Oswald thing stunk to high heaven, the whole thing . . .

Vale: What do you think of the theory that Jonestown was a CIA experiment in mass mind control—

WSB: It's conceivable, conceivable. We *know* that they've performed such experiments in countries like Brazil . . . and Athens, the whole junta was CIA-inspired. In Brazil all these experiments in control and torture, etc. were definitely CIA organized—we *know* that. They sent all these torture experts down to South and Central America. Did you see *City Under Siege*—I think that was the name of it. It was about . . . one of these CIA torture experts was kidnapped by the Tupamaros in Uruguay. He was sent down there as a police advisor. So they kidnapped him and they finally killed him. And then—at the end of the movie—you see another one getting out of the plane . . .

Vale: Do you think they could take a disoriented person out of prison and program him to become an assassin and the person wouldn't really know exactly what he's doing?

WSB: I think it's possible, but it seems to me it's more trouble than it's worth. If you really want the job done you don't want a disordered person—of course you've got an *alibi* there, no one can pin it on you, but . . . still, it's an around-the-world-oxcart way of doing it! But it's certainly within the range of possibility.

Vale: What about telepathic suggestions to subjects while they're asleep?

WSB: Well they wouldn't have to be telepathic—they could do that with microphones, sort of *subliminal* microphones. As to how effective the suggestions would be I just don't know. All these people are talking about hearing voices, telling them to do these things. Now where do the voices come from? Well this is one of the symptoms, of course, of schizophrenia, and we know now that the voices come from a non-dominant brain hemisphere, whichever that is. In fact you can *produce* voices by electrical stimulation of the non-dominant brain hemisphere in normal subjects. So that's the line to take—if you can get it into the non-dominant brain hemisphere, then it has this terrific power: people can't disobey it. But only certain people would be subject to that sort of conditioning . . .

Vale: How can we strengthen our psychic defenses?

WSB: There are whole books on that. Dion Fortune wrote a fairly good book, *Psychic Self-Defense*. It's not a bad book—old-fashioned—but there's some good tips in there. How to know when you're under psychic attack, what to do about it, and so on. There are quite a few—that's a *fairly* good one.

There's something by David Conway called *Magic: An Occult Primer*— that's a very good book.

Vale: Have you heard anything new in the field of biologic warfare?

WSB: Well, we know that the English had what they called a doomsday bug in World War II—which was created by exposing viruses to radiation and producing mutated strains. That's more than *forty years ago*—they've come a long way since then! And also there are ethnic weapons that would attack only whites or blacks or Mongoloids or whatever because of racial enzyme differences. So they can devise a plague that would attack only one ethnic group. That also is pretty old; the first statement about that was about fifteen years ago. So they've come a long way on that one.

Vale: What do you think of the hardcore survivalist movement in this country? Stockpiling dried food, weapons . . .

WSB: It could be I suppose, a good idea, but then there's the question: You might not be able to get to your stash! [dryly] And then you gotta be able to defend it and all that! I remember we had the bomb shelters, and then that sort of blew over. But I'm sure a lot of people are doing it . . .

You have several priorities: your first priority is weapons, second is drugs, third is tools. Antibiotics . . .

Vale: When you say tools, do you mean like water purification devices—?

WSB: No no no. I mean *tools!* Hammers, saws. If you don't have them, it's very bad!

Vale: By the way, do you still record your dreams?

WSB: Oh, *of course!* I'll write down a few notes, and then if it's worth bothering with, I'll write it out in a diary form . . .

The Electronic Scalpel of William S. Burroughs

Uri Hertz / 1982

This interview was originally published as "Interview with William S. Burroughs" in *Third Rail: A Review of International Arts and Literature* (Los Angeles) 1984: 6, 52–53, 94. Reprinted by permission of Third Rail and Uri Hertz.

Hertz: The effect of word-combinations on the human brain and nervous system is a concern you've dealt with at different times in your work. Would you describe how you see that as operating?

Burroughs: Well, we know the effect of slogans, for heaven sakes, whether advertising slogan, military slogan and so on. It's very powerful. Whatever your slogan, you can get it to be something that goes around and around in the brain.

Hertz: Is one of the functions of the *cut-up* system to break up syntactical and discursive ordering of concepts?

Burroughs: With the *cut-up* system, I've said that the function of art is to make people aware of what they know and don't know that they know. I mean, life is a *cut-up*. Every time you walk down the street, look out a window, your consciousness is constantly being cut by random factors. All we did was make this process explicit with a pair of scissors, this process which goes on all the time. That leads to a general increase in awareness. Galileo told people the earth was round. They knew it if they lived on the seacoast. You can't tell anybody anything they don't know already on some level. Cézanne showed people what a fish looks like from a certain angle and under a certain light. Joyce made people aware of their stream of consciousness on one level. Now, at first there's always some angry protest, rejection, and then the change, the expansion, is accepted and becomes part of the general awareness. Any child can see a Cézanne at the present time. But when his paintings were first exhibited, people looked at them and didn't see a fish or whatever. They thought it was a meaningless dance. So that's what happens as *cut-up* is becoming a more accepted instrument and technique. Of course, it's been in films for a long time anyway. It was used in *Performance*. It's been used for a long time in music . . . John Cage.

147

Hertz: Are you using *cut-up* in *Place of Dead Roads?*
Burroughs: To some extent.

Hertz: Have you worked with Joyce's stream of consciousness?
Burroughs: I don't know what stream of consciousness means. Everybody works with it. Any writer who's typewriting, you know, who's writing a scene, has a film in mind and is transcribing from that film.

Hertz: You've said that writers do not yet know what words are.
Burroughs: Not only writers, nobody. They're probably asking the wrong question as to what words are, because it implies something they essentially are. It's like, "What is electricity?" Who cares? What we're interested in is how it functions, how it can be used, rather than trying to arrive at what electricity is. The same way with words.

Hertz: You've said that censorship is mind control.
Burroughs: What is it but an attempt to control what people read, see, that is, their whole input? It certainly is aimed at controlling the mind.

Hertz: Do you equate sexual censorship with political censorship?
Burroughs: Yes, I think they're all one. Wherever you find strict political censorship, you find strict sexual censorship as well, as in Russia.

Hertz: Is humor a weapon or tool for dismantling official ideology?
Burroughs: I don't think of it in those terms. You don't sit down and say, "Now I'm going to overthrow mind control." Satire, of course, is traditionally associated with attacks on the establishment: Swift, Voltaire . . . Laughter is essentially rejection. You look at something and say, "Oh, my god," and laugh. You're rejecting it.

Hertz: You've said there are certain formulae, word-locks, which will lock up a whole civilization for thousands of years.
Burroughs: "Allah," "Ave Maria" . . . Millions of people look toward Mecca and pray at certain times of day. That tied the world up for thousands of years . . . and still does. They're all looking in the same direction doing the same thing at a certain time and saying the same words. Prayer call.

Hertz: Do you see a similar principle at work in electronic media, mass communication?

Burroughs: No, it's not real definite. I see something more similar at work in the Catholic Mass. The electronic media is too diffuse. It isn't a word-lock.

Hertz: And yet at the same time it's an instrument of conditioning which attempts to render human behavior predictable. Take advertising . . .

Burroughs: Only to some extent. The press is a very two-edged instrument in America. If you have government control of the media, that's another story. And America has far less government control of the media than other countries. There's always someone who will print a story. The whole alternative press grew up here.

Hertz: With the rapidly increasing sophistication of the techniques used by advertising propaganda through mass communications, doesn't this heighten the necessity for the independent writer or artist to blast open the ideological structures being reenforced?

Burroughs: But he really isn't attempting to do that. He's primarily engaged in creation. It may happen as a byproduct, but if he sets out to do that, he's a propagandist.

Hertz: Family and State form a major part of the institutional basis of the dominant ideology. Do you see any means of changing this?

Burroughs: There are factors within the individual which correspond to these structures, or they wouldn't exist at all. As for the possibility of altering them I just don't know. It would have to be a very drastic procedure. You have these political changes, like the Russian Revolution, which didn't accomplish that much in the way of actual psychological changes. My guess is that for any changes to be effective, the alterations would have to be so drastic that no politician would dare even contemplate it.

Hertz: You've said that politics means force.

Burroughs: Politics doesn't mean anything without police or armed forces . . . in other words, someone who enforces rules. That's what politics is. Of course, if you wanted to install electrodes in people's brains so they'd be completely controlled, you wouldn't need police.

Hertz: This might be in the works.

Burroughs: They've got it. But it has very definite dangers for the controller. You see, if control is complete it ceases to be control. You control a dog, you control a sermon, but you don't control a tape recorder. If you reduce people to tape recorders, you have nothing to control. The big drawback would be that they'd have a pile of corpses and that's all. I don't think the organism would survive being completely controlled. Control must always be partial. It can't be complete or it defeats itself.

Hertz: What are your primary sources as a writer, literary or otherwise?
Burroughs: Newspapers, magazines, other books, dreams . . . total input.

Hertz: What writers have influenced you over the years?
Burroughs: Denton Welch, Joseph Conrad, Graham Greene, Rimbaud, Shakespeare, Saint-John Perse . . . a wide gamut of writers.

Hertz: Do you continue to see the gap between words and the objects to which they refer as a problem in conceptualization and communication?
Burroughs: Well, yes. People don't know what they're talking about. They've got a word like communism, justice, capitalism . . . anything. It means as many things as there are people that use it. Have you read the semanticist Korzybski? (motions to the table) Whatever you say, this isn't a table. It isn't the label we give it. Okay, we call it "X" or anything. But when you come to an abstract work like communism, justice, capitalism . . . what the hell does it mean? Very little. It's much better, instead of using the word "communism," to talk about very definite political and social configurations, so you know what you're talking about.

Hertz: Does the same problem extend to the way we conceptualize the field of human possibility as dictated by society?
Burroughs: Well, it doesn't even approximate it. That's the whole point; the gap between potential and performance. The potential is there and the performance is almost nil. This is partly due to the *either/or* error which sees something as either intellectual or emotional. This is nonsense! Everything is both. In other words, you are instinct and intellect. As if there's some sort of dividing line. This is an absurdity. This dichotomy doesn't exist in the actual human nervous system, so it's completely arbitrary and is not approximating the functioning of the visible universe on the nervous system.

Hertz: What would you say is at the root of this misconception?
Burroughs: It's Aristotelian thinking: *either/or* . . . the proposition is either true or false. It goes back to the whole academic way of thinking which derives from Aristotle.

Hertz: Where do you see American writing going? Do you see any break-throughs?

Burroughs: No, I don't see any essential changes.

Hertz: Do you mean that methods and techniques used before will be recycled through new generations of writers?

Burroughs: I don't see that writing is going to undergo any drastic changes. It hasn't . . . and indeed, it's hard to say how this could even happen. The medium has very definite limitations.

William S. Burroughs Interview

Barry Alfonso / 1984

This previously unpublished interview is used by permission of Barry Alfonso. © Barry Alfonso.

My William S. Burroughs moments took place on February 15, 1984 at the NuArt Theater in Santa Monica, CA, ten days after his 70th birthday. He was in town to attend the Los Angeles premiere of Howard Brookner's documentary about his life and times. Through the help of a mutual friend, publisher V. Vale, I had made arrangements to speak with him that afternoon in a corner of the theater lobby. This interview has gone unpublished until now.

My post-interview notes describe Burroughs's appearance that day thus: "Dressed in a conservative, old fashioned suit: grey jacket, slacks and vest. Cream-colored tie, which he fiddled with during the interview. Kept his beige felt hat on the entire time. Dark sox, brown soft leather shoes. Had a cane, which he held onto continuously. He appeared nervous and distracted at the beginning of the interview, looking away, shifting his hands on the cane a great deal. For much of the interview, he looked straight ahead when being asked a question, then would turn to me to give an answer."

While I wouldn't say that I cracked Burroughs's wall of reserve, I did manage to touch upon his views on everything from evolution to Egyptian hieroglyphics. His comments regarding what it takes to become a commercially-successful novelist are especially interesting.

After 40 minutes or so, Burroughs concluded our conversation. What remains are the following scattered insights from this late, great Dark Genius of American Letters.

Question: With *Cities of the Red Night* and *Place of Dead Roads,* you're writing in a more narrative way than you have in the past. How does that square with your opinion that words have become outmoded? Is that at all contradictory?

William S. Burroughs: No, there's no contradiction involved. I set out to write straightforward books, and the content required that. I don't say, "I have to do this" or, "this has to square with that" at all. Every book requires something different.

Q: In *Cities of the Red Night,* you touch upon the virus concept—you indicate that humanity itself began as a virus. . . .

WSB: Oh yes, that's the viral theory of evolution. It's finding more and more credence. The virus changes in several generations, which would then be genetically conveyed. It's quite a respectable theory of evolution at the present time. They're getting further and further away from Darwin, and coming to the tentative conclusion that evolutionary change is biological mutation [over] one or two generations, possibly through a virus. No virus we know at the present time acts in this way—that is to say, would affect biologic alterations, then genetics. But such a virus may have existed in the past.

Q: That sounds a bit like Lamarck's theory of evolution, where the animal stretches its neck to reach the fruit on the tree and then passes on this characteristic to its offspring.

WSB: Of course, that's the biologic heresy of the inheritance of one characteristic. That's quite different. [The virus theory] is more Darwin. The Darwin theory would be that the virus occasioned certain biologic changes, which then were genetically conveyed.

Q: I've been interested in your "cut-up" theory of writing for a long time, ever since I read *The Job* some years ago. . . .

WSB: It's simply the old montage method that's old hat in painting applied to writing. It's closer to the facts of human perception, because whenever you walk down the street or look out the window, your consciousness is affected by random factors. In other words, life is a cut-up.

Q: In *Cities of the Red Night,* you deal with cut-ups as a form of psychic research. Is that based on any research or experience of your own?

WSB: Oh yes, it's based on research of my own, naturally. If you take say, a time segment and start cutting it and playing around with it, often quite interesting things will emerge.

Q: The method in the novel was to read and then have sounds interspersed. . . .

WSB: Yes.

Q: What would be the theory behind that? Synchronicity?

WSB: No theory behind it, it's just a fact. Just a phenomenon.

Q: In *The Job,* you cited a case where you displaced a restaurant that had served bad food by your use of tape recordings. How did that work?

WSB: I don't know why it works. You simply make recordings in front of the restaurant, and you take pictures as you make the recordings. Then you play the recordings back in front of the place and take more pictures. . . .

Q: In front of the owners, or the workers?
WSB: It doesn't matter.

Q: Is it necessary to distort the recordings?
WSB: Not necessary at all. What you're doing actually, you're sort of making a hole in time. People are hearing what happened yesterday, and they think it's happening right now, so it makes a hole in time through which something can cause a disruption.

Q: How did you stumble upon this method?
WSB: It came from a series of experiments with actual street recordings, making recordings and playing them back in the streets. When you do that, you find that very interesting things will happen.

Q: I think people are still uncomfortable with this sort of acausal view of the world.
WSB: I've never subscribed to cause and effect.

Q: In *The Job,* you seemed optimistic that the world was changing for the better. That was in the 1970s. Are you disappointed with what has happened since then?
WSB: Well . . . it's been small changes. Like the fact that many of the objectives that people, the hippies, were trying to attain in the '60s have been attained: end of the Vietnam War, legalization or decriminalization of cannabis, minority rights, the end of censorship. [These are] very important gains.

Q: I actually didn't expect you to say that. . . .
WSB: Well, why not? That's happened. . . .

Q: Well, somehow I thought you were concerned with something more fundamental, such as the power structures, and how they weren't brought down by the generation that came of age at that time.
WSB: No, no—any political change [comes] in small gains. Gains like that are valuable.

Q: Are you sympathetic to libertarian ideas? Does the Libertarian Party hold any attraction for you?
WSB: I don't even know what that is.

Q: They believe in as few laws as possible across the board, even down to building codes.

WSB: That's sensible enough, of course. The fewer laws, the better.

Q: By the way, do you mind me asking you about your opinions from the '70s?

WSB: No, but opinions are meant to be changed. It's very unlikely that an opinion wouldn't have undergone some alteration.

Q: Back then, you discussed restructuring society to phase out the family. If that actually happened, what would form social bonds in its place?

WSB: Well, there isn't any clear-cut substitute for that.

Q: That was a utopian speculation?

WSB: Yes.

Q: It's something you can envision, but not in the near future.

WSB: It's not easy to envision. I mean, OK, you can have people brought up in some kind of state institute, but then you're back to the same thing. That wouldn't necessarily be any improvement.

Q: What about the segregation of the sexes? Is that an idea that still appeals to you?

WSB: Yes, I would say so. Evolutionary mutations can occur quite rapidly in small, isolated groups. They took a small group of fish and put them in an entirely different environment, and over several generations they got quite different biologic changes. So I'd like to see more small, isolated groups with very different orientations.

Q: And one way of breaking that down would be male/female systems of groupings?

WSB: Yes, that would be one way. Of course, the very contrary is happening. You've got less and less of that, and more uniformity and standardization. But biologically, ultimately the only possibility for any species to survive is mutation. All species are doomed like all individuals, but the point is, can they change?

Q: Another point you've touched upon a great deal is dualism, which I guess in part means male/female, yes/no, right/wrong and so forth. Do you see any progress being made overcoming that?

WSB: No, I don't.

Q: It seems like a lot of your ideas are concerned with unity of some kind. . . .

WSB: Yes. Like the dominant and nondominant brain hemispheres. It would be biologically desirable if they could somehow merge instead of posing a duality.

Q: Some people would call that a spiritual idea. Do you think of yourself as a spiritual writer? Does that word give you any problems?

WSB: No, it doesn't give me any problems at all. There's no distinction—in other words, any problem is a spiritual problem.

Q: Do you think that your views on drugs have been misinterpreted at all by your fans?

WSB: I don't know. What views?

Q: I believe that you've said from time to time that harder narcotics are not good for the human body and don't produce any desirable effects. . . .

WSB: I would certainly say that's true of cocaine.

Q: What about heroin or morphine?

WSB: No, there's a place for heroin and morphine. The ill effects have been vastly overestimated.

Q: I think you made the statement at one time that "junk is death." Am I taking that statement out of context?

WSB: Probably. I may have made such a statement, but we do know that people live to a ripe old age on it.

Q: I think what I was getting at was that people may have misinterpreted what you've written on the subject, that they should emulate your entire life to get to the point where you are now. Would that be misconstruing your experiences and your thinking?

WSB: Well, yes. I don't see any reason why they should.

Q: Has it ever crossed your mind that people may misinterpret what you've written?

WSB: Well, that's inevitable that they'll misinterpret a great deal of it.

Q: It seems that drugs across the board are still identified with rebellion, and that may be a naive idea.

WSB: A very naive idea indeed, but all sorts of problems are created by legislation [against drugs].

Q: An awful lot of your ideas have been appropriated into a pop context, especially by musicians and writers. Is that a compliment, or does that make you feel uncomfortable?

WSB: I don't react to that in any way. If pop groups want to make use of them in any way they want, I consider that for the good.

Q: Have the popular arts—particularly pop music—progressed from the time that you were in your 20s? I mean people who have been influenced by your ideas, like Patti Smith and Jim Carroll. . . .

WSB: Well, in my 20s, musicians only played in night clubs and road houses and maybe made $100 or $200 a week. Playing to mass audiences in places like Shea Stadium is an entirely new phenomenon. It began really in the late '40s—I'm really talking about the beginnings of pop music, the skiffle groups and that sort of thing.

Q: A lot of these people have learned from you and honor you. Do you hold any of them in high esteem?

WSB: I don't know much about pop music. I'm not very knowledgeable about it. I don't normally go to performances.

Q: Do you think what motivates you to write has changed over the years from your earliest writing days?

WSB: I don't think a writer knows his reasons for writing at all. As you grow older you regard it more as a job.

Q: It seems that over the years you've written about many of the same things.

WSB: All writers tend to write about the same thing.

Q: In the introduction to *Naked Lunch,* you stated that one of your goals was to "wise up the marks." Is education a goal of yours in your writing?

WSB: No, except that the function of art is to make people aware of what they know and don't know. To extend the peripheries of that, in that sense, yes.

Q: You use your novels to introduce certain ideas into your plot lines. . . .
WSB: Yes, of course. There's no distinction between novels and ideas.

Q: I remember reading in the book that Victor Bockris wrote about you [*With William Burroughs: Report from the Bunker*] that you've made attempts to write straight commercial sorts of writing. Is that the case?

WSB: No. It's not possible. People may think they can sit down and write a bestseller, but you can't do it. A bestseller is written up to the level of a man's ability. You can't write down to the reading public.

Q: For instance, Mickey Spillane wrote on the level he was on, and it just happened to be something people liked.

WSB: Yeah. But that's the best he can do—that's the point. There's two kinds of bestsellers. One is something that people know something about and want to know more about, like the Mafia, how a hotel works, and so forth. If they don't know anything about it, then it's no good. And the other is the challenge posed by the menace, like *Jaws*—the menace can be an epidemic, a shark, rats, whatever. Those are the two main forms.

Q: It would seem that you would be eminently qualified to write either of those if you wished to.

WSB: No, you can't do it. You can do it, sure, but it won't necessarily work as a bestseller. Another rule of the bestseller is that you do not ask people to experience anything they find difficult to experience. Well, I always do ask people to experience things that are quite difficult to experience, and if I didn't, I wouldn't be writing up to the level of my ability.

Q: That shows a sense of responsibility to your own talent, if nothing else.

WSB: Yes. Every serious writer has that obligation to do a good job of writing.

Q: Was that a conscious decision of yours?

WSB: No, that's just the way it works.

Q: Was your first book [*Junkie*] written that way? For you, I guess, it was a fairly dashed-off project. . . .

WSB: It was. I set myself a very simple objective—simply to put down what I remembered about experiences with addiction. I didn't set myself very much of a task there.

Q: A lot of your characters seem to come from experiences earlier in your life, and you still seem to draw upon them to some degree. Have you experienced anything in the last ten years that has been as inspiring?

WSB: Well . . . other writing, movies, there's continually input. It can be anything. Books—they can be absolute trash, but they can have good ideas.

Q: Are you still doing sound cut-ups with tape recorders?

WSB: I'm not doing anything with tape recorders [now].

Q: Did they outlive their usefulness to you?

WSB: As far as I'm concerned, yes. I never used a tape recorder to compose onto it—it's a waste of time. It's more trouble to take it off a tape recorder than it is to put it on a typewriter to begin with.

Q: Have you any interest in making films? I would think that dealing directly with pictures would have a lot of appeal for you.

WSB: Hmmm . . . there are things you can do in films that you can't do with words, but there are lots of things you can do with words that you can't probably do in films. Take the end of *The Great Gatsby*—it's great prose, and you can't put it into film. Voice-overs are very, very awkward.

Q: What I was thinking of was, in *The Job,* you talk about your interest in hieroglyphics, unambiguous images that can only be interpreted one way. . . .

WSB: But that's not true, you see. If you actually study hieroglyphs, you find they can be interpreted in many ways. And also, a lot of it is purely arbitrary. How do you say "but," "who," "what" in hieroglyphs—the answer is, you don't. You're using arbitrary symbols. So there isn't any really complete pictorial language. How do you indicate tense, if something's happening in the past, present or future? You do it by purely arbitrary conventions. The grammar of a pictorial language like hieroglyphs is very cumbersome.

Q: I think you know the section of *The Job* that I'm referring to [pp. 204–211], where you laid out those five or six images. . . .

WSB: Yeah. That's all very well, but if you're gonna really write in it, it becomes extremely cumbersome.

Q: In some of your writings, you've made reference to Robert A. Monroe, the sound engineer [author of *Journeys Out of the Body,* which describes how certain sound frequencies can induce astral projection]. Have you used his methods and had positive results with them?

WSB: No, not positive. Neutral, I'd say. Nothing very startling.

Q: Are you working on anything presently?

WSB: Yes, I'm working on a novel now, a sequel to *Place of Dead Roads* entitled *The Western Lands.* A lot of it will take place in ancient Egypt.

Q: Norman Mailer had his own version of that [*Ancient Evenings*]. . . .

WSB: Yes. It was very good. I thought it was a magnificent piece of work.

Mapping the Cosmic Currents: An Interview with William Burroughs

Peter Von Ziegesar / 1986

Originally appeared in *New Letters* (53:1) Fall 1986. It is reprinted by permission of *New Letters* and the Curators of the University of Missouri-Kansas City.

William Burroughs now lives in a small one-story frame house not far from the center of Lawrence, Kansas. It is an older neighborhood, somewhat outside of the college scene, which is Lawrence's main industry. At first, the house seems deserted, something out of, say, *Naked Lunch*. Then James Grauerholtz comes to the door. Behind him, stands William S. Burroughs in silhouette.

Burroughs, 72, is stooped at the shoulders and has a restless way of turning to and fro, lifting up pieces of paper and putting them down. He seems older than the recent photographs; his eyes are sunken, and the flesh under his eyes has slipped. The famous Burroughs voice is intact, though, deep and vibrating, and his mind remains restlessly alert, continuously ferreting out facts in the conversation, trundling along on unpredictably fruitful sidetracks.

Burroughs smokes incessantly as he talks, beginning with his long, distinguished and controversial writing career that includes *On These Desert Roads, Naked Lunch, The Soft Machine, The Yage Letters, Nova Express,* and the recently published *Queer.*

New Letters: Why is *Queer* being published now, rather than 30 years ago?

William Burroughs: Well, it wasn't publishable 30 years ago. Mr. A. A. Whims of Ace Books said: "I'd be in jail if I published this." That shows you the change, since the book is very mild indeed. No, it wasn't publishable at that time, and then it was in an archive or left in a trunk somewhere. It was a fragment, I wasn't too anxious to publish it. But then the current publisher looked at it and said that he was impressed, and if I would write an introduction, he would issue it. That was how it came about. And the reason for the delay.

NL: How do you feel about it now? Are you happy that it was published?

WB: Well, I think it forced me to sort of look at things that I wasn't too anxious to look at, but that's always good for a writer, to be maneuvered into a position where he has to see things that he would rather evade. *Queer* is about a very specific phenomenon—the phenomenon of withdrawal. That's what the book's about, about a month of withdrawal. In which, of course, you get people disintegrating. The booksellers in New York report that it's selling well.

NL: Do you recognize an evolution in your style? It seems apparent, between your introduction and the manuscript itself.

WB: Oh, *yea!* See, I didn't start writing until I was 35. And so a lot of the book reads quite amateurishly in a way.

NL: When did you actually write *Queer?*

WB: About 1950 or thereabouts. It was not all written, you see, in one piece as it were. There were a number of sections, and I can't trace all the times.

NL: What's really striking about *Queer* are the *routines.*

WB: Which of course continued and formed almost the basis of *Naked Lunch* and other books I've written.

NL: Did you have any notion at that time that they would become so important to you?

WB: Well, no, because I was just starting to write. I didn't know whether I could publish anything further. *Junky* was published in 1953, and I was in South America at the time. And then there was a long period from 1953 to 1959 in which nothing was published, until *Naked Lunch* was brought out in Paris in 1959 by Girodias.

NL: What strikes me about the routines is that they always emerge in images of real horror.

WB: And humor! Humor and horror combined.

NL: But the horror seems stronger, and that is the sort of humor you seemed to have emphasized and developed. Why that and not another kind of humor?

WB: Well, I don't think a writer has much more chance than someone with smallpox. In certain cases he's going to encounter certain features, certain manifestations which he can't control at all. For example, he doesn't sit down and decide what he's going to write about, it's decided *for* him. That famous quote of Norman Mailer, "The only American writer that might conceivably be possessed by genius," is quite correct, at least in its form. You don't *possess* genius, you are possessed *by* it. Henry Miller says, "Who writes the great books? Not we who have our names on the covers." The writer is simply someone who turnes in to certain cosmic currents. He's sort of a transcriber, an explorer, a map maker. Naturally he wants to make an accurate map. That's his job, his function. But he can't arbitrarily control the area he's mapping.

NL: Do you feel that you have happened to tune in on a particularly vicious channel?

WB: No, no, I don't see it that way. Laughter is, of course, rejection, and also therefore a way of dealing with impossible situations, such as everyone finds themselves in at the present moment.

NL: Is your idea to expose evil in the world?

WB: Well, another function of art is to make people aware of what they know and what they don't *know* that they know. Because you can't tell anybody anything they don't know already on some level.

NL: You wrote once in a letter to Ginsberg that there is a space within "B" movies where sex passes the censor, where America's rottenness spurts through. Is that part of the terrain you are mapping?

WB: Marginal really, but part of it.

NL: To go back to *Queer,* it seems to me that the relationship described between you and Allerton immediately becomes one where you are trying to buy his affection by taking his camera out of pawn. I mean, Lee takes his camera out of pawn and then essentially hires Allerton as a paid companion.

WB: Exactly, exactly. Well, that's a very common situation, that someone wants to impose obligations. Which isn't a good approach at all, it's a bad one. But it's very common and I am, shall I say, mal adroit. But I've always been very mal adroit in amorous areas, oddly enough. Doing the wrong thing, saying the wrong thing.

NL: Well, I bring it up, because you are always talking about "Control" in your books.

WB: Well, this is an integral part of most intimate relationships. One is always trying to "control" the other. The way women are always trying to manipulate men to get them in a position where the men will depend on them. It's just an integral part of the whole sexual comedy.

NL: You have called love a virus.

WB: Yes, well what is the essence of virus? It's repetition. If you meet something often enough, it wears out, like an old joke.

NL: But you seem to have expanded the notion of personal control to cosmic control. Do you feel that there are tremendous forces of "Control" in America today?

WB: Well, the whole species is in the grip of Control. Headed for biologic suicide through standardization. That is, tending to rule out any possibility for change and mutation. Which is, of course, the only hope for any species, because all species are doomed from inception, as are all individuals.

NL: You mean that a species must grow, evolve and change in order to survive?

WB: Of course.

NL: And you've linked that to space travel. Why is space travel necessary?

WB: Only way to go is up. We've got no place else, having burned down this planet.

NL: Isn't space travel just going to bring more people to destroy more planets?

WB: No, because space is literally another dimension. Once the transition to space is made, I see it as a transition as drastic as the transition from water to land, with all sorts of new experiences, new fears. You see, the fear of falling would have no meaning for a fish. But as soon as he gets upon land, it will soon *have* meaning. So I think it's as drastic a change as that. So far, we've sent people into space in an aqualung. They haven't gone into space at all. Well, to make the human artifact suitable for space conditions is going to require biologic alterations.

NL: Space has never been a place where much life has existed.

WB: We don't know. We think of life as being something exactly like us. Don Juan speaks of the possibility of *inorganic* beings. And now we find that down at the bottom of the ocean are what's known as "Black Smokers" where hot gases bubble up. Now, this is two miles down, there's no light and no oxygen. And according to all our definitions, life couldn't exist there. But very plentiful life exists, the big clams and crabs and worms. And they eat minerals and sulfur dioxide. So there we have creatures living under what would seem to be impossible conditions.

NL: You've described growing up in Missouri as a "Midwestern, small town, cracker barrel, pratfall type of folk lore" and said the experience was the source of the routines that were in *Naked Lunch.*

WB: Oh yes, lots of them. Oh yes, well, that includes the whole area of the Midwest.

NL: Which you live in now. Do you still see remnants of the old midwest here?

WB: Of course the landscape is still here, what's left of it. But no, the culture's all gone. This is a whole other era.

NL: Missouri has turned out a few men who seem to have sort of an ironic, sarcastic twist, maybe a habit of saying that things aren't necessarily so. Mark Twain might be mentioned, as well as Thomas Hart Benton and Harry Truman—even T. S. Eliot.

WB: Well, they had their motto, "I'm from Missouri, you'll have to show me." But as to what influence that had on me personally, I don't know. I think you'll find that just as many people with the same turn of mind came from somewhere else.

NL: Perhaps when you went East from St. Louis to attend Harvard, you had a different frame of mind than people who grew up there.

WB: Well, that's obvious. I mean anyone is going to have the frame of mind of where he came from. But St. Louis is not quite like any other town. It's not quite South, it's not quite Midwest. It was divided in the Civil War, and the line went right through St. Louis.

NL: It seems to me you eulogized the western point of view as well as the western landscapes in *The Place of Dead Roads.*

WB: Oh, certainly, certainly.

NL: The degree of violence at the time also seems to fascinate you, seems to have become an integrated part of your writing. Has suicide ever seemed a possibility?

WB: Never! Never! No, God no! I was just thinking, the idea of shooting myself gives me the horrors! I do have a 45 in the other room, but the idea of shooting myself is appalling.

NL: But isn't the act of taking drugs, especially heroin, a suicidal act?

WB: I didn't think so at all. People live to a ripe old age on drugs.

NL: But I mean, when you're on the drug, it's a substitute for life.

WB: Well, that depends entirely on the amount. If someone lets their habit get away from them then they can sort of be a vegetable. But people often do control the drug so that it becomes a very minor factor—like doctors. I know a doctor who took a grain and half of morphine a day for twenty years—never raised the dose. Of course he probably functioned very well.

NL: But you seem to at least enjoy *describing* the act of killing and shooting in a variety of ways, linked to a sexuality and all sorts of things. How does that fit in with your world view?

WB: I've been principally attracted to the Ishmaelites and Hassan I Sabbah, and assassination as a way to salvation. The idea that everyone has to encounter and kill his own death, personified in an enemy.

NL: Have you ever had the urge to actually, physically do that? To fight a war, for instance?

WB: Oh, certainly, certainly.

NL: Some of the scenes in *Dead Roads,* particularly, seem Blakean. They seem visionary and just worlds apart. Were you influenced by Blake?

WB: To some extent, yes. He is one of the prime influences on me, through Allen Ginsberg. But I have read Blake.

NL: These days you have quite a following. There's a movement called Punk or New Wave that might be said to look to you as a mentor.

WB: Yes, I've gotten very positive reactions, and had relationships with some of the people in punk music. Patti Smith's a good friend of mine and David Bowie has always been very friendly. We're moving in sort of the same direction—they want to get further out, to explore new things, increased awareness, and that is a point of contact, of common interest. There's a group here called "The Micronauts" that Bill Rich, a friend of mine, manages.

NL: I've heard that you wrote a song for them.

WB: Well, I wrote a song . . . I had this silly old rhyme and they wanted to take it to music, so they did.

NL: There seems to be a trend in art and literature now—sort of post-apocalyptic. I'd say Keith Haring and some of those other painters . . .

WB: Keith is great. You see his exhibit? I had seen only his small drawings, and well I saw, you know, something there, but I didn't really *see* him, his paintings, until I saw the big paintings on exhibit in New York—as big as that wall—just jumping with vitality and life—it's the real thing. He's great.

NL: His images present mutations?
WB: Oh, all kinds of weird mutations, weird figures. Yea!

NL: What do you think of the recent fame that you've accumulated? How does it affect you?
WB: I don't think anything in particular about it. It's all to the good, naturally. It sells books.

NL: Is it well-deserved, is it on time, is it too late?
WB: Well, certainly it is well deserved. I won't say it's on-time *or* too late.

NL: For quite a while you must have felt very isolated.
WB: No, no, you must remember that I was living outside of the United States for the most part, and the people that I was in contact with were friends and supporters. So there was no feeling of isolation particularly. Nor does it make any difference whether one is widely accepted or not, so far as one's immediate life goes. I don't *contact* people who don't accept me. Naturally increased acceptance, being in the Academy and all that sort of thing, is always good. It gives you leverage in any situation. That is, you find it easier to get something done by the consulate or by officials and so on and so forth. It's an advantage, and in this life you grab every advantage you can. Hang on to it.

NL: As you say, you're with friends who accept you, but when you step outside of that, suddenly do you get the feeling you have to control yourself?
WB: No, I don't have to control myself. I just act the way I act. I don't have any difficulty with acceptance. A person can be fully accepted by people around them, even a whole town and be rejected by, say, the media. The media seems to be a sort of an entity in itself in some ways. They have opinions which don't necessarily reflect a majority at all. For example, the whole media is anti-gun. Even in places like here in Kansas or in the Western states, where such a stand is completely unpopular, completely against the culture, the newspapers are still anti-gun.

NL: But you think the people are pro-gun?
WB: In the Western states, sure they are. But the press consistently all

through the country is against guns. I could understand this bias if it was limited to the Eastern seaboard, but it isn't.

NL: Well, I would say in contrast that the people of the Midwest are anti-homosexual.

WB: How are you going to say that? I mean, where are your statistics? Have you asked everybody?

NL: No, I don't have statistics. My point is that the people in the West don't necessarily believe in "live and let live," in every sense of the word.

WB: I don't think they do. But you cannot generalize. I mean, what people are you talking about? Are you talking about academics, construction workers, the wealthy, the ghetto-dwellers? It's such a heterogenous bunch of people in the U.S. It's really difficult to generalize about what *they* think, because there *is* no *they.*

NL: Is that part of what you were talking about—things getting standardized? Is your feeling that they've not *yet* standardized?

WB: Yes, but everything is moving in that direction. There's a new theory of evolution, the theory of punctured equilibrium, that changes can happen quite rapidly in small, isolated groups, whose equilibrium is suddenly punctured, so they have to adjust to drastically new conditions. Well, everything now is geared to prevent that from happening. The few isolated groups that are left are being sort of steam-rollered out of the way. In South America, what little rain forest is left is going—to make way for more and more *people.* Counterfeit human stock, not worth the flesh it's printed on.

NL: It's implied in the introduction to *Queer* that there's one kind of therapeutic value in writing. You said you had to "write my way out of it." Does that mean self-therapy?

WB: Well, yes, certainly. In a general way, work is the best therapy. Gertrude Stein always said the worst misfortune anyone could have is not to have a *metier,* a trade. So work in one form or another is salvation for millions of people. This is just my particular, particular job.

NL: In the introduction to *The Place of Dead Roads,* you wrote "Happiness is a by-product of function," and you described the earth as a spaceship in which everyone might have a place, something to do.

WB: Well, it *is* a spaceship, obviously. In fact, at one time each person *did* have something to do, but less and less as time goes on. You now have one role and a million applicants, and not a very good role at that.

NL: You mean, to be a writer?

WB: To be anything. Millions of people want to be gangsters, for example. They've got a miserable objective, those millions of people trying to squeeze themselves into one wretched role. They'll never make it of course. You know, the sort of unprivileged slum people, they all want to be gangsters. One of the principal ways out of the ghetto is crime, and mostly drug-pushing now.

NL: What is the most important aspect of your being accepted now? Your skill being accepted?

WB: You just do the best job of writing and that's it. You hope, naturally that you'll be read, and you hope that people will realize what you're doing, will understand what you write, that's all.

NL: Do you feel an important mission?

WB: No, I don't feel a mission *or* a responsibility. It isn't what writers do.

NL: Well in some sense you seem to have a mission to explain the idea of standardization and control.

WB: Well, sure, that's what you're writing about. The areas that you're writing about, sure, from that aspect, yes, very definitely.

NL: What is your present relationship to contemporary writing?

WB: Lots of writers have influenced me, particularly Denton Welch, and also Conrad, Graham Greene, Kafka, Paul Bowles, D. H. Lawrence—*The Plumed Serpent.* So I've got all these influences. Other authors are an important part of a writer's input. Some of them may be good and some of them may be trash, but there's a continual input from that sort of reading.

NL: Where do you stand in contemporary literature?

WB: I don't think there *is* any such thing at the present time. Of course, we've never had literary movements in America like in France, so you could say, oh, this is surrealist, or this is this and this is that.

NL: What about the Beat movement?

WB: The Beat movement was more sociological than literary. Of course the Beat writers have something in common, but not a great deal from a literary point of view, despite a certain continuity of ideas. Corso, Kerouac, Ginsberg and myself, we knew each other, we were all friends. Still are. Except for Kerouac.

NL: I've wanted to ask you something about *Naked Lunch*. Your famous introduction says, "I awoke from The Sickness at the age of forty-five, calm and sane, and in reasonable good health. Most survivors do not remember the delerium in detail. I apparently took detailed notes . . . I have no precise memory of writing the notes which now have been published under the title *Naked Lunch*." Yet your letters to Allen Ginsberg dating from this period showed you taking your career as a writer very seriously, even to the point of preparing magazine articles about Tangiers.

WB: Well, that is uncalled for, really. It's not true, when you come to think about it.

NL: So it was hyperbole?

WB: It's just hyperbole, yes. Because I had quite precise recollections. I was somewhat surprised when I finally saw the Allen Ginsberg letters, because I hadn't seen them in years. Alan Ansen, a friend of mine in Athens, had them, and I went and got them in 1973. I was surprised to see how much material is *in* the letters that later went into *Naked Lunch*. That I'd written a great deal of *Naked Lunch* during this seemingly unproductive period. But most of it—well not *most* of it, but part of it—was written in 1957 and '58 after I'd taken a cure with Dr. Dent in London.

NL: You stood against the conformity and boredom of that time?
WB: Exactly.

NL: Do you feel that the facade of middle-class morality masks a really horrifying American character?

WB: Well, that's much too general a concept. There's the whole nuclear situation. We're sitting here on a bomb at all times, you know. God, yes.

NL: And yet you continue to write. What are you working on now?

WB: It's an extension of *Cities of the Red Night* and *Place of Dead Roads*. The final book of the trilogy will be called *The Western Lands*. I'm talking about the western lands of Egypt, not the old west here. And that is a direct continuation of *The Place of Dead Roads*.

NL: Do you have a broader audience than you had before?

WB: Well, yes, certainly. It's obvious that I'm selling more books now than I did 20 years ago.

NL: And whom do you think they are?
WB: Oh, well, I *know*. Because I've given about 300 readings. So, well,

they tend to be more young than old, university people, but not entirely. Quite a lot of older people show up as well. Yes indeed, that was one of the gratifying things about giving readings, that you actually get to *meet* the people who read your books.

NL: Do you keep them in mind when you're writing?

WB: No, that's not the way you write. You might think of this person or that person, but you don't sit down and project an audience and write for it. Oh, no, you don't do that at all.

An Interview with William S. Burroughs

Larry McCaffery and Jim McMenamin / 1987

Great authors have a way of creating texts that defy categorization and assimilation. Typically, a full literary generation elapses before the true significance of a radically new imagination can be seen in useful critical perspective; usually it's even longer before such an imagination begins to influence other writers. Consider Jorge Luis Borges, Jack Kerouac, Samuel Beckett, and Thomas Pynchon—authors who changed our notion of what fiction can be. William S. Burroughs has played a similar role in post–World War II American fiction. While Burroughs's seminal influence on the Beat generation, particularly Allen Ginsberg and Jack Kerouac, has been widely (though often cursorily) noted, the full extent of his pervasive influence on contemporary art—which extends to experimental cinema, poetry, performance art, jazz and rock music, as well as fiction—is just becoming obvious now, some thirty years after *Naked Lunch* appeared with perhaps more fanfare than any novel since *Ulysses.* Nowhere has the influence of Burroughs's radical approach to style and content been more apparent than in the work of urban-technoguerrilla artists such as punk and "industrial noise" musicians, Mark Pauline and the Survival Research Laboratory, and cyberpunk SF writers.

Not surprisingly, Burroughs's work has had its biggest influence on the radical fringe of SF—on those authors who are most concerned with formal innovations, and specifically with presenting visions of urban despair and victimization that share some of Burroughs's nightmarish intensity, black humor, and sense of dislocation. Like J. G. Ballard, Philip K. Dick, and Thomas Pynchon—three other authors who have had an analogous impact on SF in the '80s and who were also operating at the intersection of SF, the avant-garde, and "serious" fiction—Burroughs is a savage, wickedly humorous satirist. Even in the early works that are grounded most clearly in the imagery and clichés of SF pulp fiction (including not only *Naked Lunch* but also his trilogy, *The Soft Machine* [1961], *The Ticket That Exploded* [1962], and *Nova Express* [1964]), Burroughs displays a literary imagination that had fully assimilated the implications of an array of avant-garde artists, ranging from Rimbaud to T. S. Eliot (who lectured at Harvard while Burroughs was an undergraduate there), James Joyce, Samuel Beckett, and the surrealists. His most famous stylistic innovation—the "cut-up" or "fold-in" method of constructing new texts—was developed by his friend and collaborator, the painter Brion Gysin. His success in using this device as a means of short-circuiting the usual linguistic pathways has tended to obscure the fact that Burroughs is also one of the most skilled and eloquent modern prose stylists, a writer whose remarkable ear for the full range of colloquial American idioms is probably unmatched since Mark Twain's.

Burroughs is also a quintessentially postmodernist artist. Indeed, fully twenty years before the term "postmodernism" achieved critical ascendancy, Burroughs was working out implications today associated with postmodernist aesthetics that remain unsurpassed in their originality and the relentless nature of their application. The postmodernist quality of his work derives principally from the formal methods he has devised to assert that the central threat facing modern humanity involves the control of individuals through an increasingly sophisticated system of technologically produced words, images, and other dangerously addictive substances (with drug addiction being an all-pervasive metaphor throughout his work). Burroughs seeks to willfully subvert such power-wielding in part through an "innoculation program" in which readers are presented with montages of pop cultural images, fragmented texts culled from a bewildering variety of sources (Shakespeare, Kafka, scientific textbooks, '30s pulp SF authors, T. S. Eliot, Denton Welch, etc.), snippets of Burroughs's daily journals, and other materials. All these are transformed into texts whose progress is tied less to narrative continuity than to principles of poetic association.

Burroughs's fiction is utterly contemporary in its formal emphasis on fragmentation, its blending of pop and serious forms, its emphasis on the transformative process of experience, and its insistence that "meanings" are always provisional, that even the most sacred texts can be (and *must* be) continually deconstructed and reconstituted. Equally contemporary—and of particular relevance to Burroughs's role in the evolution of SF—has been his thematic preoccupation with reality-as-film, drug addiction, information control, and the technological/biological/psychological manipulation of people who have grown addicted to words, images, sex, and other thanatological substances.

Despite being firmly embedded in postmodernism's dystopian present and near future, Burroughs's work is equally significant in its exploration of universal issues. The human tendency to control and destroy others for greed and sexual gratification; the ongoing human need to resist the destructive impulses of others and themselves; a common search for some means by which to transcend our personal, biological extinction—these and many other timeless issues are examined in a body of work that is "science fictional" in the tradition of Jonathan Swift.

Jim McMenamin and I interviewed William Burroughs in July 1987 in Boulder, Colorado. Several years earlier, he had moved from "The Bunker" (his Manhattan residence) to Lawrence, Kansas, but each summer he has been a regular participant at the Naropa Institute, where he gives readings, addresses the audience, and assists young writers. The previous evening he had delivered one of his patented readings, full of playfulness and discomforting obscenities, pointed social and political commentary, and tall tales. We met Burroughs in the sparsely furnished apartment where he was staying during the conference; the only visible reading material was the *National Enquirer.* At seventy-three, Burroughs appeared healthily cadaverous, and he was spry enough to sprint up and down the stairs several times when he needed to check a reference. Later, when we glanced back at him standing in his apartment balcony, we felt certain we were experiencing something of the same exhilaration that Kerouac must have felt forty-five years ago in Manhattan, when he had just left Burroughs's apartment for the first time.

Jim McMenamin: You've just completed *The Western Lands.* Did writing this novel become a way for you to explore your own views about death and a possible afterlife?

William Burroughs: Naturally. All my books express what I actually believe in, or I wouldn't be writing them. *The Western Lands* also goes into the possiblity of hybridization, the crossing of man and animals. This goes against one of the basic taboos: that the species must remain separate. But there must have been a time in the past when hybridization was rampant. Otherwise why would we now have this terrific variety of species? This means there must have been some factors operating then that are not in operation at the present time—some radiation affecting things, or who knows what. This is, of course, related to various theories of evolution. There's the virus theory of evolution, which is one I've always been interested in. If you have a virus producing biological changes that are then conveyed genetically, you can have an entirely new species in a couple of generations instead of it taking millions of years. There's also the punctuational view of evolution, which says that if you take a species of fish from one place and put them in a completely foreign environment, they will mutate very rapidly. Alterations occur in response to drastic alterations in equilibrium in small, isolated groups. So that's another possibility. It's interesting because the evolutionary trend toward standardization will tend to rule this out. There aren't any isolated groups in which such changes could occur. The only thing is that no virus we know of right now acts in that way. Of course, this idea is a version of the Lamarckian heresy of the inheritance of acquired characteristics.

Larry McCaffery: It sounds almost like the biological equivalent of entropy—the idea that things would spread out in a random way so there could be no interaction, the end result being total chaos or death.

WB: Or total lethargy.

JM: What have you been reading recently?

WB: I read a lot of doctor books and spy books. Not much that you would call serious fiction—for that I usually go back a ways. Right now I'm reading all of Conrad. He's the greatest novelist who ever lived, far and away. You can see a lot of Conrad in my recent work. And Graham Greene, too.

LM: After spending all that time in places like London, New York, Paris, and Tangier, what made you decide to move to Lawrence, Kansas?

WB: Out of all the questions in the world, I've been asked that one so many times recently that I'm sick of it. People act as if there must be something very portentous behind moving to Lawrence. Well, things just don't work that way. James Grauerholz was living in Lawrence, and I had visited there several times. I wanted to get out of New York anyway, for a number of reasons. I'd looked at Boulder as a possibility, and I decided I didn't want to live there. Lawrence just worked out. It's a university town—nothing very special—it's all right.

JM: Do you miss the sensory bombardment that you had in New York, or is it something you don't need anymore?

WB: I didn't have it in New York. My working habits are about the same in Lawrence as they were in New York. I didn't got to parties or discotheques. I've never been to Studio 54. I didn't go to various celebrity in-spots. I didn't do any of those things. So, there wasn't any bombardment. Only in Lawrence I can get out of doors and row, and shoot, and keep cats, and things that I can't do in New York.

LM: Have you been watching the Oliver North testimony and other aspects of the Iran-Contra hearings?

WB: I've watched about five minutes of it, just enough to get a vague idea of what's going on. I'm not interested in all the intricacies. It's clear that the '80s will go down in history as the Lie Decade. Ferdinand Marcos, of course, gets the undoubted prize as the most flagrant and outrageous liar of the Lie Decade. But he's got some competition.

JM: I heard you had met with David Cronenberg to discuss a movie version of *Naked Lunch.* How did that come about—were you already familiar with his work?

WB: No, although when the possibility of doing *Naked Lunch* came up, I made a point of seeing some of his films, and I liked them. I saw *The Dead Zone*—that's the one he did from the Stephen King book—and a few others. I haven't seen *The Fly,* which was apparently very successful. Cronenberg approached us about doing the film, so we met in Tangier. That was two or three years ago, and nothing definite has occurred. Nothing happens until it happens in the film world. Actually, I haven't been paying much attention to films recently. I go very occasionally. About the last film I saw was *Brazil.*

LM: Do you think the media's willingness to offer the public all this excessive violence—on the news, in films, on MTV—will eventually desensitize people to violence?

WB: To some extent, naturally. It's bound to happen. Like the first time you go on a roller coaster, it scares you; the second time, not so much; the third time, not at all.

JM: There seems to be an ambiguity in your presentation of violence—a combination of horror, black humor, grim fascination, maybe even sympathy. Do you see your portrayal of brutality and violence as being primarily an exorcism or a celebration?

WB: Neither. There's a lot of violence in my work because violence is obviously necessary in certain circumstances. I'm often talking in a revolutionary, guerrilla context where violence is the only recourse. I feel a degree of ambivalence with regard to any use of violence. There are certainly circumstances where it seems to be indicated. How can you protect people

without weapons? If you're interested in protecting, you can't. I was very
much a fan of the Guardian Angels. That's the answer to violent crime, right
there. They should have regular patrols in all cities, and that would eliminate
the whole crime situation. But nobody—particularly no politician—wants to
eliminate any problems. Problems are what keep them in there. Anyway,
some system of organized patrols is the obvious answer to that problem.

JM: Obviously, an outfit like that would need to be formed locally.

WB: It would have to be local. But, of course, the last people who would
want to see something like this come into operation would be the police.
They would become redundant. All these big problems we suffer from are so
absurdly simple. Like the drug problem: maintenance for those who can't or
won't stop, and effective treatment for those who want to stop. There isn't
any effective treatment at the present time, and the government is putting no
money into researching the basic mechanisms of addiction. None of the endorphin research is funded with government money. Endorphin is one of the
keys to addiction, and it could lead to really effective treatment.

JM: You used to say that apomorphine could be a major breakthrough for
treating heroin addicts. Do you still feel that way?

WB: It's been more or less confirmed now that apomorphine stimulates
the production of endorphins, just as acupuncture stimulates the body's natural pain killer(s) under certain circumstances. I've got a file like the Manhattan telephone book of inquiries from probation officers and prison officials
about apomorphine research. But when I write them back, the first thing you
know they're being threatened with the loss of their jobs.

JM: What's behind the lack of governmental research into this area—Drug
Enforcement Administration repression?

WB: Certainly. The DEA doesn't want to see an effective treatment for
narcotics. My God, where would they be if there weren't any drug addicts?

LM: The public's negative attitude about drugs today seems dangerously
simplistic. There was a period back in the '60s when it seemed as if a genu-
inely enlightened attitude might be evolving.

WB: Yes, it seems like all the ground gained in the '60s—in all sorts of
areas—is now being lost.

LM: Is this rightward swing an inevitable reaction?

WB: No swing is inevitable. I'm not even convinced that what we're seeing is necessarily a swing. What we're seeing with drug attitudes is certainly engineered by the administration. They're the ones orchestrating this whole antidrug nonsense, and this hysteria could turn the whole planet into a police state. Hell, probably the biggest danger we face today is a fascist takeover under the guise of this colossal red herring of the drug pretense. Narcs roaming around free from all restraint.

LM: How might things develop if the governments (and whatever multinationals are calling the shots behind the scenes) can maintain the current hysteria level?

WB: My God, it's appalling. Urine tests. What bullshit. Our pioineer ancestors would be pissing in their collective graves at the idea that urine tests should decide whether someone is competent to do his job. Or these sobriety checkpoints on the highways. It's performance that should count. When someone told Lincoln that Grant had a drinking problem, Lincoln said, "OK, let's distribute his brand of whiskey to the other generals and maybe they'll get the lead out of their britches and do something about winning this war." We are being bullied by a Moron Majority committed to enforcing their stupid, bestial, bigoted opinions on everybody else—so you've got all this unthinking adherence to these standards that have nothing to do with the survival of the species. These are the guard dogs who will keep the human race in neoteny until this experiment is finally buried. We've even got brats turning in their parents. If things keep going this way, Reagan and Meese will have turned America into a nation of mainstream *rats!* And if this pretense of the war on drugs—which no one really wants to succeed—allows this fascist takeover to go global, there's going to be a real nightmare. Narcs will be kings! You can already see where this is heading. In Malaysia right now they have the death penalty for possession of more than half an ounce of heroin or morphine, and you can be hanged for more than seven ounces of pot! Anyone even *suspected* of trafficking can be held for two years without a charge or a trial. Anybody on the street who even *looks* like a user can be brought in and held until he gives a urine sample, and if it's positive he can be sent to a rehab center for two years.

LM: Do you think there was ever a practical chance back in the '60s to effect real change? Or was that just a lot of hippie nonsense?

WB: Well, you never know. You can look back on what's happened and you can see various points where a wrong turn was made, an opportunity lost. And these wrong turns weren't just taken in America. The same thing was happening in France, for example. It looked like the students were really going to take over, but then they began falling out among themselves. I'm not saying now real progress was made. Prior to the '60s minorities had no rights at all to speak of, and four-letter words could not appear on a printed page. But considering what the opportunities were, where we are now is pretty discouraging.

JM: In *Cities of the Red Night* you use the familiar SF motif of the alternative universe—with the Captain Mission experiment in Madagascar, and so on—to deal with this idea of the "lost turns."

WB: Yes, what happened with Mission in Madagascar was another possibility. Of course, you had just a small colony of three hundred there, but if it had spread it could have been a whole different ball game for people, a new option. But it didn't spread. They were overwhelmed by a native uprising, probably orchestrated by the British.

LM: You could look at what happened after the Revolutionary War as being another one of those turning points.

WB: That's one reason why it's a pity these pirate colonies weren't able to maintain themselves. If you'd had these kind of movements operating on a worldwide scale, people might have seen what the actual practice of freedom meant. That might have forced the American Revolution to stand by its words. The French, too. But everybody came over here looking for money, money, money. Nothing else on their minds. The American Dream has always been money, not freedom. But you must remember that these situations aren't comparable; people were pouring into the United States, while in Madagascar—and in the other pirate colonies that were formed on Tortuga Island and in the West Indies—there was just a small colony of three hundred people.

LM: Once you get more than a few people involved in any idealistic project it's inevitable—

WB: *Nothing* is inevitable, except possibly the speed of light. That's what the scientists say.

LM: Did the idea for developing a "road-not-taken" premise in *Cities of the Red Night* derive from your readings in science fiction?

WB: It came from various sources. A lot of it came from my sense of the actual possibilities of those real colonies at the time. I was familiar with the way SF had used that idea, but certainly I'd say my handling of it comes more from actual materials than from SF. You can see the appeal of going back and rewriting history from certain crucial junctures. One of the things that interested me in *Cities of the Red Night* was seeing what would have happened if you could get rid of the Catholic influence. Even after the Spanish were kicked out of South America by the liberal revolutions of 1848, their whole way of doing things—the bureaucracy, the language, the calendar, the Church—was still in effect. What would have happened if that influence had left with the Spanish? There must have been a number of crucial junctures in the Russian Revolution, too; depending on how you look at it, other paths that could have been fortunate or unfortunate.

LM: Other paths like what—Lenin not dying as soon as he did?

WB: I'm more interested in what would have happened if Stalin hadn't grabbed the whole thing and held it together. Without Stalin, the whole thing might have foundered into a number of separate, warring factions; then they would never have been able to establish a strong central government and set up the phony, so-called communist state. That state was Stalin's doing.

LM: Several recent SF writers, like Gregory Benford, in *Timescape,* and John Varley, in *Millennium,* have developed ingenious novels purporting to present time travel as being feasible based on what we now understand about physics. If so, maybe things really can evolve differently.

WB: Perhaps, but what we know about biological mutations indicates that certain changes can happen only in one direction. This doesn't necessarily apply to time travel, but as far as we know evolution remains a one-way street. You can see this illustrated in the newts. Newts start their life cycles in the water and they have gills. After a certain time they shed the gills and come up onto land and get lungs. Then they go back and live in the water—but they never get their gills back, even though gills might be convenient. And we know that whales and dolphins must have lived on land at one time, which is why they now have lungs. Obviously, it would be very convenient if evolution would allow them to go back and have gills again, but the whole evolutionary process seems to make this impossible. What this means is that a biological mutation, once established, becomes irrevocable. I'm not sure, but maybe this kind of irreversibility applies to time travel in a general sense.

LM: It's interesting to speculate on how we've now developed the capacity to start tinkering with these basic processes. Biological mutations or evolution may be a one-way street in nature, but perhaps we can intervene in this by surgery and cybernetic engineering to biologically alter ourselves in some favorable ways.

WB: Obviously we could do this, but the social and political difficulties are enormous. Alvin Toffler, the fellow who wrote *Future Shock* (which is a great title), has pointed out in a much better book, *The Third Wave,* that a lot of things like this are not two hundred years away but ten or twenty years away. The problem is that these things could not be absorbed by our increasingly creaky and unstable social system. We have all these people who are really unnecessary, and supposedly we're going to be made more biologically efficient and more intelligent. Well, who's going to make the definitions of intelligence and efficiency? Who's going to implement them? As transplant techniques are perfected so that we theoretically have the dream of immortality within our grasp, who's going to decide which applicants get the transplants? There simply aren't enough parts to go around. Is this going to be a sort of rule by scientists? Politically and socially speaking, we don't have any answers.

LM: You've said that our sociological chaos may really reflect a biological crisis—that is, maybe the human species is the end of an evolutionary line; and if we don't find a way to adapt ourselves somehow to conditions in outer space, we're going to die as a species. Are you seriously talking about our living in outer space?

WB: Certainly.

LM: Isn't that going to require basic changes in our bodies?

WB: Of course. Very drastic changes. It might even require eliminating our bodies altogether. This isn't really so farfetched. You can say that the body is automated by an electromagnetic forcefield, and that forcefield possibly can be separated from the body and transported. One of our big drawbacks is weight—weight and then, on top of that, having to transport the whole environment around something that's already fairly heavy (the human body). But the dream or astral body is virtually weightless (not completely so, but pretty nearly), so that would be the obvious way to go. Of course, the Russians are doing a lot of work on adapting to space, trying to overcome the decalcification problem, but that's just tinkering.

Then, of course, you have another question entirely: the conditions on another planet, or in a space station. I know some people at the Ecotechnic Institute, which is based in Fort Worth, Texas, backed by oil money. They're building an ecosphere near Tucson. It'll cover over two acres, and it has an artificial ocean (a small one), fish ponds, and intensive agriculture. Eight people are supposed to live in there for two years. The system must be a self-perpetuating environment. About $30 million has gone into the thing already, and space people and foreign scientists are very interested in the results. The idea is to see whether you can take a unit like that and put it down any-where—put it down on the moon, put it down on Mars or any other planet. I don't know how far along the thing is right now. I've been meaning to go down there and look at it.

LM: That's like your analogy of the fish inventing an aquarium it can take up onto land.

WB: Sure, that's exactly what it is—a giant aquarium. And there are so many technical difficulties involved. They've got a lot to think about: temperature control and all that, sewage disposal.

JM: As far as you know, is any serious research being done in the other direction—things like astral projection?

WB: I don't think so. If there is, it's not being done overtly. Of course, Bob Monroe, who wrote *Journeys out of the Body,* is still experimenting down in Afton, Virginia; he's got machines to facilitate leaving the body, I think. But I haven't heard any results from that. He teamed up with Kübler-Ross for a while. But having Kübler-Ross at your bedside is about as ominous as having a priest. Or a vulture.

JM: What about government funding for that type of thing?

WB: Not that I know of. There might well be, but if it's being done, it isn't overt. I should imagine the Russians are more likely to be into that. They're really much more practical than we are, you know.

LM: Do you think the fact that we're not conducting serious research into these areas has to do with the empirical biases of thinking over here?

WB: The scientists may take it seriously enough. But remember: when it comes time to allocate money for it, politicians are going to say to them-selves, This is fine, but what are our *constituents* going to think if they find out about this? Jack Anderson brought out that a lot of psychic research has been done by the CIA secretly in the Nevada desert somewhere. They couldn't justify the appropriations to Congress, and Congress couldn't justify them to their constituents. Well, the Russians don't have to worry about their constituents. That's a big advantage in getting anything done.

LM: Were these the CIA experiments involving the use of LSD?

WB: These experiments were more involved with ESP and trying to set up a way to control and contact agents using ESP. Far-seeing was one of the things; the CIA has done a lot of experiments with far-seeing. The idea was that agents could go and see enemy encampments and emplacements. I've read a number of books on the subject. Quite interesting, well documented. I used the idea in *Cities of the Red Night* with the character Yen Lee.

LM: You had your first hallucinatory visions when you were only about four years old. What kind of experiences were these?

WB: I wouldn't call them hallucinatory at all. If you see something, it's a shift of vision, not a hallucination. You shift your vision. What you see is there, but you have to be in a certain place to see it. There were two that I remember. Little gray men playing in my block house, and green reindeer. I didn't dream up the whole concept of the gray men or the small green reindeer subsequently. I think everyone has one or two of these experiences at one time or another. I think an actual shift of vision is involved. I'm doing some pure chance paintings now that seem to produce these perceptual shifts. For example, you take a piece of plywood and a spray-paint can and stand back and shoot the can with a shotgun. The can explodes—it will go thirty feet. Now you look at this thing and there's a shift. You can see all kinds of things in there. Movies, little scenes, streets. Anybody can see it. They're there somewhere. So I wouldn't speak of it as a hallucination.

LM: If you take LSD and look at clouds, or at any other surface that has a lot of information on it, these sorts of images seem to jump out at you.

WB: Sure. But my point is that you don't need acid to experience these things. It's just a question of looking at it. It used to be that people would look at a Cézanne painting and not even recognize the apples or the fish on the canvas. Those things were really there, but people didn't realize they were looking at something seen by the painter from a certain angle, under certain light conditions. They had to be shown how to look. That's one of the main functions of art, or of any creative thought for that matter: make people more aware of what they already perceive but don't yet recognize. Expand awareness. There's someone in Lawrence, a photographer, who's done "cloud pictures." He waits and gets a clear image and takes that. With a lot of patience, you see, you get a number of perfectly clear faces, animals, all kinds of things. You could get the same thing with vistas, particularly lakes and mountains, but you'd have to shoot a lot of footage to get anything. This sort of thing would be very worthwhile as a photographic experiment. Clouds would be best, though. Well, sometimes leaves. I've done this sort of thing very successfully with some of these paintings. Anybody at all can look and see these images, and they often see the same things. And some of them obviously *are* the same. There'll be a perfectly clear cat, or a number of cats, when they've been on my mind.

JM: Do you think your mind in some way influenced the spray of the paint?

WB: Not in any cause-and-effect way. It's a matter of synchronicity. What you're thinking of, you'll encounter. When I became interested in cats, I began to see cats in Brion's paintings. I'm merely following in Brion's footsteps in the introduction of random factors. That sort of thing also goes on in his calligraphy. This notion that what goes on inside somebody can affect something outside goes against the dogma of scientific materialism, which would insist there can't possibly be any relationship between what you see as you walk down the street and what you're thinking. But that's obviously not true. I'm thinking about New Mexico, and I come around a corner and there's a New Mexico license plate. The Land of Enchantment. Well, that's not an example of cause and effect. I didn't put it there by thinking about it. But I was there at the same time. The whole concept of synchronicity is much more in accord with the actual facts of perception.

LM: Have you experimented with the different effects you get from different types of guns and shells?

WB: Oh, yeah, yeah. A shotgun is about the only thing that will work, because it makes interesting patterns on the other side where it emerges. Sometimes you'll get big patches of paint, and some of these are the most interesting. You actually have two sides to these things—they're not two-dimensional like a regular painting, because the plywood can be three-quarters of an inch thick. I've shot a lot of different shells through plywood, but nothing does it like a shotgun.

LM: These synchronistic effects you describe—having cat images emerge in the paint splatterings while you're thinking about cats—seem related to what's happening in cut-ups.

WB: It's the same principle of allowing a random act to produce effects that you don't know you're going to get. Or on some level you may well know and be doing it exactly right. I've had that happen several times. I'll

shoot at the plywood with my shotgun and think, Oh God, I missed. Later on
I find out I didn't really miss but had fired at where it really should have
gone.

JM: You've said that the cut-up method gives writers an access to the
materiality of language that's analogous to painters' access to the elements
of their medium.

WB: Yes. By that I mean a painter can mix his colors on his palette, and
the writer using cut-ups can do somewhat the same with words. At one time,
of course, writing and painting were one—that is, with picture writing.
They're still very close in Chinese poetry and calligraphy.

LM: The development of the phonetic alphabet in the West, so that words
are connected to objects only through these arbitrary conventions, must affect
the way we think. You'd assume it would make us feel separated from the
world around us.

WB: Yeah, but you've got to remember that a lot of the relationships
established between words and objects in a picture-writing form, like Egyptian hieroglyphs, is just as arbitrary. How do you say all your prepositions
like "before," "toward," "under," "over"? You say them in a rather arbitrary
way. And the Egyptian hieroglyphs do have an alphabet, so it's not entirely
pictographic by any means. But even so, the grammar of a pictorial language
is unbelievably complex and confusing. Egyptologists never really agree on
the interpretation of a passage.

JM: You've repeatedly attacked the either/or mode of thinking—all those
dualities that seem so essential to Western thought and language, whereas in
Chinese, for example, there's no inflection for gender.

WB: And that makes sense. Also, in Egyptian hieroglyphs, while they do
have a verb "is," it's not used the way we use the "is" of identity. They don't
say, "He is my son" or "The sun is in the sky" but "He *as* my son" or "Sun
in sky." They don't have to say "is"—they make much less use of the "is"
of identity which, as Alfred Korzybski said, is one of the big fuck-ups of
Western language. Something "is" something, with the implication that there
is some sort of eternal status being conveyed.

LM: That helps produce the basic confusion between idea and object.

WB: Yeah, or between word and object. The idea that if you have a word
there must be something corresponding to it. Korzybski used to start his
lectures by saying, "Whatever this is, it isn't a table." It's not the label.

JM: You've said that when you were writing *The Place of Dead Roads* you felt you were in spiritual contact with Denton Welch. What sort of contact did you mean?

WB: Any writer feels that sort of contact if he's serious. He's in contact— *real* contact—with his characters. As Genet says, a writer takes upon himself the very heavy responsibility for his characters.

JM: What about Welch intrigued you in the first place?

WB: He's a very great writer. I admired his work, and I thought he fitted right into this role I had in mind.

LM: Did the student rebellions taking place in France and the United States in the '60s have anything to do with your conception of *The Wild Boys?*

WB: No, not really, because *The Wild Boys* was pretty removed from any sequences occurring in reality. It was more like a children's story, *Peter Pan* or something like that.

LM: You seem to be in touch with a lot of young people today. What's your sense of them?

WB: I'm not so much in touch. I mean, I do readings and lectures and I talk to a few people, but I don't feel myself in any sense able to evaluate their *Zeitgeist*. From what I have seen, though, they certainly seem less purposeful than they did in the '60s.

LM: And less willing to take risks, perhaps? In that *Rolling Stone* article a few months ago, you describe an encounter where you offered students a chance to use a wish machine.

WB: They didn't believe it. They didn't have any wishes. I wonder if young people today *have* any wishes. No, it's not that they aren't willing to take risks, exactly. There aren't any risks to be taken. Danger is a very rare commodity in these times, monopolized by intelligence agencies and stuntmen.

LM: Maybe this is one reason why everyone seems so fascinated with Ollie North?

WB: That sort of mindless fascination has got to grow out of this general absence of danger. The middle class feels this particularly acutely. Nietzsche said, "Men need play and danger. Civilization gives them work and safety." Danger is not an end in itself, by any means. It is a conflict of purposes, or a conflict of some sort. The danger is a by-product, just as happiness is a by-product of function. You can't hope for happiness in and of itself; that's like seeking victory without war—the flaw in all utopias. Of course, since danger and happiness are by-products of function, we are in shit-shape today because very few people function in our society. There's no place for them to function.

LM: So do people today have to be more creative about inventing these arbitrary functions?

WB: I don't know what you mean by arbitrary.

LM: I was thinking of something like football, where heroism and danger are generated as by-products. Capitalism could be another example—people assess their successes or failures on the basis of definitions invented by the system itself.

WB: There's no question about that. You see, the frontier's gone, and with it disappeared all those opportunities for taking on a role that really means something. Outer space is the only place that's going to create new roles, and that's monopolized by a very, very few people in the military. So you've got millions of people and very few roles for them. That's what functioning really means: enacting a purposeful role.

JM: In the *Retreat Diaries* you include an anecdote about being asked by the Rinpoche not to take the tools of your trade—your typewriter, paper, pens, whatever—with you on a retreat. You refuse, saying you need to be open to the writing experience at any time.

WB: Right. A writer may only get one chance, so he shouldn't ever put himself in a position where he can't write something down if he wants to. That's not true if you're a carpenter, where you've got plenty of time to build something, plenty of chances.

LM: Computers seem potentially very significant for writers in that they allow you to manipulate textual elements more freely. Have you done much work on word processors?

WB: No. I'm very poor with any mechanical contrivances. I don't know how a typewriter works, for example. I can use it, but I don't know how it works. Right now word processors seem just too complicated to get into. I guess they would be helpful, save a great deal of time undoubtedly, but at this point the effort involved in learning how to use them just doesn't seem worthwhile.

LM: Have you talked with Timothy Leary about his work in designing computer software? He says if artists start designing the software, maybe computers could eventually start opening up our consciousness in creative ways.

WB: I've talked with Leary about this, but I dare say I've not seen these programs work this way. I know with some of these things you actually participate and make decisions about the plot and all that—audience participation. But audience participation has never worked very well in my experience. After all, the audience isn't necessarily coming to a work of art to participate. Brecht and the Living Theater did a lot of experimenting with that sort of thing.

LM: Of course, audience participation with computer-generated novels is limited. You can only respond to the artist's prior structures.

WB: In other words, you're only going to have the choices somebody else has given you. The experience will only be as good as the program. And, of course, once you're talking about audience participation, you've got to realize most of the audience just isn't competent.

LM: A lot of recent SF deals with things like people interfacing with machines and computers, and machines that can program themselves so they can really "think."

WB: It's quite possible people could occupy a machine. Why not? But as far as machines developing thinking capabilities, the basic problem is that nothing happens without *will*, without motivation. How do you motivate a machine? They have not, so far, developed any machine that can process qualitative data. They could simulate this in a very crude way by different charges of electricity which could indicate that, say, here you have mild annoyance, distinct annoyance, anger, homicidal rage. Those obviously are quantitative differences, but at some point all quantitative differences become qualitative. So now you have a different charge for those—homicidal rage will light up half of the machine, whereas these other states are very faint.

LM: Do you think machines may eventually supplant the human "soft machine"?

WB: Machines aren't going to supplant us without a motive. A machine isn't going to do anything unless it's motivated, any more than a person is. People don't think unless they have a reason to think—which we have at all times, of course. I'm not sure a machine can be given this kind of motivation.

How can you frighten a machine? It isn't thinking that's important in this respect—machines can think better than we can. But the machine would have to be motivated—by fear, desire, whatever—before it could ever replace us in the evolutionary movement of things. In other words, it would have to be alive.

LM: SF writers have recently been dealing with these issues about machine intelligence and fear and consciousness. I'm thinking of, say, the computer HAL in *2001: A Space Odyssey,* or Philip K. Dick's androids in *Do Androids Dream of Electric Sheep?* (and in *Blade Runner*). I guess this idea was already there in Mary Shelley's *Frankenstein.*

WB: This whole business about the machine becoming alive at some point has certainly been a theme throughout SF. But they're very vague as to just how this could occur. It depends on what is meant by being "alive," or what you mean by "conscious." Consciousness is always a matter of conflict of some sort.

LM: In *2001* it appears that HAL somehow recognizes the implications of being turned off—that he'll die, cease to exist. Couldn't you program a machine so it wouldn't want to be turned off?

WB: How could this be programmed? To *not want*—that's the trouble. Wanting or not wanting are the stumbling blocks.

JM: Your work has used a lot of SF motifs and imagery. Did your interest in SF (and other pulp forms) start out when you were a kid?

WB: Oh, yes, I read all the SF I could get my hands on. As I remember, there were some good stories in *Amazing Stories* and *Weird Tales,* though I can't remember who wrote them. The best of them seem to have disappeared without a trace. You don't find much really good SF because it's very hard to write; there just aren't many writers who have the imagination and know-how to make you believe this or that could actually ever take place. So you're lucky if you find more than a few good sentences in an SF novel. Every now and then you find a whole good paragraph, or even a chapter. I think Eric Frank Russell is pretty good. His *Three to Conquer* is still one of the best virus books I've come across. So is Henry Kuttner's *Fury.* There's some sword and sorcery stuff by Fred Saberhagen that I like. H. G. Wells's best works still seem to hold up. But I read all those adventure stories and Western stories, science fiction, the Little Blue Books, all that stuff.

LM: It's interesting that in the United States, the most technologically advanced nation in the world, SF until recently has not been taken seriously.

Up through the '30s it seems pretty much adventure-story oriented, whereas in Europe you already had this tradition of serious SF writing: Wells, Jules Verne, Olaf Stapledon, Karel Čapek, Aldous Huxley, Evgenii Zamiatin, and others.

WB: It's not so much a matter of whether you're writing something that's adventure oriented but how you handle what you're doing; how much you're able to use the adventure formula to convince the reader that you're dealing with something important and believable. You look at Wells and he's adventure oriented: *The Time Machine* and *The War of the Worlds* and all that. He was a great influence on SF at its earliest, along with Jules Verne, of course. *The Voyage to the Moon,* where they lived inside the moon, the insect creatures—that's quite a story. But you're right: SF wasn't taken seriously at first in America. We didn't have any name comparable to Wells or Verne when I was growing up. Maybe we still don't. I'm always hearing people talking about how SF is "coming of age" in America, but I don't know. The main problem with SF seems to be that even though we've had a lot of writers who are dealing with these really strange, remarkable ideas—black holes, the business about relativity and quantum mechanics, machine intelligence, the birth and death of the universe—the way they portray these ideas has been pretty old-fashioned. If you're going to treat these really far-out ideas seriously, you've got to be willing to try something different stylistically.

LM: When the SF pulps really got started in the late '20s and '30s, not only were we in the midst of a depression, which a lot of people would want to escape from, but it was also a time when scientific technology was beginning to affect our everyday lives.

WB: I remember when television was thought of as an SF idea. It seems that a lot of SF these days is really science *fact,* that is, dealing with discoveries that are already actually here. Like they actually have these brain implants you see in *The Terminal Man.* It's not future technology but present technology. Michael Crichton's not trying to *predict* anything so much as to build a story around what we already know is possible.

LM: Back in the '60s, when you started developing your SF trilogy (*The Soft Machine, The Ticket That Exploded, Nova Express*), you seemed to be borrowing some of your key motifs directly from the SF pulps—like your use of Venus and Venusians.

WB: I took that right from all those old SF novels where Venus is thought of as this teeming, dangerous jungle, with all these exotic, poisonous plants and animals. That's what Venus would conjure up for most people.

JM: In *Word Cultures,* Robin Lydenberg argues that a lot of your materials that critics have assumed were metaphors aren't metaphors at all but literal things.

WB: That's right, although we'd have to fool around with definitions of metaphor. What is a metaphor? How is it different from a simile? I don't even know. To me, a metaphor is setting up something that is similar to something else. Writers can't function without them. You can't write a single page without metaphor. (It would be interesting to try—that is, to see if you could write a book without a metaphor.)

LM: That was something that Alain Robbe-Grillet and some of the other French New Novelists seemed to be trying to do.

WB: Yeah, the new realists or whatever they call themselves now. Phenomenologists. They just dealt with certainties. But how far did they really get without metaphor?

LM: They seemed to use geometrical images to describe things, but do they really think geometry isn't metaphorical?

WB: Right away they're talking about circles, squares, rectangles, which are themselves metaphors. How would you describe, for example, a table without reference to any measurements? I mean, how big is it? As soon as you say this table is "a round piece of wood," you've already got a metaphor. How about "a piece of wood so shaped that if you walk around it you come back to the same place you started from"—that's a little awkward. That's what some of the prose of that school sounded like to me. Finally, what's the point?

LM: One significant thing that emerged from these sorts of linguistic investigations was a deeper awareness of some of the things you talk about a lot: the falsities that derive from the implications of the language system itself, like the either/or dichotomy that may have nothing to do with reality.

WB: Which is Korzybski's point. That opposition doesn't correspond to what little we know about the physical world and the functioning of the human nervous system. Every act is not either instinctive or intellectual; it's instinctive *and* intellectual, involving the organism's entire body. You may want to eat something, which most people would say is an instinctive reaction; but in order to actually eat that steak, your rational intellect may be doing things like looking at a map, trying to figure out how to read a menu in French, driving a car, or paying a cab fare. Who's to separate these responses?

JM: The virus metaphor is central to your work, and a lot of things you were describing back in the '60s seem very prophetic today. What's your view about AIDS, for example?

WB: Have you seen the flyer from that society, the United Front against Racism and Capitalism? It claims there is evidence that AIDS could have been a laboratory creation. [Burroughs goes upstairs and returns with the flyer, whose headline reads: "RUSSIA HOPES THAT THE SPREAD OF THE DEADLY AIDS VIRUS WILL BRING AMERICA TO ITS KNEES."] This business about the U.S. or the West being brought to its knees, of course, is very unlikely. The whole AIDS scare is mainly a publicity campaign on the part of Ronald Reagan and that whole Moron Majority lunatic fringe. Compared with smallpox or the Black Death, AIDS is just a drop in the bucket. Certainly, the way in which AIDS is spread in this country suggests that it was done deliberately—but probably by us, not by Russia. After all, what's Russia going to gain by killing off gays and blacks and drug users? They wouldn't be hitting at our military, our manpower, at all. On the other hand, the American government has very good reasons. They want scapegoats, for one thing. Diversions. They want a pretext for more governmental control. Addicts form a perfect conduit for introducing any biological or chemical agent. Addicts buy their needles where they buy their junk. Junk dealers have always got them there all sealed up. They sell hundreds of those things a day. Nothing would have been easier than to put a tiny, minuscule drop of infected blood in some of those needles and, *Whamo,* in a couple of days you've got the virus spread all over New York. What I'm saying is that evidence points to contamination at the source. It's inconclusive, but the circumstantial indications point in that direction. Of course, then there's the African and Haitian scene. There's an interesting article in *Life* magazine about AIDS and the Haitian connection—it's about the women and children, just a pandemic right now. So I wouldn't make any definite statements on whether or not it is a laboratory creation. But it certainly *could have been,* and it could have been spread the way I just described. And there's no question that the U.S. government is much more motivated to do something like this than are the Soviets.

LM: Are you pessimistic about the chances for the human race finding a way to avoid exterminating itself with its own technology?

WB: We certainly have a very, very dark picture here today. But I don't consider myself pessimistic, because that word doesn't have any significance; neither does "optimistic." I mean, if the planet is destroying itself and I say it is, does that make me a pessimist? The only person in the political arena with some trace of good intentions at the present time seems to be Mikhail Gorbachev. To what extent these intentions are genuine, I don't know, but they certainly seem more so than the Reagan administration's.

JM: You've suggested that the only hope for Earth to survive will be if we can get rid of nations. But, as you've also pointed out, in order to do that we'll probably have to get rid of the family system as well. There have been some experiments along those lines in China.

WB: Yes, but if there's going to be any real hope for long-term survival, there have to be some very basic biological changes. As I said earlier, maybe our best hope is to get away from this planet, with its abysmal cycles of overpopulation, depletion of resources, pollution, and escalating conflicts. Now that's going to require biological alterations in the human structure that would make us able to exist in space—that, or we go the out-of-body route, which is probably more practical. But if you look at the human organism as some kind of biological artifact created in response to some design or motive we can't fathom—and I'm convinced that nothing in this universe happens without will or intent—you can see how much is wrong with it. In fact, just about everything we know of seems to have been a basic mistake, biologically speaking. The dinosaurs were a mistake; maybe the way we've evolved sexually is a mistake; maybe the development of the human species is a mistake, and now we're about to move out of some kind of larval stage into something that's inconceivable from our present point of view.

Certainly, if we don't find some way to help evolution along, the chances of there being people around much longer can't be good. Our track record so far is terrible. Why should we think it's going to change unless something very drastic happens, like being able to make these biological adaptations? Brion Gysin says man is a bad animal—wherever he goes he destroys all the animals, then destroys the environment. The rain forests have been called the lungs of the world. What other animal systematically destroys its own lungs? I'm very much an animal activist, so it's tragic to see the destruction of, for example, the species of lemurs in Madagascar. The gliding lemurs are quite helpless on the ground, so they can't survive the destruction of their habitat. Neither can the singing gibbon, whose singing has been described as the most beautiful and variegated music produced by any land animal. They live only on one island in the Indian Ocean. The purpose of their singing is to establish a little patch of territory in a rain forest where the resources are very limited. So as soon as the rain forest disappears, they disappear.

JM: What were the origins of your interest in animal activism?

WB: It started with my interest in cats. Cats and lemurs. I prefer cats to people, for the most part. Most people aren't cute at all, and if they are cute they very rapidly outgrow it. And they're not an endangered species at the present time, except for the danger they're bringing on themselves.

JM: What do you think about the prospects for developing some means of communicating with animals—for instance, John Lilly's experiments in interspecies communication?

WB: "Communication" is a bad word to use when you're trying to describe that sort of thing, because the purpose of communication is to keep something at a distance. "Contact" is the word I use, which means *identification. The Western Lands* is very much concerned with animal contact. The title refers to the Egyptian paradise, the western lands.

LM: Your recent books rely more heavily on plotted narratives than did the cut-up books back in the '60s. Has this shift grown out of a conscious desire to appeal to a larger audience? Or have you decided that more traditional forms may be more suitable for expressing your sense of reality?

WB: Mostly it's had to do with selecting a form appropriate to what I'm saying, to my content. If you're going to have a pirate story, you have to have straight narration. It has nothing to do with the facts of perception. It's true that popular novels are usually written in the old-fashioned, nineteenth-century form, but that form is really as arbitrary as something like a sonnet. This doesn't have anything to do with "realism."

The point about cut-ups is that *life is a cut-up.* Every time you look out the window or walk down the street, your consciousness is being intruded upon by all these random factors. The idea that a writer composes in a vacuum is itself a fiction. That was the point in introducing this random factor: it's closer to the way human beings perceive things. That's why painters started using the montage method—which is what the cut-up is, applied to writing. Brion Gysin, who first thought up the cut-up idea, was a painter, and montage was already old hat when we started using the cut-ups in our work. Painters walk down the street and put what they see on the canvas—and what they see is a jumble of fragments. If they put *that* on the canvas, it's not going to look like a representational painting, because they've introduced the time and motion elements. If you sit in front of something and paint it, that's one thing; but if you try and paint what you see when you're moving, you're going to be creating a totally different landscape. You can't put that moving, perceptual landscape—particularly urban phenomena—down on a canvas using the old representational methods.

LM: Still, your recent books seem less discontinuous and "in motion" than your earlier books. Why did you feel that your SF stories back in the '60s didn't require as much straight narrative as, say, the pirate or Western stories in *Cities of the Red Night* and *The Place of Dead Roads?*

WB: This is all a matter of degree. For one thing, a lot of people who are pointing to this major break seem to forget that there was always narrative in all my books. Unless there's some narrative, a book won't hold together. And there are passages in, say, *Cities of the Red Night* that were written in much the same way I wrote in *Naked Lunch*. And there are still cut-up passages in the new stuff. I may cut up a whole page and use a sentence or two, or I may throw the whole thing away. Sometimes I just draw a complete blank. If I don't see where the narrative is going, sometimes I'll get an idea from cut-ups. But I've always believed a fiction writer can't get away from straight narrative completely.

LM: It seems as if some writers' efforts to move away from storytelling are defeating the whole impulse behind writing fiction in the first place. Some of these purely formal fictional experiments can be interesting, in the same way that minimalist painting or conceptual art is interesting. But even very radical minimalist fictions can be shown to have a narrative principle underlying them.

WB: It's important for writers to recognize that you can't apply all of the techniques used in painting to writing. For example, in painting you have minimalist expression—in a certain painting there are very slight changes in color, varying shades of white or blue. Well, if you did the equivalent in writing, no one would want to look at it. Sure, you could have one page written like this, and then another page that would be almost the same, each succeeding page just a little bit different. But no one would read it.

LM: One good thing that came out of the literary experimentalism that took place in the '60s was that writers were able to exhaust certain methods that didn't lead anywhere.

WB: Exactly. You simply reach dead ends. In painting, once you have painters starting to get off the canvas, where do they go? There were all those "happenings." A lot of that was just pretentious nonsense. Where would writing go if you threw away the book? Or got rid of the page?

JM: In your 1965 *Paris Review* interview, you talk about the possibility of people in general eventually becoming liberated from words. That basic change would seem to require a long transitional period.

WB: I'm not sure this is going to happen, but if it does, it's not necessarily going to take a long time. If it happens, it will probably happen quickly, just as these things always have. The beginning of words undoubtedly involved biological changes. Animals are not biologically designed to talk; they don't have the apparatus necessary, the larynx and so on. Since a biological change in the apparatus was implicit in the origins of speech, maybe another biological change could produce some other new form of communication. Words did not arise to convey information in the first place, so it's easy enough to imagine that someday information will be conveyed in an entirely different manner. No, the origin of words was probably emotional and had nothing to do with conveying information. You'd be surprised at how few words are really necessary. You go into a shop and see something you want—you don't need any words in that kind of situation. You need words for something that isn't there.

William Tells

Michele Corriel / 1988

Originally appeared in *Cover* (January 1988): 16–17. Reprinted by permission.

William S. Burroughs "A gray eminence in a leaky lifeboat." Time Magazine, 1962. Twenty-five years later the renowned author has combined a predilection for firearms with a propensity to paint. Lately, Burroughs has collaborated with Robert Rauschenberg, Jean Michel Basquiat and Philip Taaffe and will show his own work this month.

Recently Burroughs spoke to me via telephone from his home in Lawrence, Kansas.

Painting

"I started painting in '82. I didn't switch mediums, I was just sort of fooling around. I was out shooting. I just had a shotgun and a piece of plywood as a target. I didn't have a recoil. When I looked at it later I said that looks like art. I called it 'Sore Shoulder.' I never expected to sell any of them, but it went on to become more serious.

"After completing *Western Lands* I've been shifting more and more to painting rather than writing."

Final Step From Word To Image

"I don't know. Perhaps I said what I had to say in words. Now in the last six months I've been painting rather than writing.

"Some books in progress are: *The Ghost Lemurs, Of Madagascar,* and I'm doing some memoirs, *Captain Mission,* and *Interzone*—a collection of writing between *Junkie* and *Naked Lunch* containing some travel pieces and some new/vintage work."

Guns

"I wouldn't have started painting without them. If I wasn't out shooting in the first place I never would have gotten to it.

"I was brought up with guns. When I was a child, children reached a certain age, they got a certain type of gun.

"I don't hunt. The last time I hunted was forty years ago. Birds. Those wild ducks were really something. When I moved to Lawrence I resumed shooting.

"Coming to Kansas directly affected my painting. I never painted in New York. I've also become an animal activist and I'm very attached to my cats. Yes, moving to Lawrence had a terrific and very favorable impact on me."

Writing

"I started painting when I was writing *The Place of Dead Roads* and continued while I was writing *Western Lands.*

"*Western Lands* has much less sex. In fact, it is devoid of explicit sex. It is a direct carryover from *The Place of Dead Roads* and Joe the Dead.

"I don't do very much cut-ups these days. Sometimes I will make a cut-up to find something new. If I'm looking for something. Maybe I'll just throw it out or maybe I'll use it."

A Conversation with William S. Burroughs

Simone Ellis / 1990

Originally published in *Contemporanea* no. 23 (December 1990): 80–83

Acclaimed author of *Naked Lunch, Junky, Cities of the Red Night,* and many other controversial novels, William S. Burroughs has recently turned the greater part of his creative powers toward painting. Starting with a solo exhibition at the Tony Shafrazi Gallery in New York in 1987, Burroughs has gone on to have more than twenty-five exhibitions internationally. One of the most recent was at Seed Hall in Tokyo, planned in conjunction with the opening of a $13-million Tokyo nightclub. "The Bunker," which was designed to replicate Burroughs's New York loft. With undoubted renown in the literary world, Burroughs at seventy-six has now exploded into the art world with the deadly precision of one of his gunshot paintings.

Simone Ellis: *Of course, you've been known as a writer since the publication of* Naked Lunch *in 1959. Then in the early eighties you worked with Robert Rauschenberg on his series of lithographs,* American Pewter with Burroughs. *Was this the beginning of your working with images instead of words?*

William S. Burroughs: Not exactly. It actually goes back to the sixties. I was experimenting with scrapbooks with Brion Gysin, who was living in Paris at the time. We used actual pictures from newspapers, and the scrapbooks were a really weird mixture of painting, writing, and collage. We were trying to break down the barrier between painting and writing. Of course, you must remember that writing arose from painting via pictographs, and then there were Egyptian hieroglyphs. There's no doubt in my mind that the pictographs were created as magic.

SE: *Yes, and I know that you have always viewed writing as making magic. Is painting the same sort of magical act for you?*

WSB: Well, not entirely. When I am painting, I see with my hands. When you write, you can't help but see what is right in front of you. This is not true with painting—your hands do all sorts of things. For example, I read a book called *Bad Medicine* by C. Q. Yarbro, and in it someone had overdosed on anticoagulants, so that blood was coming out of his nose, through his skin, everywhere. And the drug was disguised in orange juice, because it had an acidic taste. Well, in one of my paintings, you can see the guy drinking the orange juice, which is odd because I wasn't necessarily thinking about that at the time. In other words, what I am doing is automatic painting.

SE: *When did you recognize it?*

WSB: As soon as I painted it, I looked at it and said, this is that scene. I have had several experiences like that, recognizing events in my paintings after they have been completed.

SE: *Do you think symbols come out of your unconscious mind onto the paper through your hands?*

WSB: I would never use the term "unconscious," because if it were completely unconscious, no one would ever be aware of it. Usually it is partially conscious.

SE: *So when you have your materials in front of you, what sort of state of mind do you get into?*

WSB: I try my best to make my mind a blank, but there is no such thing as making the mind a blank. The whole idea is that I try to let my hands go and paint whatever my so-called unconscious mind is aware of. I try to get my pictures to move. A face comes into focus, almost smiles, snarls, speaks. There are green monkeys, a green man, very serene. But I looked at that anticoagulant one afterwards and there was the man drinking the orange juice. Horrible death, horrible. One time I saw a bicycle accident that happened at the same time that I was painting the picture. I have seen many things in my paintings.

SE: *Do your paintings serve as oracles?*

WSB: It isn't really a question of oracles, it is a matter of the future and the past being laid out, so that you can see both the future and the past from the present. There is a very interesting book by John Dunne called *An Experiment With Time,* written in 1925. He started writing down his dreams and found that they very often referred to future events. I dream about earthquakes, and he had a very interesting point to make about that. He said that if you dream about an earthquake, you are not foreseeing the actual event. What you are seeing is the moment when you will become aware of it. That is, the moment you will see it in a newspaper or hear about it on the news.

In other words, you are moving forward on your own time track to a moment of your own future awareness.

SE: *You have spoken before about the clairvoyance of writing and art. Why do you think making art is a clairvoyant act any more than, say, laying brick or driving a cab?*

WSB: Well, art is a creative act. Paul Klee said that art does not simply render nature, it renders it visible. The artist sees something that others do not see, and by seeing it and putting it on canvas, he makes it visible to others. Recognition art. A particle physicist at the University of Texas named John Wheeler has developed something that he calls "recognition physics." Wheeler says that nothing exists until it is observed. Well, the artist as observer is like that. The observer creates by observing, and the observer observes by creating. In other words, observation is a creative act. By observing something and putting it onto canvas, the artist makes something visible to others that did not exist until he observed it.

SE: *And by observing it, he takes part in its coming into being.*
WSB: Exactly.

SE: *You have called your artistic process "nagual art," after Carlos Castaneda's books, referring to the concepts of the tonal (predictable) and the nagual (unknown) universes. So, by extension of recognition physics, is it the nagual that you are observing?*

WB: Yeah, the unknown, precisely. I am observing the unknown.

SE: *And that is not the kind of art that paints the cow in the field?*

WSB: Well, no. The cow in the grass is another sort of painting, and it is terrific. But now it can be done so much better with the camera. The next step was collage, which introduced the element of time. Someone walks around the block, comes back, and puts down on canvas what he is seeing. He is seeing a medley of fragments, which is much closer to the actual facts of perception. He is seeing someone's face in a shop window, a dog, a cyclist, but it's going to be a medley, and it will be much more real than sitting down and painting that static moment of the cow in the grass.

SE: *There is no such thing as that frozen moment in time.*
WSB: There is no such thing.

SE: *Furthermore, unlike the cow painters, you are not looking at the outer landscape.*

WSB: No, I am looking into an inner landscape and, to the best of my ability, rendering it.

SE: *And somehow these figures continue to rise out of the ink.*
WSB: Yes, through my hands.

SE: *Have you ever considered yourself an expressionist, or do you think in those terms at all?*
WSB: I never think in those terms. I just follow my hands. Sometimes they do not do anything interesting at all, but sometimes they do.

SE: *And then there are the gunshot paintings. You have always been known to experiment with random selection, such as the cut-up method of writing. How do the gunshot paintings fit into that aesthetic?*
WSB: When I make the shotgun-blast paintings, I am usually not thinking about the painting but about hitting the can. I line it up, and you get this explosion of color. Then the gun whams against your shoulder, but not hard at all.

SE: *And that is the split-second of creation?*
WSB: Yes, it happens only once. If you miss it, it is gone.

SE: *Like the burning-out of a star.*
WSB: Exactly.

SE: *Do you get a rush out of this moment of creation? Out of creating these works of art and then having them look back at you?*
WSB: Yes, absolutely.

SE: *How does painting affect your emotions, your state of mind? Do you take it seriously enough to get depressed by a painting that does not turn out?*
WSB: I take it completely seriously, but it is something to be absorbed and realized into yourself, for god's sake.

SE: *It allows you to exist on another level? In another dimension?*
WSB: Exactly.

SE: *You went through an obscenity trial over* Naked Lunch *in the sixties. Do you think that we are entering a new age of censorship?*
WSB: Yes. It has not reached the written word in the United States yet, but it has definitely reared its head in the visual arts. I have very few overtly

sexual pictures. I have one collage painting with pictures of Bosch's *Garden of Delight,* but I do not think that anyone will be bothered by that. For one thing, it is protected by age. As Henry Miller pointed out, if it is old, then it is all right. Something that is perfectly acceptable in a museum may meet with opposition when it appears in new work.

SE: *Do you think that the rise of censorship could in fact further the evolution of freedom by inspiring the artist to stretch boundaries, to make more cutting-edge art?*

WSB: Well, that is the whole idea of opposition giving impetus. I say that it does. But any new school of art always comes about as an opposition to something that has been petrified.

SE: *So along those lines, censorship in the United States may further the cause of creative art, however backhandedly?*

WSB: Yes, but I do not see where it could go along those lines. There is nothing new about sexually explicit content.

SE: *So where do you go from here?*

WSB: Well, I have been working with the gunshot paintings, and with India inks and watercolors on slick paper. I have also been making Rorschach monoprints that have produced some interesting results, but I think I will try oil on canvas next. I have not done that yet. And, of course, I will continue to let the picture see me. If you try this method, you will always notice that some little detail in the picture is looking back at you—seeing you, coming alive in your presence. For instance, look at this one, which I did with my suction-cup method—dipping a rubber suction cup into ink and then sticking it to the paper and moving it across it.

SE: *These look like aliens.*

WSB: They are. They are supposed to be aliens. Here's one that I like very much—they are the Root People. I recognized them the moment that the painting was finished.

SE: *Do you feel that you have checked into the unknown—the nagual—and come back out again?*

WSB: I do indeed, at least sometimes. You know the story about the Zen master who appeared before the emperor with his painting, bowed three times and then disappeared into it?

SE: *Will that ever happen to you?*
WSB: I hope so.

Mind Set: No One Gets a Free Lunch

Regina Weinreich / 1991

This previously unpublished interview is used by permission of Regina Weinreich. © Regina Weinreich. Annotated, June 1996, Montauk.

William S. Burroughs had been to Tangier with director David Cronenberg, producer Jeremy Thomas, and a film entourage poised to replicate the exotic environs, if need be. They went to see Paul Bowles, and what is left of Burroughs's old haunts, the Hotel Muneria where *Naked Lunch* had been assembled and so named in favor of *The Sargossa Sea*.

After a decade of Burroughs interviews, I had been asked to go on a press junket to Tangier by the pop publication *Entertainment Weekly,* incha' Allah. The press junket had been aborted by the Gulf War. Was it fate or the will of Allah? Journalists and critics came instead to Canada. And thanks to the prescience of David Cronenberg and his able crew, Tangier was brought— rather recreated, donkey and mint smells, cobbled Medina streets, rug vendors hawking goods, and all—to a Toronto warehouse.

William was holding court in a hotel suite, seated on a couch in a conservatively appointed space and wearing a dark suit, white shirt and black tie with gold, hand painted brushstrokes. Two buttons were affixed to his lapels: one from the American Academy and Institute of Arts and Letters, the other, the Commandeur de l'Ordre des Artes et des Lettres, a French citation. He was obviously proud. "Jerry Lewis got one too," says William. "There's a plaque that comes with it, that you can wear around your neck. They've awarded it to two of our best humorists. That's fantastic."

While we smoked a bit of a joint we made small talk. "That's a gorgeous tie," I tell him. "Oh. Steve Low brought over about 100 of them which I hand painted. The motif is oriental geisha house." I told him about the 1988 shooting of my documentary on Paul Bowles; he wondered whether Mohammed Mrabet, a Moroccan storyteller from the Rif who was also Bowles's homme d'affaires, displayed his characteristic anti-Semitism. No, indeed, when I first met him in 1983, Mrabet had proposed that I become his second wife and appeared on best behavior. (The proposal took place at a dinner at Paul's with Francine du Plessix Gray as the fourth guest seated on cushions around the low table a la marocain. Paul suggested I say no.) It was the first time in all my years of knowing William though, that I was aware of his awareness of me as Jew. Perhaps, thought William, now with the Gulf War, Mrabet would have greater license to unleash his anti-Semitism. That goes for everyone, methinks.

In due course, we begin our interview:

RW: Why didn't earlier attempts to film *Naked Lunch* lead to anything?

WSB: Money. Now that the people involved are both dead, I can speak. I was not pleased with the film script. Brion Gysin and Antony Balch worked on it together. They wanted Mick Jagger to star.

RW: Do you think that Jagger was a good choice to be in it?

WSB: I don't know. Their idea was sort of a 1940 musical. As I said, I was not too keen on the film script.

RW: Was *Towers Open Fire* an early attempt at *Naked Lunch?*

WSB: No. It had nothing to do with *Naked Lunch*. It was just a short, experimental film using some of the techniques that Anthony Balch was developing with Ian Sommerville and Brion and myself.

RW: How do you feel about David Cronenberg's script?

WSB: I like it very much. It is quite different from anything I would have thought of, which is good. There are so many things in it—that's very valid—ideas I would never have thought of like the concentration on the typewriter, the instrument of writing. The typewriter as having a life of its own is something I would never have thought of. Of course you can make many films out of *Naked Lunch*. You can make one on the death of Joselito, for example.

RW: What about the use of pieces of your biography in the film?

WSB: He had a free hand. The whole film is so bizarre, so far out, so beyond the parameters of reality, so I didn't feel like it was an invasion of privacy. It is beyond the concept of privacy.

RW: Even though it has the cataclysmic event of Joan's death?

WSB: Some parts of this work are from other works, *Exterminator,* for example. Some parts are biographical. You'll have to ask David Cronenberg about the Joan character. Because of David's surreal structure, no parts of the film are related to anything real. So the Joan character is okay. Because it is a fantasy film.

RW: Did the thought of having you in the film come up? You were a great cinematic presence in *Drugstore Cowboy.*

WSB: Both David and I felt that I should not take any part in it. David did not want anything real. If you have me in it, people can relate it to reality. [He is comparing Cronenberg's decision to Bernardo Bertolucci's in casting Paul Bowles himself in the role of Invisible Spectator in the 1990 film *The Sheltering Sky*. A big mistake, according to Cronenberg.] As soon as you put something in there and people know who it is, the whole bizarre fantasy collapses.

RW: Here is my toughest question: why shouldn't we take this as just another way of making your life more important than the work, since *Naked Lunch* is so hard to film?
WSB: I didn't get that.

RW: You know, historically all of your writing has been overshadowed by the so-called life of the writer. Why shouldn't we take this as just another attempt to make the life more important than the work?
WSB: It has to be seen in the first place as something in its own right. It is not the book. It's not supposed to be. It has to stand if at all on its own special merits. That is one consideration. People will tend to emphasize the life of the writer, but anyone who has done a lot of writing knows that writing is more important as far as the writer is concerned and occupies more of his time. Writers don't have time to do many strange and outlandish things that people like to think of them doing. Most of their time is spent alone at a typewriter.

RW: Yeah, but your life is not like anyone else's life!
WSB: Most of my time has been spent at a typewriter, not engaging in flamboyant episodes.

RW: What about the early years?
WSB: They like to think that's what you do all the time. For example, when I was living in New York I never went to Studio 54. Now, if I meet David Bowie or someone, they assume this is a nightly occurrence, that I do this all the time. If I have a birthday party at Limelight [which he did at age 70], this is something that may happen once or twice a year that I would go there.

RW: David Cronenberg made up a whole bunch of drugs for *Naked Lunch*. You told me you made up a whole bunch yourself and imagined withdrawal symptoms. Could you mention one or two?

WSB: Yes. There are various metal drugs. People took on metallic qualities. The withdrawal symptoms were excruciating because they had to reconvert from a metal metabolism back to mammal metabolism. Some drugs
where people were getting a stonelike immobility. Quite a few were mentioned in *The Western Lands* and *The Place of Dead Roads.*

RW: Is there anything from *Naked Lunch* which you wish had not been
left out of the film?

WSB: No. You have to consider the structure and what he felt fit in and
what didn't. In other words, he had complete control of the script. It was up
to him to decide what belonged and what didn't.

RW: You and David seem to share a preoccupation with conspiracies,
hallucinations, and centipedes.

WSB: He got the centipede motif from me. I don't remember centipedes
in previous films. Of course there are some insect references like the fly. That
was certainly a point we have in common. Also, special effects and people
turning into insects. [Cronenberg had made *The Fly* in which a young scientist played by Jeff Goldblum is transformed into a fly.] That was a good start
for working together on the film. Although, as I said, the script was entirely
his.

RW: Conspiracies come up in his work.

WSB: Well sure. Conspiracies are one of the leitmotifs of modern life.
Everytime we turn around there's a new one.

RW: Mugwumps.

WSB: I like them. They're different from my concept because they are
bigger and they have a much more benevolent aspect than mine. They certainly are extraordinary: They have these beautiful blue eyes. They look helpless and slow-moving. They don't look menacing. Their lips move. They can
breathe. They don't look like anything human. I have one. They sent me one.
It's huge.

RW: How did it arrive?
WSB: In a box.

RW: How did it get through customs?
WSB: I don't think they thought anything of it—just a prop made of latex.
Some have all this machinery inside of them. They can smoke. Their lips
move. They can move their things on top—tentacles and antennae—they have

an extraordinary gamut of actions they can perform. They have to be controlled by about ten people, pressing buttons and all this has to be synchronized. I've seen them in action in the film. It's quite impressive.

RW: Do you know how to operate them?
WSB: Oh good heavens no. Mine doesn't have any insides. I'm no good at that sort of thing. I haven't any mechanical aptitude is all.

RW: How are you getting along with your seven deadly sins project?
WSB: It's finished.

RW: Tell me about the process.
WSB: You'd have to talk to James about that. It's so complicated. All I did was paint on a certain medium and then paint on something else and shoot. I took 50 shots at seven boards. I'd hit it here with the gunshot and hit it there, following instructions.

RW: What instructions?
WSB: He's given instructions. On the plywood. I was doing the shooting. He wanted it to fit into a certain framework. Each sin a different color: envy green, lust red, avarice gold, anger black—extremes.

RW: What's the relation to Shakespeare?
WSB: (quoting): The expense in spirit and waste in shame is lust in action. Lust is one of the 7 deadly sins. Pride. Proud man like an angry ape . . . doth play such fantastic fix before fantastic heaven make the angels weep. I did a short piece of prose to go with every sin and sometimes I used quotes like that.

RW: And aren't you also putting together a book of dreams?
WSB: Yes. I get up, make breakfast and jot down pertinent dreams, dreams I remember intact. I wake up and remember them straight. I dream about different places with completely different rules. The more inexplicable a dream is, the more interesting. You feel it comes from something distant, a completely different reality. There's no relation at all to present day or your regular life. Those are the most interesting dreams. I always keep a pencil by the bed. I can go over it several times in my mind. There must be a physical difference the brain is in when you dream. I always make a note of my most interesting dream: I found that I could levitate. Now I've had lots of flying dreams. I just get off and dive and fly. I'm not going to rocket up—flap and keep above ground—but this one I found that I could levitate. Strange place

in a haze but I could see through the haze. I saw a billboard down the street. No one in sight. I came down in front of a hotel, a yellow light was coming out and I realized that this was the only light in the area. In a nondrinking place they will have liquor in the bar and on the way in I saw what is known as a weathercock. I could levitate to the room. It was very sleazy. It had an old ceiling. I flew up and bumped against a tin ceiling. Someone came in to fix something at the foot of the bed. An iron thing. I was debating whether I'd go out through the window and see this show I'd seen advertised. Then I was afraid that I would wake up and find out I was in a dream and couldn't levitate but not wake up in Kansas but in that hotel in that bed. It had nothing to do with what I read. Completely unrelated. That's what made it interesting. Not a Freudian dream, the ones that are so obviously some kind of sexual fulfillment. I've had several in the past six months of that caliber. I was myself. The only thing was, I couldn't see myself in the mirror.

Which Is the Fly and Which Is the Human? Cronenberg/Burroughs Interview

Lynn Snowden / 1992

Originally published in *Esquire,* February 1992, p. 112–16. Reprinted by permission of Lynn Snowden.

Deep in Kansas, darkly dressed, William S. Burroughs, a man who shot his wife in the head and waged war against a lifetime of guilt, who has sucked up every drug imaginable and survived, and who has made a fine career out of depravity, can't on this particular afternoon take another moment of a simple midwestern housefly buzzing around his head. "I can't stand flies," grumbles the seventy-seven-year-old author in that distinctively sepulchral voice, which retains a vestige of his St. Louis roots despite his many years on another planet. The fly swoops down onto Burroughs's plate of cookies. "Terrible," Burroughs exclaims, exasperated, attempting to backhand the fly into oblivion.

"William, that's my pet fly!" cries David Cronenberg, a man who may love insects but not necessarily people, the director who is perhaps best known for turning Jeff Goldblum from scientist into bug in the 1986 remake of *The Fly.*

"Now, Julius, I told you not to bother people," Cronenberg commands the fly. "Not everyone likes flies."

Not everyone likes giant meat-eating Brazilian aquatic centipedes either, but they're featured prominently in Cronenberg's current film of Burroughs's chilling masterpiece of a novel, *Naked Lunch.* Now that the movie is in the can and Burroughs is out of the hospital after having undergone triple-bypass surgery, Cronenberg has showed up in Lawrence, Kansas, Burroughs's hometown of the last ten years, to pay his respects to the laconic sage. With two exemplars of evil incarnate wandering around town at the same time, Lawrence suddenly seems like a haven for drug-crazed refugees escaping the Interzone, the fictional horrorscape of Burroughs's *Naked Lunch.*

In the Interzone, we are told, "nothing is true, and everything is permitted." In Lawrence, however, not nearly so much is permitted, but if everything I've heard about William Burroughs and David Cronenberg is true, then

the next couple of days will severely test my capacity for revulsion. Burroughs's books, for example, are phantasmagorias of buggered boys, bloody
syringes, talking assholes, and vaginal teeth. The old gun-toting geezer himself has been referred to as "a green-skinned reptilian" by no less an authority on manhood than Robert Bly.

"Well, I don't think you'll find him to be that bad," said Cronenberg, the
forty-eight-year-old Canadian director who has known Burroughs for seven
years. Of course, this is *David Cronenberg* talking, the creator of such lyrical
films as *Scanners* (exploding heads), *Dead Ringers* (gynecological horror),
and *Videodrome* (sadomasochistic public-access TV), who last night giggled
while telling me, "I would like it if you could say that I was the embodiment
of absolute evil."

But with both Cronenberg and Burroughs in the same town, let alone the
same room, and with so many disgusting, revolting visions between them,
how's a woman to choose? No, perhaps it is better to simply enumerate *their*
revulsions, because if William Burroughs and David Cronenberg are aghast
at something, then the odds are the rest of us will be a little queasy, too.

Revulsion No. 1: *Shooting Joan*

In 1951 Burroughs was living in Mexico City with his wife, Joan, and young
son, Billy Jr., after a heroin and marijuana possession charge against him
back in the States had been dropped. One September afternoon, Burroughs
and his wife dropped by to see an acquaintance and a few other friends who
had gathered to enjoy some drinks. Burroughs was packing a Star .380 automatic. At one point in the festivities, he said to his wife, who was sitting in a
chair across the room, "I guess it's about time for our William Tell act."
They'd never performed a William Tell act in their lives, but Joan, who was
drinking heavily and undergoing withdrawal from a heavy amphetamine
habit, and who had lived with Burroughs for five years, was game. She placed
a highball glass on top of her head. Burroughs, known to be a good shot, was
sitting about six feet away. His explanation for missing was not that his aim
was off, but that this gun shot low. The bullet struck Joan in the head. She
died almost immediately.

The judge in Mexico believed the shooting to be accidental, as the other
people present in the room asserted that this was the case. And so after paying
a lawyer $2,000 and serving thirteen days in jail, Burroughs was allowed to
post $2,312 and was freed.

Eight years later, Burroughs's first novel, *Naked Lunch,* was published. One of the last books in America to be the cause of an obscenity trial, it is a biting, hallucinatory work that Norman Mailer described as having been composed by a genius. But Burroughs might never have written a word of it had he not shot his wife in the head. "I am forced to the appalling conclusion that I would never have become a writer but for Joan's death," Burroughs has said, "and to the realization of the extent to which this event has motivated and formulated my writing. I live with the constant threat of possession, and a constant need to escape from possession, from control. So the death of Joan brought me in contact with the invader, the ugly spirit, and maneuvered me into a lifelong struggle in which I have had no choice except to write my way out."

This is exactly what the film *Naked Lunch* is about. It's not so much a re-creation of the book itself, but a story of how William Lee, played by Peter Weller, came to kill his wife (Judy Davis) and write a novel called *Naked Lunch.* "It's Joan's death," explains Cronenberg, "that first drives him to create his own environment, his own Interzone. And that keeps driving him. So in a sense, that death is occurring over and over again." We both look at Burroughs, relaxing in his modest Kansas house, years away from the charged tropical dream of Mexico City. Although the home seems at first glance fit for a preacher, a quick look around reveals a human skull sitting stolidly in a bookcase and a drawing hanging on the wall of Burroughs throwing a knife. Burroughs considers Cronenberg's theory. How many times has he gone over this same, excruciating terrain? He says only, "That seems quite valid."

"What caliber of gun was it exactly?" I find myself asking. An abrupt transition, maybe even horrifying, but it's practically a relief to bring up the grotesque particulars, and indeed, with these two such a query actually seems to lighten the mood.

"A three eighty," Burroughs shouts out, speaking of the actual event. At the same time, Cronenberg blurts out "a thirty-two!" referring to the movie. It's a confusion of real life and fiction, not unlike the film itself.

Revulsion No. 2: *Cobras, Puffers, and Blue-Spotted Octopuses*

Burroughs leads the way into his backyard, using his cane to rustle weeds, flip over likely rocks or boards while I stand poised to grab whatever might slither out. Earlier he'd displayed the cane as proudly as a schoolboy at show-

and-tell. Inside it is hidden a sword. "I just had it sharpened," he said. "Feel that edge!" He reinserted the blade into the cane. "Don't want it to come apart in the supermarket," he said.

Now he is stirring at something in the grass with the cane. I ask him what we are likely to turn up.

"Garter snakes," he says.

At one point in the snake hunt, Cronenberg sees some sort of insect hovering over nearby tall grasses and cups his hands to try and gently catch it. Burroughs waves it away with his cane.

"William, are you interested in insects?" says Cronenberg, mostly for my benefit, a question that causes Burroughs to regard the two of us warily. "Not entirely," he finally says. After a few minutes of completely addled discussion, Burroughs exclaims, "Oh, insects! I thought you said *incest.*"

"The most awful creature to me is the centipede," he says. A number of them crawl slimily through the movie version of *Naked Lunch.* "I don't go into hysterics or anything, but I look around for something to smash it with. I used to live out in the country when I first moved here, and there were a lot of centipedes in the house, and I set out to kill them all. A program of genocide. I'd wake up in the middle of the night, and I'd know there's a centipede in this room. And there always was. And I couldn't go to sleep until I killed it." Although he never hunts mammals and is even somewhat of an animal activist, Burroughs is quite an expert on killing bugs, having once held a job as an exterminator.

"William's use of insects as metaphors is generally negative," Cronenberg points out. "When he says someone has insect eyes or an insect voice, it's not a compliment. Now, in my movie, you can tell I'm a little more well-disposed toward insects, because the typewriters, which are insects, are almost like cats, really. They came about because when I write at night with the light on, insects come and land on the page." This is clearly a fond memory. "They're relating to you somehow. People are obsessed in a public way with life on other planets," he says, a subtle reference to Burroughs, who is so interested in the idea of alien visitation that he has struck up a friendship with *Communion* author Whitley Strieber. "I'm saying that right here on earth we have the most alien life-forms we'll find anywhere, and most of them are insects! How they survive and what their life cycles are like is incredible."

Burroughs is unmoved by this aria for bugs. "Your insect typewriters are kind of fun," he concedes. But touching bugs in general is not his thing at all. "I hate the touch of spiders," Burroughs says. "A biology teacher at school had a tarantula, and I couldn't touch the thing, even though tarantula bites are not dangerous. The most deadly spider is the funnel web spider of Australia." This leads to the two trying to one-up each other on ghoulish facts of nature.

"There's a spider in Virginia called a brown recluse," says Cronenberg. "And when you're bitten, the tissue just starts to deteriorate and spread. It's very dangerous."

"Brown recluse!" says Burroughs as we continue our stroll through the yard. "There are cases of people who have these huge lesions down to the bone. I'd much rather be bitten by a black widow. They make you desperately sick, but at least it's not deadly for a healthy adult." As long as we're on the subject, I ask them to choose the best method of death in the animal kingdom.

"Well, you'd want it to be quick," says Cronenberg, "and as painless as possible. So, what, a Gaboon viper?"

"I wouldn't choose a viper at all. Any of the vipers are apt to be painful, they have both hemo- and neurotoxins. Cobras have neurotoxins." Burroughs indicates that this is preferable. Cronenberg shakes his head.

"Cobras are not very good at getting it into your bloodstream," he says. "They don't have injector fangs." His hand mimics a snake repeatedly biting his other arm. "They actually chew, and dribble it into the cut."

"They have plenty to dribble, believe me," says Burroughs. At this point, I've stopped looking for snakes. "With the blue-spotted octopus, people are usually unconscious."

"That sounds good," says Cronenberg, beaming.

"It's a tiny little thing only about that big. No one's ever survived it. DOA in one hour. Puffer fish have the same venom, and it's also used to make zombies. The flesh of a puffer fish is supposed to be an aphrodisiac and a gourmet sensation, but one tiny part of the liver, one milligram . . . there are several accidents a year."

"Well, that's the obvious choice then," says Cronenberg. "Strangely enough, we have puffer fish in our movie. Hanging there in one shot."

As long as we have death by nature settled, I ask them by which weapon they would choose to die. "I don't think about dying by a weapon," Burroughs says as we walk back to the house. "I think about killing someone else with a weapon!"

"I guess that's the difference between an optimist and a pessimist," says Cronenberg with a giggle.

Revulsion No. 3: *Sucking on Mugwumps*

The film that would showcase addicts hooked on insecticide, lizardlike aliens
known as mugwumps who suckle humans on mugwump jism, and Roy
Scheider, had its genesis when the director and the writer met in 1984 at
Burroughs's seventieth birthday party in New York City. Cronenberg visited
Burroughs a few times in Kansas, discussing how to approach their project.
"I wanted William's blessing, because basically, there was nothing he could
do for me, I had to do it myself." Cronenberg finally wrote the script in 1989.
"I sent it [to Burroughs] to see what his reaction would be. He hated it and
threatened to sue." Burroughs smiles indulgently. He actually liked the
script, but a Japanese backer pulled out after reading a translation of the
screenplay. "It could have been something as simple as talking assholes,"
says Cronenberg with a shrug.

For years, there have been other attempts to get Burroughs's books, including the notorious *Junky,* to the screen. Among the people rumored to star in
earlier incarnations of *Naked Lunch* were Mick Jagger, Dennis Hopper (who
also wanted to direct), Jack Nicholson, and David Bowie. Chuck *"The Gong
Show"* Barris wanted to produce; Terry Southern was supposed to write the
screenplay. While these projects fell through, *Naked Lunch* had nevertheless
penetrated the public consciousness in one way or another long before now.

"One of the problems I had when I said, 'Okay, how am I going to do this
movie,' " says Cronenberg, "was that a lot of the book, and Burroughs's
writing in general, has been absorbed into the culture."

Indeed, he has revealed that when he wrote his first commercial horror
film, *They Came from Within,* his favorite book was *Naked Lunch.*

Originally released in 1975 in Canada as *Shivers,* the film concerns a venereal parasite that infests an apartment complex, causing some rather grisly
deaths. Burroughs has lately been credited for graphically predicting in
Naked Lunch what is now known as AIDS, when he wrote of a venereal
disease that would originate in Africa and afflict homosexuals. "Males," he
wrote, "who resign themselves up for passive intercourse to infected partners
like weak and soon-to-be purple-assed baboons, may also nourish a little
stranger." Cronenberg in his own right earned the title of *King of Venereal
Horror.*

"It's a limited kingdom," Cronenberg says with a proud smile, "but it's
mine. One of the reasons Burroughs excited me when I read him was that I
recognized my own imagery in his work," he says. "It sounds only defensive

to say, 'I was already thinking of a virus when I read that!' But there is a recognition factor. That's why I think you start to feel like you're vibrating in harmony with someone else. It's the recognition, not that they introduced you to something that was completely unthought of by you."

"Here's my conceit," says Cronenberg. "Burroughs and I have been fused in the same telepod together," he says, referring to *The Fly,* where Jeff Goldblum and a housefly are fused at the molecular genetic level. "And what you've got now is the Brundlething, which is my and his version of *Naked Lunch.* It's a fusion of the two of us, and it really is something that neither one of us would have done alone. Now I don't know which of us is the fly and which is human."

Revulsion No. 4: *Jerry Lewis*

There's not much in this world left to horrify William Burroughs, but being told at this same meal that he, Cronenberg, and Jerry Lewis have each been elected members of the French order of Arts and Letters is nearly enough to send him on another heroin jag. "We need to vote him out, then!" shouts Burroughs.

"Yeah, we can all get together and expel him from the order," says Cronenberg, "because everyone always says, 'Yeah, but so is Jerry Lewis.' It's an embarrassment to the order. And what about this: Jerry Lewis's movies are dubbed in France, and no one ever heard his real voice. When the guy who always dubbed his movies died, the next three movies of Jerry Lewis bombed in France because it was the wrong voice! So it isn't even the real voice they're responding to!" They both shake their heads.

"And," Burroughs adds disdainfully, "they *loooove* Damon Runyon over there. Now, good God!"

Revulsion No. 5: *Yage Till You Puke*

It's been half a day and no one has taken a hit of anything stronger than the vodka and Coke Burroughs is nursing. These days, at seventy-seven and post-triple bypass, Burroughs is taking a break from the opiates. The conversation, however, is free to range where Burroughs no longer does.

It takes a brave man to try and trade drug stories toe-to-toe with William Burroughs, and Cronenberg makes only a perfunctory attempt. "I tried opium once, in Turkey, and there I felt like I had a hideous flu, you know? It was like I was sick."

"You probably were! It can be very nauseating. You had just taken more than you could assimilate."

"I did take LSD once," Cronenberg responds. "It was a great trip. It was a very revealing experience to me, because I had intuited that what we consider to be reality is just a construct of our senses. It shows you, in no uncertain terms, that there are any number of realities that you could live, and you could change them and control them. It's very real, the effects it left."

Burroughs nods patronizingly, although he was more of an opiate man. "Yes. I've taken LSD, psilocybin, mescaline. My experiences with yage were"—he thinks of the South American medicine-man drug mixture that caused him to puke violently, suffer seizures, and almost die—"mixed, but on the whole, good."

Talk then shifts to over-the-counter drugs one could abuse, which included the availability of codeine in Canada, opium cold-and-flu tablets in France, and "in England," says Burroughs, "they used to sell Dr. Brown's Chlorodine. It was morphine, opium, and chloroform. I used to boil out the chloroform."

"I was chloroformed once," says Cronenberg, "as a kid, when they took out my tonsils. I still remember what happened when they put this mask over my face. I saw rockets shooting. Streamers of flame, rockets. . . . I can still see it. And that sickly smell." He makes a face. After discussing insects, gunshot wounds, and snake bites all day, we're finally onto something that can gross out Cronenberg.

"I hate general anesthesia," says Burroughs. "Scares the hell out me. I had to have it when they did the bypass, but I knew where I was. I knew I was in the hospital having an operation, and there was this gas coming into my face like a gray fog. When I cracked my hip, they put a pin in with a local. A spinal. Of course, it ran out and I started screaming."

"I was in a motorcycle accident where I separated my shoulder," says Cronenberg. "They took me into the operating room and gave me a shot of Demerol."

"Demerol," says Burroughs, brightening a bit. "Did it help?"

"I loved it. It was wonderful."

"It helps. I had a shot of morphine up here somewhere," he says, pointing to the top of his shoulder near his neck, "from my bypass operation. She said, 'This is morphine.' And I said, 'Fine!' " Burroughs drags out the word in a sigh of bliss. He closes his eyes in an expression of rapt anticipation. "Shoot it in, my dear, shoot it in." I ask Burroughs if the doctors and nurses at the hospital knew who he was. "Certainly," he drawls. "The doctor wrote on my chart, 'Give Mr. Burroughs as much morphine as he wants.' "

Revulsion No. 6: *Possession by Demons*

There's no question that in one way or another both men are absolutely possessed, but only one of them believes in evil as an actual presence, in fact, in demons themselves. "I would have to say yes, evil exists, definitely," says Burroughs. "I'm very interested in the whole matter of possession and exorcism." He's said in the past that he felt that the dark presence that possessed him on the day he shot his wife had never left him. "I asked myself," he goes on, "why do these demons have such necessity to possess, and why are they so reluctant to leave? The answer is, that's the only way they can get out of hell—it's sort of like junk. They possess somebody and they want to hang onto it because that's their ticket out of hell."

"Do you believe in a literal hell?" asks Cronenberg somewhat incredulously. He is, as he puts it, "not just an atheist, but a total nonbeliever."

"Certainly," says Burroughs, as if it's the most obvious thing in the world. As to the existence of a literal heaven, Burroughs says, "Heaven is the absence of hell." Earlier in the day he had remarked that pleasure was the absence of pain and that pleasure in morphine lies in the absence of the pain of withdrawal.

Revulsion No. 7: *The Horror of Female Genitalia*

Mary McCarthy once wrote a review comparing Burroughs to Jonathan Swift because of, among other things, their shared "horror of female genitalia." It was a phrase that naturally came to mind as I watched some of Cronenberg's films. "I'm interested in the aesthetics of revulsion," Cronenberg explains. "I'm showing not only female genitalia but the equivalence of male genitalia also, insects and diseases, gooey icky stuff, and I'm saying—or as I had Elliot Mantle [in *Dead Ringers*] say—We are so unintegrated, we have not yet developed an aesthetic for the insides of our bodies. It's my attempt to say, What is ugly and what is repulsive?"

Burroughs is looking tired this evening. In this, his era of clean living, it's his habit to turn in early. He sees Cronenberg and me out, and as we drive back to Cronenberg's hotel, we see Burroughs, frail and courtly, waving from the front porch. In his suite, Cronenberg continues his defense. "I find the whole idea of revulsion quite strange, actually," he says. "I could easily imagine a human species where revulsion was not a response to anything. It's a specifically human thing. Does your dog have that response?" he asks.

And in which scene, Cronenberg wants to know, does he actually show a horror of female genitalia? I point to *Videodrome* when James Woods looks on in fear as he grows an enormous vaginalike slit in his abdomen. "He seems to like it!" Cronenberg laughs. "It's almost like he's proud of it and happy to have it!" Yeah, and then he loses a gun in it? Isn't that highly symbolic of a well-known male fear? "Well, I've known some women who thought they lost their Tampax and were just as freaked out as anybody else."

He tells a story from the making of *Videodrome,* when Woods is forced to spend days with rubber appliances glued to his chest to attain the previously mentioned orifice. "And he turns to Debbie Harry and says, 'When I first got on this picture, I was an actor. Now I feel like I'm just the bearer of the slit.' And she said, 'Now you know what it feels like.' So I'm forcing him to be the bearer of the slit! Reality is what he perceives it to be."

Cronenberg is becoming increasingly unnerved by the topic. His rebuttals grow more animated. His chief concern is that his art might be seen to reflect his life. "If you buy into an autobiographical thing between the filmmaker and a character that he portrays, you then make it impossible for an artist to create characters that are literally not him," pleads Cronenberg. "Martin Scorsese was terrified to meet me! He expected to meet a guy who was like Renfield from *Dracula,* a drooling maniac." Scorsese, he points out, would be dismayed if anyone thought he was Travis Bickle. "I found it hard to believe that the guy who made *Taxi Driver* would be afraid to meet me. And that someone in the business himself could still fall prey to the same things that I'm ranting and raving about right now.

"What can I say! It's not true that I have a fear of female genitalia! But how can I prove it without getting into very personal stuff? What level are we talking about, I mean . . . in the dark, with women . . ." He's referring now not to his movies, it seems, but to himself. Here Cronenberg adopts the skeptical tone of a documentary film voice-over. "Does Cronenberg have this horror of female genitalia or doesn't he?"

If my take on Cronenberg's films is accurate, perhaps we've arrived at the last outrage: female genitalia. Oh, the horror!

But narrowing this particular revulsion to include only women may be too limiting. Given the progression of revulsions we've discussed, I realize that there's something worse, something in Burroughs's estimation that is even more horrible, the final atrocity: humanity. Just a few hours before, Cronenberg, trying to prompt Burroughs for my benefit, had said, "I once asked William about women. He said something that is in the script, about how it's conceivable that men and women are different species, and they have different wills and purposes on earth. I think it's a very interesting proposition."

Burroughs sat silently on the couch as his theories were recounted, then nervously cleared his throat. "Valerie Solanis"—the woman who shot Andy Warhol—"in her manifesto, gets around to the position that females are almost as bad as males. And that's much closer to my position, where it's all a bad idea. Male and female. You know, let's call the whole thing off." I looked at Cronenberg, whose intrigued expression seemed to indicate that he suspected Burroughs might be onto something.

And perhaps, in some perverse, exhilarating way, he may well be. It's a character-building march, that icy trek from misogyny to misanthropy. After all, there's something a little too parochial, too narrow-minded, about hating only one gender. How much better, really, to be disgusted by us all!

Grandpa from Hell

The L.A. Weekly / 1996

From *The L.A. Weekly* (19–25 July 1996), 21, 24. © *The L.A. Weekly*.
Reprinted by permission.

Artist Robbie Conal and *Weekly* arts editor Tom Christie each spoke
by phone last week with the self-described "Grandpa from hell." What
follows is a synthesis of their interviews.

L.A. Weekly: "Ports of Entry," at the Los Angeles County Museum of Art
reveals the full extent of your visual art. Were you painting before you were
writing?

William S. Burroughs: No, I did quite a lot of graphic work with Brion
Gysin, scrapbooks, image montages and one thing and another. I remember
I once came back from lunch with two reporters from *Life, Time, Fortune,*
David Snell and Loomis Dean. Brion had a lot of magazine and newspaper
articles and stuff that he had cut up, it was on the table, and Loomis Dean
and Snell got an eyeful too. There were really some lifted eyebrows. Dean
was the photographer and Snell was the reporter. They worked together like,
like Snell went, "Yes, yes, Mr. Burroughs, when we finally found old Burns
he was eaten and skinned alive and rolled in broken bottles." And Dean
would be photographing my reaction to that, you see.

Weekly: I see.

Burroughs: Yeah, they did it all the time. That was years ago . . . when
Naked Lunch came out . . . 1959.

Weekly: And when did you actually begin to paint?

Burroughs: July 14, 1986, the day Brion died. Bastille Day. I couldn't
have competed with him. I would not have competed with him. I'd done
wood before that, you see? Wood shotgun paintings. I just shot a charge of
shot through a piece of plywood and I looked at the other side and saw some
very interesting patterns. I began experimenting with painted surfaces, shooting painted surfaces, and I got some rather surprising results, that is to say,
very clear scenes. And so then I went on to paper. I couldn't have made the
further step to paper painting unless Brion was dead.

220

Weekly: One of the shotgun paintings, *Sore Shoulder,* is more like a . . a port of exit. Was that part of your intention?

Burroughs: Well, I didn't have much intention. I was just amazed when I looked at it. You see, I never went to art school, I had no draftsmanship, so I don't know what I'm going to paint until I've painted it. I don't set out to paint something. I paint it and then decide what I've painted and give it a title.

Weekly: So you just start and whatever happens, happens, it's kind of an organic, random process?

Burroughs: Well, yes. The question is how random is random? *[Chuckle]* I'd say it's an emergent painting. You look at it and then things come out with photographic clarity. You see faces, feet, shoes . . . various objects, but very clear. These emerge.

Weekly: They emerge from the process?

Burroughs: They emerge when you're through. When the process is through.

Weekly: How important is the random factor?

Burroughs: I think it's essential. Otherwise it becomes just sterile repetition. Besides which, life is a cut-up. Every time you look out the window, walk down the street, receive a phone call, your consciousness is being cut by random factors. In other words, the cut-up is much closer to the facts of human perception. And any representational approach explodes the myth of the omniscient writer or painter operating in a vacuum, or purely representational paintings. Cows in the grass, you know.

Weekly: Cows in grass?

Burroughs: "Cows-in-the-Grass" painting. It's beautiful . . . I've seen it beautifully done in the museums in Holland, but it can't be done now.

Weekly: We're beyond that?

Burroughs: Of course. Besides, photography can do it better.

Weekly: So this is part of the evolutionary process?

Burroughs: I don't know, it's just . . . Remember that at the turn of the century there was an exhibit of photography that said photography is the death of painting. Well, it wasn't true. But they had to go . . . they went on to montage, which is very much cut-ups, and then Cubism and various other forms.

Weekly: Where would you say we were when you began, and where are we today?

Burroughs: I don't know where we are. I can't understand the lingo of art criticism. What is deconstructive postmodernism? Do you know?

Weekly: No.

Burroughs: Neither do I. *[Chuckle]* It really gets pretty arcane.

Weekly: Do you notice a feedback between your art and your writing?

Burroughs: Oh sure, sure. Remember that, at one time, painting and writing were one. Cave painting. They painted what they wanted to happen. The original purpose was magical, evocative magic. But yes, I would find that I was dreaming about paintings, and sometimes what I saw in the paintings would give me ideas for writing, and vice versa. And then I would find that my writing was showing up in my painting. Or someone else's writing. For example, I suddenly found that I had a picture that I had painted, I looked at it carefully and saw *The Nigger of the Narcissus* by Conrad, the burial of the mayor. I didn't know how it got there, but there it was.

Weekly: Do you consider yourself a writer who paints, or would you prefer not to make such distinctions?

Burroughs: Writers paint, and painters can write. Although Brion, I know, had the experience that he did do many things. People don't like it when you are trying to make your way as a painter and you also write. And so they don't know how to classify you, you see, and that can be an impediment to one's career. Which it was with Brion, I know.

Weekly: Now, some folks might say that this show coming up at the County Museum has been given to you because you're a well-known writer. What do you say to them?

Burroughs: I don't see that there's any contradiction there. Not at all. And also, I say that in this life you gotta play the cards you got. If I derive attention to my painting from the fact of being a well-known writer, I say fine. You got some aces, you don't turn 'em down.

Weekly: Similarly, is that how you feel about the Gap ads and the film work and things like that?

Burroughs: Sure thing, sure thing.

Weekly: How do you mesh the notion that you're subverting pop culture while at the same time taking part in it?

Burroughs: What do you mean, "subverting it?"

Weekly: Well, haven't you, in your work, tried to undermine the power of word and image?

Burroughs: So what? There's no contradiction to subverting something and profiting by it at the same time. I say, you gotta play the cards you got.

Weekly: Do you have any spiritual inclinations?

Burroughs: Of course. I believe in God . . . or gods, rather. Egyptian and so on. This sort of gives an out to these people who say, "How can an all-powerful and all-knowing God permit my wife to have hemorrhoids?" That kind of talk, you know. Well, of course, you've got a lot of gods, and then you can say, "Well, we've got a famine here, Osiris." "Well, what the hell, you can't win 'em all," says Osiris. "I'm hustling myself." He was one of the gods of youth and regeneration, very much corresponding to the young corn god in the Mayan pantheon.

Weekly: Speaking of the Mayan pantheon, you've said that our culture is related more to the Aztecs and the Mayans than we understand, in terms of time and control.

Burroughs: Yeah, oh well, they were obsessed with control, and they predicted millions of years in the future. That is like you'd say, "What day of the week would Christmas fall on a million years from now?" It seems to me rather a sterile preoccupation. It took a lot of their time. They conceived time as having a definite beginning and a definite end.

Weekly: You've also said that people who lived in the Middle Ages understood that the Earth was round and the only reason they believed it was flat was because the church said so.

Burroughs: Well, I was talking about people on the seacoast. They knew the Earth was round, like in seeing the ships come in; they believed the Earth was flat because the church said so. And it wasn't healthy to disagree with the church, so they wouldn't allow themselves to know what they knew. I've always said that one of the functions of art, or of any creative thought, is to make people aware of what they know and don't know that they know.

Weekly: And do you think that that applies to the average person?

Burroughs: Oh yes, they know much more than they think they know.

Weekly: You're interested in the occult, aren't you?

Burroughs: Certainly, I'm interested in the golden dawn, Aleister Crowley, all the astrological aspects. I'm interested in all that whole level of meta-physics and occultism, magic . . .

Weekly: Scientology?

Burroughs: Oh no, no. *[Chuckle]* I left Scientology way back there. It had some ideas, but Hubbard just cribbed these ideas from everywhere. Someone in the movement told me he steals and curses the source. He's dead now.

Weekly: You knew Timothy Leary?

Burroughs: Yes, I knew him for years. And I think he accomplished a great deal, really. I talked to him the day he died. His son called me and said that he was slipping in and out of the coma. But I talked to him. He said, uh, "Is it true?" I didn't know exactly what he meant. Well, I guess it's true. *[Chuckle]* It's true, Tim. And then he just said, "Well I, I love you, Bill," and I said, "I love you, Tim." He died about four hours later. That was all there was to it.

Weekly: What was Leary's accomplishment?

Burroughs: He had a worldwide impact on young people, leading men to question what they had taken for granted, and to experiment. And to increase awareness. But it's obvious, I think, that the old, the old gods have fallen, the old beliefs are gone. Gone, crumbling before our eyes, of their own inertia. And when that happens, you look for something new.

Weekly: Have you ever studied with any sort of guru?

Burroughs: Never. I haven't encountered anyone that I felt could tell me anything that I couldn't find out on my own . . . yet. The one who taught me more than anyone else was Brion Gysin, the only man I ever truly respected.

Weekly: In "Ports of Entry," there are photos of you and Brion that have been combined to make one image, one man. Is that an accurate. . . . ?

Burroughs: Yes, he always said that he was my conscience.

Weekly: Do you think that's true?

Burroughs: I think it is true. I can't . . . it's too complicated to elaborate on.

Weekly: There's one thing that you have said about silence that's wonderful, about turning off the muttering and the noise. Has aging helped you to be able to stay in this silent state?

Burroughs: Well, yes, it has. It's just a matter of inner control, this letting anything come through. And after a while there are these periods of silence.

Weekly: And you have techniques for blocking out the noise?

Burroughs: The only technique . . . well, it depends on how noisy it is . . . but generally speaking, you know, I think that you should just let it, let the noise go through. I remember that some time I was kept awake all night by the dogs barking in some village. In Tangiers. It got on my nerves terribly. You'd almost go down, and then one would start way over there, and then they'd suddenly all be barking. And a guru said, "Well, if you just let them bark through you it won't bother you."

Weekly: That's brilliant. Here's a little L.A. question for you: Have you seen any good movies lately?

Burroughs: *Twister* was the last one I saw. That was fun. It was really so appropriate to Kansas. Two tornadoes since I've been here. And I've seen tornadoes in St. Louis—I was there for the 1927 tornado, which was a major disaster. I was in school. It's a little outside of St. Louis, and we didn't see the whole works, but there were these great gangs of girls wandering through the hall screaming. Extraordinary sight. *[Chuckle]* Well, it was a good movie, I enjoyed it. And no long, boring love scenes. Twisters here and twisters there.

Weekly: Do you watch television?

Burroughs: Oh yes. I watch *The X-Files.* And on Discovery, they often have good natural-history programs. There's the leaping lemurs and madagascars and, uh, Easter Island.

Weekly: Are you still interested in drugs?

Burroughs: Well, in a way, yeah, certainly it's always been one of my interests—that is, the whole chemistry of drugs. How strong do they make a drug? Could they devise a drug that would be 20 times as habit-forming as heroin? *[Chuckle]* So on and so forth.

Weekly: Are you still able to handle drugs?

Burroughs: Well, alcohol, that's about all.

Weekly: Getting back to your art: Is it true you've stopped painting?

Burroughs: No . . . I've paused.

Weekly: Why is that?

Burroughs: Well, I've got quite a backlog. You don't keep pouring 'em out and just pile and pile 'em up, you see?

Weekly: How do you feel about having this retrospective at LACMA?
Burroughs: It's very gratifying, of course. The catalog's beautifully done.

Weekly: In terms of your life's work, do you feel that the show represents . . .
Burroughs: My last words? *[Chuckle]* I hope not, I hope not. That's all I can say.

Index

Ace Books, 60, 91
African Genesis (Robert Ardrey), 70
Alfonso, Barry, xii
Algeria, war in, 29, 75
Amazing Stories (magazine), 188
American Rifleman (magazine), 143
Anderson, Jack, 181
Anderson, Poul, *Twilight World*, 83
Ansen, Alan, 80, 169
Aristotle, 150
Ashbery, John, 95

Balch, Anthony, 52, 115, 204
Ballard, J. G., 171
Barris, Chuck, *The Gong Show*, 214
Barthes, Roland, xi
Basquiat, Jean Michel, 196
Bayley, Barrington, *The Star Virus*, 83
Beat Hotel, xii; Brion Gysin on, 64–67
Beckett, Samuel, 82, 104, 136, 171, 172
Beilles, Sinclair, 71
Benford, Gregory, *Timescape*, 179
Benton, Thomas Hart, 164
Bertolucci, Bernardo, *The Sheltering Sky*, 205
Biological Time Bomb, The (Gordon Rattray Taylor), 49, 88
Blake, William, 165
Bly, Robert, 210
Bockris, Victor, *With William Burroughs: A Report from the Bunker*, xiii–xiv, 118, 157
Bog People, The (Professor P. V. Glob), 107
Borges, Jorge Luis, 171
Bowie, David, 165, 205; early plans for film version of *Naked Lunch*, 214; *Ziggy Stardust*, xii
Bowles, Paul, xii, xiv, 137, 168, 203
Brazil (Terry Gilliam), 175
Brean, Herbert, *How to Give Up Smoking*, 100
Brecht, Bertolt, 187
British Broadcasting System (BBC), 67
Brookner, Howard, 114–15, 152
Brownjohn, Robert, 78
Brownstein, Michael, 95
Buful Peoples, 53
Burroughs, Edgar Rice, 83
Burroughs, William S.: Academy Series, 73; as activist, 24; on acupuncture, for drug treat-

ment, 84–85, 111, 125, 176; on addiction, 12, 14, 91, 94, 95, 101, 110, 158, 172; addiction, on cures for, 44, 111 (*see also* acupuncture; apomorphine); on addiction, government responses to, 44, 125; on advertising, 149; advertising, employed in, 222–23; on aging, 224–25; on AIDS, 191, 214; on alcohol, 63, 93, 111, 225; on alcoholism, 111; on aliens, visits from, 46, 212; on the American Dream, 178; on American youth, 4, 73–74, 185; on amphetamines, 63; on animal activism, 193; on apomorphine, 40, 44, 45, 61–62, 64, 84, 101, 111, 125, 176; on Arabs, 4, 8; on the army, 28, 136, 149; on art, affective quality of, 201; art career, xiii, 196, 198, 220, 225; on art, purposes of, 107, 124, 157, 162, 182, 199, 223; on artificial intelligence, 188; on the artistic process, xiii, 182, 183, 199, 200, 201, 202; on assassination, 36, 128–29, 143–44, 145; on astral projection, 159, 181; authorities, problems with, 87; authority, opposition to, 11, 14, 21, 37; autonomic shaping, 42, 44, 45, 47, 48, 52, 58, 73, 93; on the avant garde, 124–25, 133; on the Aztecs, 223; on barbiturates, 63, 64; Beats, connection to, ix, 65, 94, 130, 131, 168, 171; on bestsellers, 119, 158; biographical information, 7, 16, 90, 119–22, 132, 161; biological alteration by surgery and engineering, 180; biological and chemical weapons, 76; biological warfare, 76–77, 135, 146; on Blacks, 4, 20; on bodyguards, 144; the Bowery, 108, 141–42; on the brain, use of, 45–46; on breakdown of bourgeois values, 33, 35, 169; on Buddhism, 83, 138; the Bunker, 109, 113, 134–35, 141–42, 173; on bureaucracies, 62, 136; on California, 91–92; on cancer, cure for, 127; on cannabis, 63, 64, 93; on cannabis, legalization of, 64, 131, 154; on cannabis, use of in writing *Naked Lunch*, 93; on capital punishment, 4; on capitalism, 72, 186; on Catholicism, 149, 179; on cats, 193, 212; on cave painting, 222; on censorship, 14, 130–31, 136, 148, 162, 201, 202; centipedes, Burroughs and Cronenberg on, 206, 212; chemicals, used to control, 31, 40; civilization, decay of, compared to Rome, 69; cobras,